What's Wrong with "Globalization"!?

What's Wrong with "Globalization"!?

Thomas C. Fischer

FORMER DEAN AND PROFESSOR OF LAW EMERITUS,
NEW ENGLAND SCHOOL OF LAW, BOSTON;
DISTINGUISHED ACADEMIC IN RESIDENCE,
SEATTLE UNIVERSITY SCHOOL OF LAW

CAROLINA ACADEMIC PRESS

Durham, North Carolina

Library of Congress Cataloging-in-Publication Data

Fischer, Thomas C. (Thomas Covell)
  What's wrong with "globalization"!? / Thomas C. Fischer. -- 1st ed.
    p. cm.
  ISBN 978-1-59460-665-6 (alk. paper)
  1. Foreign trade regulation. 2. Law and globalization. 3. Law and economic
development. I. Title.

  K3943.F574 2008
  337--dc22

                                    2008049675

CAROLINA ACADEMIC PRESS
700 Kent Street
Durham, North Carolina 27701
Telephone (919) 489-7486
Fax (919) 493-5668
www.cap-press.com

Printed in the United States of America

Say not, the struggle naught availeth,
The labour and the wounds are vain,
The enemy fails not, nor faileth,
And as things have been they remain …

For while the tired waves, vainly breaking,
Seem here no painful inch to gain,
Far back, through creeks and inlets making,
Comes silent, flooding in, the main.

Arthur Hugh Clough (1862)

Contents

Foreword

Professor Thomas Fischer has written a worthy successor to his two previous books, *The Europeanization of America* and *Allies or Adversaries?* Whereas the earlier books were concerned principally with Europe and its relations with the United States, this book is about the entire world emerging around us and our relationship to it. *What's Wrong with "Globalization"!?* is a rhetorical questioning of contemporary attitudes, many highly skeptical, towards globalization. The book is a masterful review of the many elements of globalization, of trade in goods and services, of investment, capital markets and reserve currencies, of the position of China, Russia, Japan, the EU, and really every country and region in the world, and the world's principal international organizations. There is a feast of knowledge to be enjoyed.

But there is more here, much more. To the title question, Fischer answers with a broad and fair review of what is wrong, and also what is right, with globalization. As I write, a Wall Street "crisis" is upon us, and the institutions of our government and others are seeking to grapple with it. Professor Fischer has of course touched on the relevant financial issues. And, rightly in my view, sees the march of economic globalization as having enhanced human standards of living and the quality of life for countless individuals in a way unimaginable in the past. And there is no reason, whatever the challenges, that the same cannot spread to everyone. Thom Fischer has a justified faith in the unlimited promise of free trade and open institutions and markets, if properly governed and regulated. But he also appreciates the political dimensions and difficulties.

This is a book recommended to the thoughtful reader, curious for knowledge and a chance to think deeply about possibly the most important, if often misunderstood and sometimes distorted and abused, phenomenon in the world today.

Don Wallace, Jr.
Professor of Law, Georgetown University Law Center
Chairman, International Law Institute
Washington, D.C.

Foreword

Globalization, as we are reminded in the final paragraph of this wide-ranging and perceptive study, "has the potential to grow diverse economies in an equitable manner.... What is lacking is vision, political will and leadership." The problem was highlighted in July 2008 by the collapse of lengthy negotiations (on the Doha round) aimed at securing a global agreement on trade.

Professor Fischer has an established reputation as a writer on global or international trade, and in what is his latest analysis of the many problems and issues involved he succeeds in identifying the challenges faced by the United States, by the European Union, by the emerging economies of Brazil, Russia, India and China, and by many other countries and organisations. Globalization is not confined to questions of trade, of course, and in chapter after chapter Thom Fischer examines a variety of issues. We even learn (from chapter 8) that multinationals "that engage in outsourcing and offshoring" have been attacked as "Benedict Arnold" corporations, a term which may require some explanation for non-US citizens!*

From the start of his work Professor Fischer favours a positive approach to globalization, but he is fully aware of its numerous negative factors. He examines areas such as regulation, intellectual property, the protection of the environment, the maldistribution of resources, the "sub-prime loan mess," standards of accountancy, problems of health and disease, private philanthropy, the production of energy, over-population, graft and corruption, and the importance of the Rule of Law. He recognises the importance of the World Trade Organisation to global trade and supports many initiatives from numerous other bodies and from individuals.

This is an important study, presented in a clear, often conversational style. Professor Fischer has succeeded in bringing us up to date on so many aspects

---

* Initially a hero at Ticonderoga and Crown Point in the American Revolution against the British, Benedict Arnold (1741-1801) later turned traitor and offered to assist the British side. John Garraty and Mark Carnes, eds., AMERICAN NATIONAL BIOGRAPHY (Oxford, 1999) Volume 1, pp. 629-631.

of globalization, and his itemization of those aspects is valuable in dispelling over-optimistic expectations while at the same time underlining the need to move ahead. He deals with globalization in a scholarly and clear-minded work which deserves to be widely read and widely consulted.

Professor Sir David Williams, QC
Fellow of Emmanuel College
Emeritus Vice-Chancellor of the University of Cambridge
Cambridge, England

Preface

This is the third in what was never intended to be a trilogy of books. The first, *The Europeanization of America*,[1] undertook to assess the political, economic, and military impact of the rapidly-maturing European Community on America; as a result of the Single European Act and its 1992 Program.

The second book, *Allies or Adversaries?*,[2] asked why the United States and European Union, as the world's two economic superpowers, with around forty percent of global domestic product between them, did not collaborate more in setting the standards of global trade. The third chapter of that book, "An Economic Map of the World", handicapped the role of the major world economies at that time in the global sweepstakes. It predicted the decline of Japan, the rise of China and Southeast Asia, and the emergence of Latin America. This last book builds upon that theme by assessing more generically the hallmarks of globalization, and their virtues and vices.

I was upset that so much of the existing literature viewed the globalization process uncritically, as if it were inevitable and chiefly positive.[3] Or, condemned it as altogether bad.[4] I felt that the globalization process had many vices, but also many virtues, and that the vices could be modulated so that the net effect could be positive for developed and developing nations alike.

I am no Pangloss. Getting the most out of globalization requires energy and application; too often absent in today's sound-bite world. However, a sound global community cannot be built on ignorance and emotion. It takes reasoned, rational thinking. I hope this book contributes to that.

Acknowledgments

A book of this sort, so long in gestation, owes a debt to many people. I cannot mention them all, but they know who they are, and I thank them.

Of those I mention, I begin with my original mentor, Professor Kurt Lipstein of Clare College, Cambridge University, who first schooled me in the subject. Sadly, Kurt passed away in 2006, aged 98, but will always be remembered by me and many others as a true gentleman and scholar. My wife, Brenda, has suffered my projects bravely, although we both regret their intrusion on our time together.

Among others who have most encouraged and informed my work are: Professor Sir David Williams, QC, Vice-Chancellor Emeritus of Cambridge University, Alan Dashwood, formerly Director of Legal Services for the European Council and past Director of Cambridge's Centre for European Legal Studies; Catherine Barnard, its present director; Takis Tridimas of Queen Mary College, London; Professor Sir Francis Jacobs, QC, formerly Advocate General to the European Court of Justice, Luxembourg, and presently at King's College, London; the late David Lord Renton and Baroness Elles, both of Lincoln's Inn and the House of Lords, London, and Lord Peter Goldsmith, QC, formerly of Fountain Court, Temple, and UK Attorney General, now with Debevoise & Plimpton, London.

Further afield, were Professor Francis Snyder of the European University Institute, Florence, the London School of Economics and the University of Aix-en-Province; Werner Ebke of the University of Heidelberg, Germany; Gordon Walker, Canterbury University, Christchurch, New Zealand, and Aneurian Hughes former European Commission Ambassador to Australia and New Zealand, Canberra.

All of their input, and that of many others, has passed through a prism of my own making. So I alone am responsible for its accuracy and interpretation.

I have also been blessed by the assistance of stalwart research associates, Michelle McKiernan, Ingrid Gude, and James Thurman at New England, Tracy Sarich, Rachel Landsee, Bob Zierman, Mark Rose, Jason Salvo, Greg Hitzel, Karen Skretkowicz, and Brendon Taga at Seattle; outstanding librarians, Barry Stearns at New England, Guy Holborn at Lincoln's Inn, Jules Winterton at the Institute for Advanced Legal Studies, University of London, David Wills at the Squire Law Library, Cambridge, and Bob Menanteaux at Seattle. Finally, I am indebted to my hard-working secretaries, Elisa (Xiao Ying) Wu, Season Holloway, Erin Espedal, and Nanette Bradshaw.

Acronyms

ABAC	APEC Business Advisory Council
ACP	African, Caribbean and Pacific Countries (mostly less-developed, former colonies of EU member states)
APC	Advance Purchase Commitment (of drugs for poor countries)
APEC	Asian Pacific Economic Cooperation forum
ASEAN	Association of South East Asian Nations
AU	African Union (57 African countries allegedly pledged to better governance and economic growth)
BRICs	Brazil, Russia, India, and China (rapidly-developing, large-market economies)
BSE/CJD	"Mad-Cow" Disease; animal and human forms
CAFTA	Central America Free Trade Association
DDA	Doha Development Agenda
DSU	Dispute Settlement Understanding (under the GATT treaty)
ECB	European Central Bank (manages the Euro)
EIB	European Investment Bank
EU	European Union
FDI	Foreign Direct Investment
FTAs	Free Trade Agreements
FTAA	Free Trade Association of the Americas (proposed)
G7	Group of Seven Industrial Nations (Canada, France, Germany, Italy, Japan, the United Kingdom, and the United States)
G8	The G7, plus Russia
G20	Twenty or so emerging economies acting as a negotiating counter balance to the G7; chiefly China, India and Brazil
GATT	General Agreement on Tariffs and Trade
GDP	Gross Domestic Product
GMOs	Genetically Modified Organisms
HIV/AIDs	Auto-Immune System Disorders
ILO	International Labor Organization

IMF	International Monetary Fund
IP	Intellectual Property
IPO	Initial Public Offering (of stocks or bonds)
LDCs	Less (or Least)-Developed Countries
M&A	Mergers and Acquisitions
MAI	Multilateral Agreement on Investment
MTAs	Multilateral Trade Agreements
NAFTA	North American Free Trade Agreement
NAMA	Non-Agricultural Market Access (of GATT)
NATO	North Atlantic Treaty Organization
NGOs	Non-Governmental Organizations
NTBs	Non-Tariff Barriers (to trade)
ODA	Overseas Development Assistance or Aid
OECD	Organization for Economic Co-operation and Development
PLA	(China's) Peoples Liberation Army
R&D	Research and Development (of new products/services)
S&D	Special and Differential Treatment (for less-developed countries, under the Doha Development Agenda of GATT)
SED	Strategic Economic Dialogue (between U.S. and China)
SMEs	Small and Medium-Sized Enterprises
SOE	State-Owned Enterprise
TABD	Transatlantic Business Dialogue
TRIPs	Trade-Related Intellectual Property Agreement (of GATT)
UN	United Nations
U.S.	United States of America
WTO	World Trade Organization

What's Wrong with "Globalization"!?

Chapter I

Globalization

A. Globalization Defined

Many people use the term "globalization," but few undertake to define it. From the context in which the term is used, it is clear that it has several meanings. These include international trade in goods, that is, the production of a good in one country to be sold in another, or the purchase of a good in one country for resale in another. But there is nothing unique to this age about these practices. They have been going on since the time of the Phoenicians.

As I use the term "globalization" in this book, it means one of two things. First, the harmonization of standards or practices across national borders. And second, the co-venturing of public—but especially private—entities across state borders.[1] The latter takes several forms, notably; foreign investment, licensing, or production in a foreign country for sale or distribution there. Although these phenomena are not unique to this age, their incidence has increased dramatically in the past fifteen years, and seems destined to continue, indeed accelerate.

More important, the acceleration of these phenomena has produced an entirely new paradigm in international trade; hence the term "globalization." Rather than the old trade paradigm that assumed that one trader could win only if another lost, the new paradigm holds that cross-border or multi-national enterprises can win together; and, as recent events reveal, lose together.[2]

While this new paradigm does not eliminate competition in the marketplace, it does encourage collaboration among nation states and enterprises involved in globalization. It is this rapidly growing interdependence of nations, private businesses, and individuals that has created the great opportunities, but also the great concerns, associated with globalization.

One reason for the latter is the assumption that the global economy is a zero-sum game. Hence, if one nation's economy grows rapidly, another nation's economy must necessarily shrink. But the global economy is *not* a zero-sum game.[3] Otherwise, the American economy would have grown much less than it has—or even shrunk—as emerging Asian and Latin American countries have doubled their gross national income in the past fifteen years.[4] Should Americans be concerned if developing nations' economies grow if our economy continues to grow as well? It is the economies that are most-isolated from global trade that grow most slowly.

Nevertheless, the warp-speed emergence of a more-integrated global economic system, assisted by information technology, cross-border ventures, and capital flows, has seemed to marginalize the nation state and individual. To some extent, this is so. Globalization involves a substantial melding of interests across national borders, so that regional and global solutions gradually eclipse national ones. The process stresses interdependence over a potentially divisive independence. In doing so, it elevates economic concerns over political concerns and collectivism over individualism. This can lead to a feeling of helplessness and fear of change; a fear of globalization.

But the facts are irrefutable. Globalization is having a profound impact on national economies, both developed and developing. No large national economy can suffer a significant shock without its impact being felt in other markets. The most powerful and wealthiest nation in the world cannot set market conditions on its own. No national economy of any size is unaffected by global events.

B. The Impact of Globalization: Some Numbers

The many statistics that illustrate the process of globalization could fill this book. A few examples will have to suffice.

To illustrate both the size and acceleration of the globalization process, consider that, in 1950, the U.S. exported only $10 billion worth of goods and imported $9 billion worth. By the year 2000, our exports of goods and services had grown to $1.07 trillion and imports to $1.44 trillion; a 17-fold increase in exports and 27-fold in increase imports in real terms; well ahead of the growth in gross domestic product (GDP). More importantly, in the last two decades of the 20th Century, exports and imports doubled or nearly doubled every ten years.

Export/import trade, as a percentage of U.S. GDP, reflects similar growth. In 1950, exports and imports amounted to a mere 3.6 and 3.1 percent of U.S. GDP, respectively. By the year 2000, they amounted to 10.4 and 13.3 percent, respectively. That would mean that, at the turn of the century, nearly one-quarter of the U.S. economy depended upon trade, whereas only one-fifteenth did in 1950. Once again, most of this growth occurred in the last two decades.[5]

Please do not misunderstand me. Domestic consumption still represents the largest proportion of the U.S. economy, as is the case with all developed economies. My point is that trade is of increasing importance to all economies, and is growing much faster than domestic consumption. In other words, trade is today's engine of economic growth.[6]

Finally, there is the matter of foreign direct investment (FDI), a measure of the interdependence of various economies. Not surprisingly, developed economies invest most heavily in one another. The U.S. and European Union have the largest two-way FDI of any of the world economies.[7] But it is the growth of FDI and where it goes that illustrates globalization most clearly. In decade-on-decade comparisons, U.S. FDI abroad grew $211.4 billion from 1980–1990, but by $705.6 billion between 1990 and 2000, (a 230 percent increase). FDI into the U.S. grew from $326.6 billion to $591.9 billion during the same periods; a lower but still substantial growth.[8] But developing economies also attract FDI; particularly those that have growth prospects, are reasonably stable, and are semi-transparent (see Chapters IX and X).

The numbers cited above make globalization seem like an irrepressible force. That is not necessarily so. One might ask therefore: can globalization be stopped or, assuming it can, *should* globalization be stopped? Its virtues and vices are discussed in Chapter II, but it is worth saying here that, whenever FDI and technology transfer reach developing economies in Asia, Latin America and even Africa, generally living standards are raised, human rights and the rule of law improved, and disease, crime, and warfare reduced. Trade cannot proceed in the face of insecurity, however. The cross-border initiatives that lie at the core of globalization require a stable economic and political environment.

Finally, globalization is not a one-way street. Whereas it has the potential to reward all who participate, it is also a two-edged sword. It can have negative as well as positive consequences.

C. Stopping Globalization

There are some who would ring-fence the United States to keep local industries and jobs from migrating. Even if this were legal—and successful—we would be casting away one-eighth of our economy, and the fastest growing sector at that. We could no longer import products upon which we rely. And our businesses would miss out on opportunities abroad.[9]

Globalization has been good for America, in the form of expanded markets, inexpensive imports, and foreign investment that creates jobs here. Most important, our industries would lose their competitiveness in the rarified air of a hermetically-sealed economy in which the quality of their outputs are not tested.

Of course we need to be concerned about outsourcing. But jobs are created and disappear all the time. Where, after all, are the hearty coal miner, wheelwright, and blacksmith of yesteryear? All gone. Modern technology and the globalization process permit some jobs to be exported, although nowhere near the number that hysteric media stories suggest. (When was the last time you heard about jobs being created?)

Rather than try to stem their outflow (a doomed effort in my view), the challenge is to create new and better jobs, and to become more competitive. In time, improved working conditions and wages in developing countries will narrow the wage gap.

Change is frightening, but inevitable. Of FORTUNE's top 100 firms in 1957, only seventeen remained on the top 100 list 50 years later. Moreover, the 1957 list contained a large number of manufacturing firms, while the 2007 list was mostly services.[10] Conditions are not static: capital flows around the globe in search of opportunity; there is political upheaval; markets inflate and deflate; industries and jobs migrate. One of the reasons the U.S. economy boomed in the 1990s was the painful "right-sizing" it underwent in the late 1980s. But many industries in Europe, Asia and Latin America have yet to make that adjustment. Paradoxically, much of the change in the global marketplace is driven by consumers; the very persons who—as workers—most fear globalization.

Better than anxiety and resistance, I think, is to accept globalization for what it is and is not; neither to embrace it mindlessly or fatalistically, nor to shrink from its challenges. It is not an unvarnished blessing. Virtually every opportunity has a downside; some need to change, some loss of control. Rather than rejecting globalization totally (which strikes me as short-sighted, if not impossible), we should bend it to our advantage.

The numerous bilateral and multilateral meetings that characterize the globalization process are extremely positive. They involve ever larger numbers of nations, the private sector, and non-governmental interest groups. Although the volume of participants may slow the process somewhat, more inclusive meetings mean better outcomes. However, no one should suffer unnecessarily on account of globalization. Simply put, globalization needs to be better understood.[11] And that is what this book is about.

Chapter II

The Pros and Cons of Globalization

A. Reactions to Globalization

There are so many advantages and disadvantages to globalization that it would be impossible (not to mention mind-numbing) to list them all here. Because the globalization debate is so divisive, however, a short list of some of its most obvious—and frequently voiced—virtues and vices is in order.

Globalization's proponents, sometimes called free-traders, believe that open markets stimulate competition, producing a wider variety of better-quality and lower-cost goods and services and distributes them around the globe thereby improving conditions for producers, consumers, and local economies. Capital and technology are also allowed to move freely, seeking the best returns. For example, foreign affiliates doing business in the U.S. employed some 6.4 million American workers in 2001, which doesn't include the additional jobs created to meet those workers' consumption needs.[1] U.S. foreign affiliates in Europe sold $1.5 trillion in goods and services in 2001; with their income rising more than ten-fold between 1990 and 2003.[2] Foreign investment in U.S. government securities helps us to pay our debt service. And inexpensive foreign imports have helped meet America's consumption demands without higher inflation.[3]

The opponents of globalization, sometimes called fair-traders, believe that the globalization process allows the rich to get richer while leaving people in less-developed countries as poor as ever. Competition among large multinational corporations is thought to fuel a race to the bottom in which jobs and industries migrate from developed countries to developing ones. (This is the "giant sucking sound" that Ross Perot felt would result from Mexico's entry into NAFTA). Once there, it is feared these corporations will exploit the local labor force and despoil the environment, leaving the countries essentially bankrupt. In addition, "western" merchandisers will homogenize the marketplace, destroying unique social and cultural differences.

To some extent, all these things are true but not to the degree that either the proponents or opponents of globalization would have you believe. There are virtues and vices in every globalizing step. The real question is to what extent the former might outweigh the latter, whether market intervention could produce a better result, and how that might be brought about.

Globalization is a process that can be distinguished from its impacts, however. I doubt that the process can be stopped, far less reversed. But its negative impacts can be anticipated and minimized, or corrected and compensated. Some may require only short-term adjustments. Others, unaddressed, could prove toxic to an economy, region, or the entire trading world.

Proper analysis of globalization's pros and cons requires an understanding of its benefits and liabilities, especially in light of economic and political realities. Some things can be controlled more easily than others, while some cannot be foreseen or will affect some economies more than others. All involve some degree of economic or political inertia.

In Chapter III, I will look at some alternatives to globalization. But here I plan to set forth its major pros and cons in seven fields that broadly cover the areas it impacts: maldistribution of resources; differences in political and market structures; trade; capital; labor, health and environment; capacity building; and peace and security.

B. Pros and Cons

1. Distribution of Resources

Resources (natural, capital, labor and technical) are needed to build an economy. They are essential to economic growth and poverty reduction. But resources are not uniformly distributed around the world. Can globalization help adjust the imbalance and its effects?

Pro:

Today, resources move around the globe as never before. So those countries with abundant resources: for example, oil, capital, and know-how, have a unique opportunity to profit from globalization. And indeed most foreign direct investment goes to better-developed countries. But emerging economies also have a better chance today to attract the capital and know-how they need to develop their own resources or to trade for those they need.[4] Obviously, there is a benefit to maximizing resources, whatever their nature. Doing so creates wealth and builds economic stability.

Con:

There are many developing countries around the world that do not have vast natural, capital, or human resources. What natural resources they do have could be quickly and unprofitably exhausted by local and foreign speculators, and the environment degraded in the process. Less-developed country work forces are also open to exploitation in the globalization process. A poor country could reap some short-term benefits from globalization, but the gap between rich and poor economies seems likely to increase.[5]

2. Differences in Political and Market Structure

Pro:

Markets need some oversight to function fairly. But resources are generally used most efficiently in a liberalized market (where there is not too much government interference). Countries that have embraced trade liberalization—including China, India, many formerly communist countries of Central and Eastern Europe, Argentina, Brazil and Mexico—have experienced rapid economic growth. It was the dismantling of a failed command economy, and not capitalism or liberalization, that left many of these countries with large numbers of underemployed workers engaged in unproductive, unprofitable pursuits.[6]

For example, Poland's exports rose by more than 30 percent in the first nine months of 2004, following its entry into the European Union (EU). A major reason for this was the abolition of market restraints.[7] There have been similar changes in China and India, especially compared with economies which that remained closed, such as North Korea and Cuba.

For much of the 20th century, developing countries favored a socialist ideology. Governments relied on central planning, state monopolies, punitive taxes, and grandiose programs of public spending. They rejected liberalized trade, which was deemed exploitative and unfair. The drawback was that these countries stayed poor. Toward the end of the 20th Century, many developing countries threw off this victim's yoke and began to embrace capitalism, both in the way they organized their domestic economies and in their approach to international trade. All of the sudden, they are a lot less poor, and it hasn't cost the West a cent.[8]

Overregulation stifles economic growth. Overall, businesses in poor countries pay three times the administrative costs and struggle through twice as much paperwork as their counterparts in rich countries. As a result, businesses in poor countries do not flourish and foreign investment is discouraged.[9]

Efforts at self-sufficiency on the other hand, practiced by India for more than three decades, produced abysmal growth rates. Only when India began to globalize did it manage to reduce poverty in a sustainable way. This is because multinationals usually pay more than the going local wage to both skilled and unskilled workers.[10]

In liberalized markets, governments generally play an effective role in protecting consumers and promoting competition, since they are not market participants. Consumer behavior is the engine of growth, not government regulation.

Con:

When resources are scarce, there is greater need for government regulation. And resources are scarce in most developing economies. Small wonder then that emerging economies have tried to regulate themselves into competitive market positions. Excessive government regulation creates opportunities for fraud and corruption, however, which is more common in developing economies. China's state-owned enterprises, for example, are loss-producing and stifle innovation and competition, while the private sector is starved for capital because capital is largely controlled by the government. When governments perpetuate unneeded jobs and dispense patronage, efficiency is undercut and skills acquisition discouraged.[11]

However, the General Agreement on Tariffs and Trade (GATT) and similar agreements that aim to stimulate trade are viewed by developing nations as devices employed by developed economies and multi-national corporations to restrain poorer signatories. Setting market regulations beyond the nation state level means that market forces cannot be controlled by governments, particularly those of smaller, weaker states. And these countries have not the skills and resources to participate fully in international negotiations.[12]

3. Trade in Goods and Services

Pro:

Truly open markets encourage competition. Globalization benefits the consumer by offering a greater variety of goods and services at a lower cost. With lower labor costs and less regulation, less-developed countries can compete more effectively and increase their share of trade. Increasing income from trade builds wealth and increases tax revenue. Increased government revenues allow greater investment in infrastructure, education, and health, leading to economic growth and stability.[13]

The principle of comparative advantage suggests that all countries can raise their living standards through specialization and trade. Even if one country could make everything it needs, it still gains by focusing on the goods and services it produces most efficiently. This distributes the best goods and technologies around the world.

Countries change their comparative advantage as they develop, generally moving from an agrarian economy to manufacturing, then to light industry, and finally to a service economy. This economic "ladder" is how the lower-cost-producer benefits exporters and consumers. A service economy, like that of the United States, wastes resources propping up its agricultural sector because it is cheaper to import agricultural goods from developing economies.

Trade creates jobs and enhances the quality of existing jobs. Many workers in developing countries need and want work. Multinational corporations, on balance, pay more, have better working conditions, and are more likely to remain in business than local firms.[14] Given time, the gap between wages and working conditions in developing and developed countries will shrink, and competition will promote best practices in both.

Technology transfer improves productivity in developing countries. Plus, the number of jobs outsourced is small. Most outsourced jobs go to other developed countries, not to developing ones. Nearly half of corporate America's overseas workforce is employed in Europe, rather than low-wage countries like Mexico, China or India.[15] The transatlantic economy generates roughly $2.5 trillion in commercial sales every year and employs over twelve million workers in mutually "insourced" jobs—jobs that pay good wages, have high labor and environmental standards, in a largely barrier-free market.

Con:

Developed countries' workers are said to be losing their jobs to less-developed countries primarily because of wage differences. The latter's workers are thought to be exploited; paid low wages, in poor working conditions. Large corporations are the big winners. They profit from the low wages and lax environmental standards, and then leave. The wealth gap widens.

Globalization also causes the marketplace to become homogenized, destroying unique cultural differences.[16] Conversely, some markets are controlled by a market-dominant minority, which profits at the expense of "indigenous" majorities. The Chinese are a market-dominant minority throughout Asia. Whites are a market-dominant minority in South Africa and much of Latin America. Globalization concentrates wealth in their hands and marginalizes the impoverished majority, creating hostility and sometimes bloodshed.[17]

The ease of intellectual property theft across borders and the lack of international laws to prevent it decreases the incentive of inventors to invent; and discourages technological transfer. But, until developing nations can develop competitive industries of their own, they might be forgiven for being protectionist.[18]

4. Capital and Investment

Capital is an essential building block of economic development, job creation, and trade. But, like other resources, capital in developing economies is often limited. And, like other resources, capital is not uniformly distributed, nor necessarily attracted where it is most needed.

Since developing countries have a small tax base and many pressing social needs, public money to build a stable, growing economy is often insufficient. Hence, foreign direct investment (FDI) is needed to promote development. A stable infrastructure helps to attract business and withstand economic shock, whereas an unstable, non-transparent, ill-regulated economy, or corrupt government, does not attract FDI.[19]

Pro:

For many multinational firms, FDI has become a substitute for trade. For example, a German car manufacturer will produce in America rather than export to America. In 2002, European firms' dollar sales from their American subsidiaries were four times larger than their exports to America.[20] When investment and trade are taken together, one sees that U.S. economic engagement remains overwhelmingly focused on Europe.[21]

However, less-developed countries are attracting more FDI, including from one another.[22] Most important, the amount of private money that multinational corporations invest in the world is far greater than the public money from sources such as the International Monetary Fund (IMF), the World Bank and national foreign aid packages. One Washington D.C. think tank estimates that currency trading alone amounts to $3 trillion a day.[23]

We have now undertaken to forgive the massive debt of the world's poorest nations, both because they cannot reasonably repay it, and debt service siphons off capital needed to improve their economies. However, this encourages reckless borrowing and lax monetary practices. Conversely, corporations that invest in developing countries have a stake in improving of the economy they invest in.[24]

Con:

Technological advances such as the internet allow money to move around faster than ever before. The advent of capital mobility makes investment, particularly private investment, very powerful. But venture capital can lead to unwanted speculative bubbles.

The increased mobility of private capital, or "hot" money, and the ease of cross-border monetary investing can produce instability due to speculation, leading to booms and busts, particularly in poorly-regulated, developing economies.[25] Indeed, the greatest strains on the world economic system have not come from trade disturbances, but rather from speculation and volatile capital flows. Although all had different origins, the three most recent economic crises—Latin America in 1982, the Mexican peso crisis of 1994–1995, and the Asian meltdown in 1997–1998 —had in common excessive overseas borrowing, often to finance unsustainable property and investment booms; followed by equally reactionary disinvestment as lenders lost confidence. This produced an unwarranted domino effect, as the fall from favor of one emerging country drew down more-stable ones.[26] Speculation destabilizes economies, and instability makes them unattractive for future investment. The net effect is to increase the maldistribution of capital resources.[27]

So, as economic and financial interdependence increases, developments in one area will increasingly affect economies far removed. Global business cycles could become self-reinforcing, and booms and recessions more severe.[28]

To attract investment, emerging economies have to agree to absorb some corporate costs, offer subsidies, and sometimes relax environmental and employment standards, something they can ill-afford to do. Only the corporations end up more profitable.

Finally, excess capital, large capital flows, and disparate regulatory systems can lead to corruption, cronyism, and money laundering, especially if there is a lack of transparency.[29]

5. Labor and Health

Pro:

Globalization can improve conditions in developing countries by creating jobs, raising wages, and enhancing working conditions. This is especially true of emerging economies where jobs, foreign investment, and technology transfer are needed. Economic growth leads to a larger, wealthier tax base, resulting in improved skills training, reduced unemployment, improved health and education, and lower birth rate and mortality. While anti-globalizers claim that multinational firms exploit the poor in low-wage countries, there is growing evidence that they actually improve economic prospects there.[30]

Steady job creation and stability eventually lead workers to organize. Labor organizations generally improve working conditions and raise wages, and, in due course, improve the human condition. As economies improve, so do peace, security, and human rights. Economic freedom and political freedom are closely linked.

Inexpensive labor reduces production costs. This keeps companies competitive, raises profits and reduces prices as firms pass their lower costs on to customers. Low prices increase demand and keep inflation in check. Companies spend their profits to improve existing products or introduce new ones. Customers buy more, which stimulates innovation and creates new jobs to replace those that are not in demand or that have migrated. This calculation requires that the U.S. economy create new jobs of course. But America's labor market is a miracle of flexibility: it turns over nearly 30 million jobs every year.[31]

Only 3.4 million American jobs are expected to be outsourced by 2015. Although this number seems large, it implies an annual outflow of only 0.5% of the jobs in the affected industries.[32] Not only are some jobs recovered, but new and better jobs are created. If American workers are truly displaced due to foreign trade, wage insurance and skills retraining are preferable to protectionism.[33]

Con:

In their zeal for economic growth, developing nations' political leaders and multinational corporations often turn a blind eye to human rights abuses and squalid working conditions, especially for women and children. Workers are pitted against one another in a struggle for survival that pushes wages downward. Any corporation with a social conscience that refuses to engage in these practices must absorb higher production costs. So it is said that globalization may favor the producer and consumer, but *not* the worker.

The U.S. job market, somewhere between 130 million and 140 million workers depending on your source, changes constantly. The Bureau of Labor Statistics divides it into nineteen major industry groups. From 1992–2002, twelve showed employment gains. But large losses hit other sectors. Farm workers went from 2.1 percent of the total to 1.6 percent and manufacturing workers from 13.6 percent to 10.6 percent. Big gains occurred among education, health, and professional and business service workers, however. And by 2012, the number of computer programmers and software engineers is expected to grow from 1.2 million to 1.6 million.

An expanding economy constantly demands new skills, but this is of little solace to workers whose jobs are eliminated or transferred. In 1870, almost half of the U.S. work force was in farming.[34] 300 million Chinese workers shifted from farms to factories in the past 25 years and many more are expected to do so by 2020.[35]

Ill health and starvation strain public resources in less-developed countries. Unless addressed, disease can spill over and threaten the developed world.[36] The UN, through its Millennium Development program, is attempting to halve extreme poverty by 2015 by changing trade policy and increasing official development assistance and technology transfer to the world's poorest people. The program aims to provide universal access to primary education; promote the equality of women; reduce infant and maternal mortality; halt and reverse the spread of HIV/AIDS and malaria; and achieve environmental sustainability through a global partnership for development.[37] Although these goals are laudable, they may be just good intentions, since the UN does not presently have the means to achieve them.

Progress is highly correlated to economic growth. East and Southeast Asia is on track to meet many of the goals by 2015. At the other extreme, the economies of sub-Saharan Africa are not likely to meet a single one. Nearly five million people were newly infected with AIDS in 2003, and in Eastern Europe and South Asia the disease is spreading more rapidly than before.[38] Lack of inertia and the selectivity of global trade is marginalizing many of the poorest people in the world.

6. The Environment

Pro:

Globalization helps protect and restore the environment by producing enough national wealth to undertake environmental improvements. Conversely, developing nations do more to pollute the environment, but less to clean it up, than developed nations that have both the will and the capacity to address environmental problems. Pollution growth is far more rapid in developing economies. Hence globalization helps to increase public and government awareness of and commitment to resist/correct environmental degradation. Developing countries with inefficient markets do more to despoil the environment than developed countries with better resources.[39] Furthermore, large multinational corporations are under great pressure from consumers and green organizations to be environmentally responsible.[40]

Con:

Developed nations, however, are the greatest net polluters by far. And their multinational corporations sometimes seek out places where environmental standards are lax or ill-enforced, thereby exploiting local environments in the quest for corporate profit while contributing to worldwide global warming.

Globalization also raises sustainability concerns. Economic growth may exceed the environment's ability to absorb our wastes, resulting in a loss of topsoil, fisheries, forests and potable water. If industrial processes exceed the atmosphere's ability to cope with harmful gas emissions, we risk further depletion of the ozone layer and accelerated climate change.

Our planetary resources are not being used to meet the needs of all people, maintain biodiversity, and assure the availability of resources for future generations. If economic growth exceeds the capacity to accommodate it, it is unsustainable.[41]

7. Capacity Building

Pro:

In the past, as one region sprinted ahead another often stumbled. Today, rapid economic growth is more evenly spread across nations and regions.[42] Recently, emerging economies have been outpacing developed ones. Since 2000, emerging economies have grown at two and one-half times the rate of the developed world. Developing economies' infrastructure has improved as well, which augments and sustains growth. Structural reforms and sounder macroeconomic policies help to lock in those gains.[43]

Less-developed countries that integrate into the world economy most speedily enjoy faster, more stable growth. Thus globalization helps emerging economies by accelerating development and improving living standards for millions of people.

Although speculative bubbles can result, recovery is often rapid. And the recovery generally brings better regulation and more openness. In a few short decades, the Asian economic miracle has lifted hundreds of millions of persons out of abject poverty by a combination of hard work, good policies and the benefits of open trade.[44] Indeed, emerging economies have begun to assert themselves on the world stage.[45]

The cultures of developing countries should find their niche in the international marketplace rather than invariably "westernizing." For all the belief that globalization leads to homogeneity, facts indicate that firms competing in global markets are often driven to differentiate.[46] Western Europeans, for example, have not become passive victims of America's "cultural imperialism." Instead, they have adapted American culture to their own needs, tastes, and traditions.[47] Other economies are likely to do the same.

Con:

Globalization causes developing countries to loose sovereignty in that they must conform to developed nations' standards and practices, including those of the IMF and the World Bank. Those two organizations, and the WTO, are said to be puppets of developed countries. This leads to homogenization and "western" conformity, forcing developing countries to change too much and too fast. Developing countries should be allowed to set their own priorities and policies, even if developed economies, the IMF and World Bank (or, for that matter, Greenpeace and Oxfam) disapprove.[48]

As they liberalize, some developing countries overstretch their government infrastructure, with disastrous results. In Russia, for example, instant capitalism failed. There was no adequate regulatory system to support it. As a result, the middle class was devastated by crony and mafia capitalism.[49]

Developing countries get too much advice from experts abroad. The gospel of market economy may not apply everywhere.[50]

8. Peace and Security

Pro:

Globalization helps promote democracy around the world. Indeed, the number of democratic governments has almost doubled in the past decade. But, to be successful, global trade requires rules and their reliable enforcement. Closed, authoritarian regimes do not attract foreign direct investment and technology transfer, so they fall behind. Contrast, for example, the conditions in North Korea and Cuba with emerging economies such as South Korea and Taiwan. Stable governments and economies are more prosperous. There is less prospect of warfare, famine or disease.[51]

Twenty years ago, democracy had barely taken root anywhere in East Asia. Now, with the exception of China, newly-planted democracies are thriving in the region. The most encouraging thing about Asia's democratic spring is the extent to which people are delivering tough messages to their rulers to punish corruption and petty politicking. Even if some of the democracies are not making good choices, they are better off than undemocratic North Korea or Myanmar.[52]

Private influence is not a reliable substitute for state power, however. Most persons would prefer national legislation to control the trade process.[53]

Con:

Democracy and capitalist structures do not automatically provide peace and security. It takes time to move from an authoritarian regime to a democracy. The latter requires the rule of law, bipartisan institutions, and mechanisms to deal with cultural differences. It is not appropriate for free market superpowers to thrust their ideas on emerging economies with different perspectives and traditions.

The aggressive exportation of free market democracy can breed ethnic hatred and global instability. In such cases, free market democracy and globalization make the situation less rather than more stable.[54]

C. Conclusion

It should be evident from the foregoing that globalization is not a one-way street. It has both virtues and vices.

The globalization process involves different political and market structures; it raises questions about how much power nations should cede to international institutions and the marketplace; and the extent to which efficiency and productivity should dominate other important political and social concerns. The debate needs to recognize the trade-offs between growth and sustainability.[55] Past industrial epochs, such as the industrial revolution and the union movement, have had their excessive and exploitive side effects. Today we are better informed and more sensitive, but the issues are more numerous and complex. As a rule, countries should pursue their own goals in ways that disrupt trade least.[56]

The question is: how do we maximize the benefits of globalization while minimizing its liabilities? Globalization has resulted in a quality of life unimaginable one hundred years ago. Continued improvements are quite likely. But now might they be managed, and what alternatives are there?

Chapter III

Alternatives to Globalization

A. Introduction

If the process of globalization is so complex and has so many virtues and vices, there must be alternatives, and indeed there are. But I doubt that some of them (for example, ring fencing) could ever succeed. And others (bilateralism) could be no more than another step, albeit modest, in the globalization process. For globalization is such a powerful force that it would be quite difficult to stop. However, alternatives should be explored for whatever they may be worth.

B. Refusal to Participate; The Ring Fence

The first alternative that comes to mind is a simple refusal to play the globalization game; to decline to deal with other traders and "ring fence" one's domestic economy.

There is probably no economy in the history of the world more capable of this than the United States of America. We have considerable natural and renewable resources, as well as significant technology and a deep talent pool. And yet we have grown dependent on raw materials and products that we either do not have, or have in insufficient abundance. Hence, it is more efficient to import them than to produce them ourselves or do without. Could we ring-fence our borders and economy and still enjoy an adequate lifestyle? Perhaps we could, but it would entail numerous sacrifices; sacrifices that many Americans—given today's consumption demands—seem disinclined to make. While it would decrease our negative balance of trade, it would bring few benefits, since trade is one of the fastest growing areas of our economy.[1]

Besides, an increasing amount of our purchasing power is due to our exports to foreign countries. If we ring-fence our economy, other nations would probably do likewise, and we would lose not just a source of resources and goods, but a source of income as well.[2] The net effect of ring fencing then would appear to be a significant reduction in the lifestyle Americans now enjoy, as well as a loss of income and influence in the modern world. Even to suggest retrenchment weakens America's traditional role as an advocate and beneficiary of free trade.[3] Refusing to play the globalization game, even if one could, is not a very attractive option. Indeed, if closed economics were productive economies, Cuba and North Korea would be among the best; which they surely are not.

C. Bilateral Trade Arrangements

A better alternative than ring fencing is a bilateral trade arrangement. These are often pursued when no better, broader multilateral negotiations are making progress; although both can be pursued simultaneously.

Bilateral trade agreements are easier to negotiate than multilateral ones because they involve only two parties, and may involve traders with very similar economies (a so-called "north-north" trade treaty). They may even involve a single item of trade. (A good example would be mutual-recognition agreements (MRA's) between the United States and European Union, involving veterinary tests and marine equipment.[4]

The problem with bilateral agreements is that they exclude all but the signatory parties, and therefore run the risk of distorting trade by giving preferential treatment to one trader and interfering with multi-national trade negotiations. This is particularly so if the treaties are between developed economies (north-north), although we are beginning to see more north-south bilaterals,[5] and even south-south bilaterals (between developing economies). The latter two can help to ease less-developed economies into the trading mainstream.[6] However, it would be unusual for a bilateral trade agreement to include a dispute-resolution and enforcement mechanism, so their terms are binding only to the extent that they are honored by the two signatories.

If such agreements are honored, they involve a modest loss of sovereignty, but not much; particularly if they are temporary substitutes for multinational agreements and are unenforceable. They advance global trade somewhat, but not nearly as much as regional or multinational agreements. Likewise, their impact on world trade is extremely limited, unless the bilateral agreement is between major traders like the U.S. and EU, in which case the pact can become a prototype for a multinational agreement. Thus, there are relatively innocent bilateral agreements and others that can have much wider trade implications.[7] However, it is easier to address entirely new trade sectors (labor, the environment) initially in bilateral agreements, and later extend them to multiparty agreements.[8]

D. Regional Trade Arrangements

Another alternative to globalization is a regional trade arrangement. They vary considerably, depending upon the region and number of traders involved, and how tightly they are bound by their agreements. The preeminent regional system is, of course, the European Community (or European Union, EU). It comprises twenty-seven states (and may enlarge further), overseen by "supranational" institutions including an executive (the Commission), a legislative branch (the Council of Ministers and European Parliament), and judiciary (the European Court of Justice and Court of First Instance). No other regional trading bloc is quite so comprehensive or sophisticated.[9]

Among numerous other regional compacts that might be listed are the North American Free Trade Agreements (NAFTA) binding the U.S., Mexico, and Canada in a reasonably-close free trade relationship.[10] With luck, this agreement may eventually, extend to most of the rest of Latin America (a Free Trade Agreement of the Americas, FTAA), but only if traditional north-south trade issues can be resolved.[11] The NAFTA and proposed FTAA are weaker arrangements than that of the European Union, but both, despite their size and diversity, seem more concrete than some, such as the new Central American Free Trade Agreement (CAFTA) and the Association of South East Asian Nations (ASEAN), because the latter do not have the size, economic clout, or interconnectivity of more established trading blocs.[12]

Large, well-connected regional trading blocs like the EU and NAFTA partners, on the other hand, can wield tremendous influence in multinational trade negotiations. But they often disagree among themselves, and do not want to be perceived as running roughshod over less-developed traders trying to get a foothold on the trade ladder. Thus, large, influential trade blocs can aid but also retard other emerging trading blocs. Among the former we could list the Asian Pacific Economic Cooperation (APEC) forum, while the Mercosur and the Andean group in South America, seem marginalized by NAFTA and the FTAA.[13]

Many smaller, regional arrangements exist or will be launched, I feel certain. But their influence on world trade, at least in the short run, will be felt only when they compete, or advance their regional groups' agenda in multinational negotiations.[14]

Indeed, it is common for regional trade negotiations to be at their lowest ebb when bilateral or multilateral negotiations hold out greater hope for progress, and then pick up if the other two initiatives stall or fail.[15] But strongly held regional positions can also stymie progress in other negotiations.[16] Thus, the advantage of regional blocs, particularly among like economies, is that they can harmonize faster (because they are smaller and generally more cohesive) and have a broader impact on trade than bilateral arrangements. But their liability is that they also have enough influence to interfere with multinational negotiations and agreements. So regional trading blocs—which account for some 60 percent of world trade—can assist in opening and harmonizing that trade, but can also serve as a barrier to globalization insofar as their agenda is purely regional and can exclude others.[17]

However, if regional trading blocs can develop market standards without interfering with or violating multinational standards, then regional solutions can point the way and serve as stepping stones to wider trade pacts. If they cannot, then regional harmony can be a barrier to better economic trade relations.

E. Multilateral Agreements

Agreements among a number of nations, including regional agreements, are of course multilateral agreements. But here I use the term to describe trade agreements among very large numbers of nations, with very diverse economies. Among such agreements we could list the General Agreement on Tariffs and Trade (GATT), the World Trade Organization (WTO), and the United Nations (UN). Because bilateral and regional trade agreements focus somewhat narrowly on the interests of their participants and exclude others, multilateral agreements are to be favored as being more inclusive. But, for that reason, they are often more generic. Their virtues and vices stem from those characteristics.

Because the affected market is so much larger, trade harmonization is expedited by multilateral agreements. They have maximum impact on global trade. They also permit more flexibility in negotiation because, with so many trade issues involved, there is more room for trade-offs and compromise.[18] Finally, at least with respect to the WTO, the agreed terms can be enforced.[19]

But, because of the number of states and multitude of issues involved, it takes many years to reconcile diverse interests and conclude a global round of trade talks. This also slows enforcement, which is sensitive to diverse interpretations of so broad a treaty. Indeed, it is my impression that the decisions of WTO dispute panels (chiefly legal) are often diluted on appeal. Appeal decisions are more political, precisely because the glue that holds the agreement together must insure balanced outcomes. Since not all traders benefit equally from the treaty and final agreement is by "consensus," less developed traders (a majority of the WTO's 153 members) retain a certain amount of leverage.[20]

Nonetheless, since the beginning of GATT rounds in 1947 (eight rounds have been concluded to date), the trade areas covered have steadily expanded, as well as the number of participating states.[21] And a number of additional trade issues, the so-call "Singapore issues,"[22] are already on the threshold of inclusion.

Until recently, global trade negotiations have been dominated by developed economies. But developing countries are more numerous signatories to the GATT, and have asserted themselves in the latest (Doha) round of trade negotiations. The most forceful group, the so-called G-20, led by Brazil, China and India, torpedoed the WTO ministerial in Cancun (2003).[23] The result was a renewed concern to involve less-developed and least-developed countries (LDC's) in the globalization process, as pledged in the Doha Development agenda (DDA) launched in late 2001 in Doha, Qatar.[24] The round was due to end in 2006, but has staggered on without agreement.

Given that LDC's proceed from a weak negotiating position, and there is considerable resistance from large agricultural producers (chiefly the European Union, United States, and Japan) to giving up their subsidy and export support programs, progress in the negotiations has been grudging.[25] And yet major concessions by both the U.S. and the EU have kept the negotiations alive. Hence, it is still within the capacity of major traders (the U.S.) or regional blocs (the EU) to influence the pace and outcome of multinational negotiations.[26] But, developing countries have solidified their negotiation position and improved their bargaining skills as well.[27] And why not? They comprise well over one-half of WTO members and WTO members account for 96 percent of world trade.[28] In addition, developing countries are certain to get some concessions from the round—called "special and differential" (S&D) treatment—that allows them to delay meeting certain obligations under the GATT treaty.[29] Developing nations also need some relief from agricultural tariffs, quotas and supports. Agriculture is the most protected commercial sector in the world, but absolutely fundamental to the economic growth of emerging economies. For example, full liberalization of agriculture would raise Brazil's real net farm income by 46 percent and GDP by $3.6 billion a year.[30]

So, despite the great complexity and long gestation period of multilateral trade agreements, they are much more harmonizing than most bilateral and regional agreements *and* they are *enforceable*. Most trade treaties are little more than gentlemen's agreements. The WTO, EU, and NAFTA offer better enforcement, which is why countries are queuing to join.[31]

Among multinational organizations, the World Trade Organization is the preeminent agency overseeing and administering the rules of global trade.[32] It assists in the smooth flow of trade among nations, arbitrates disputes among governments, and organizes further trade negotiations. It has made an excellent start on reaching its primary goals: developing a durable multilateral trading system; reducing tariffs, and other barriers to trade; eliminating discrimination in trade relationships; and expanding trade in goods and services. It is being challenged, however, to meet more difficult secondary goals: extending differential and preferential treatment to developing nations; promoting full employment; raising living standards; achieving sustainable development; and preserving the environment.[33] It is the WTO's alleged failure to meet these secondary goals, along with its leviathan nature, that foster criticism and even hostility.

Moreover, there is a belief—legitimate I think—that states are sacrificing some national prerogative to the globalization process.[34] Undoubtedly they are. But, if a state is to grow its economy in a global world, do they have options other than to participate? Is something akin to *de facto* global governance,[35] with a rich and diverse set of participants, worse than a set of protected, warring national entities? Rather than jealously guarding one's own economy, if indeed one could, isn't it better to participate in collaborative undertakings that could produce advantages for all?

All trade negotiations are good, even when they fail, because ultimately they scupper age-old suspicions and antipathies that have skewed and slowed economic growth for years. And conflicts between national laws, even if non-protectionist, limit export/import growth.

F. Conclusion

Trade negotiations move in fits and starts. History has proved that. When economies are robust, negotiations are easier. But negotiations probably are more necessary when economies are stagnant or in recession, and there is a need to restructure. Either way, I worry most when no trade negotiations are going on at any level, for that suggests that economic growth is slowing or has stopped, and that bodes ill for almost everyone. As I have suggested, a closed economy cannot be self-sustaining in our modern world.

Admittedly, not all trade agreements benefit all traders equally[36], just as natural calamities (floods, earthquakes and drought) do not strike all nations equally. But trade negotiations offer a way around these disproportionalities, more than they create them.

You would not get this impression from the news media, however. It is their persistent reporting about winners and losers that reinforces confrontation in trade negotiations, without acknowledging that there can be "balanced co-existence." The media also tends to focus on trade disputes much more than trade successes, although the latter clearly outnumber the former.[37] Bad news simply sells better than good news. But this skewed reporting encourages an "us versus them" mindset. Some market protection may be necessary, and defensible, to protect a vulnerable market sector and allow it to restructure. But a permanently closed economy is not good for itself or fellow economies.

Yes, trade negations can be frustrating. The aims can be ambitious (as with the launch of the Doha Development Agenda). The negotiations are often self-centered and conservative.[38] Moreover, the process can be exhausting, especially for developing economies with limited resources. And the payoffs can be subtle and long-deferred.[39] Major traders may stimulate negotiations,[40] but they can also slow them. Nevertheless, developing economies (notably the Group of 20) have gained significant leverage in trade negotiations following the failure of the Cancun ministerial. That leverage is limited, however, by the net influence these traders have in relation to the whole of world trade. In the end, they probably will have to settle for something less than they hope for. But half a loaf is better than none, and their prospects can only improve as they integrate further into the trading world.[41]

Multinational businesses also are more involved in international trade negotiations than ever before. Witness the Trans-Atlantic Business Dialogue (TABD) and APEC Business Advisory Council (ABAC). The roles of public and private actors in international trade negotiations are becoming increasingly blurred. The creation of a *consumer* advisory group in transatlantic trade dialogue is another example. As is the increasing attention paid to non-governmental organizations in trade deliberations.[42]

The on-going discussion about trade regulation and economic inequities attests to the fact that a growing world economy can (and should) provide for all participants. In that context, ring-fencing is simply not an option, as the rest of this book attempts to show.

Chapter IV

Maldistribution of Resources

Just about everyone knows that resources are not uniformly distributed among the nations of the world. But few people think about the consequences of that fact. Although numerous resources could be considered, I will concentrate on just four of the most important ones: natural resources; human resources; capital; and know-how. Of these, some are renewable (forest, fish stocks) and some are not (oil). Some are mobile (labor and capital) and some are not (climate).

The most obvious maldistribution involves natural resources. This is a geographic phenomenon. Some nations have plentiful water, oil, minerals, temperate climates, fertile soils, navigable waterways, and so forth, and some do not. But most of these resources are immobile. Their maldistribution is immutable. Hence, there are unavoidable inequities among states.

But the consequences of immutable maldistribution can be modulated by the aggregation of mobile resources. For example, Switzerland has a highly developed economy, despite the fact that it is landlocked, mountainous, and has few natural resources. It has exploited other resources such as skilled labor, capital, and technical know-how. These resources are more mobile and therefore could be more evenly distributed if the international economic system facilitated it. But even these resources will not travel to locations where they are not well-received.

This means that man-made conditions such as a stable government, a transparent market, and adequate communications and transportation infrastructure must exist in order to encourage and protect the transfer of mobile resources. Countries with unstable governments and primitive infrastructure are neither able to develop their own resources or attract foreign resources. Scarcity coupled with insecurity virtually doom these nations to a perpetual cycle of poverty and conflict. Sub-Saharan Africa is caught in this Catch-22; lacking natural resources or the ability to access them, but unable to attract foreign resources.

Of course, no country—including the U.S.—has all the resources it needs. Rather, countries export what they have in abundance, and import what they need. But, when resources become limited, this process breaks down. Instead of export/import trade, there is fierce competition for inadequate resources that often manifests itself in religious or ethnic conflict. We have seen this repeatedly in Africa and the Middle East. But it is also evident in Asia and South America.

Personally, I think these conflicts are less about ethnic or religious differences than a scarcity of resources. The former rationales are used to justify hoarding by and for one group or another, until it is overthrown and the process is reversed. The failure of developed nations to intervene in these conflicts generally compromises even more resources (destruction and rebuilding), until they finally do so or the conflict is resolved.

Even those less developed countries that have resources can dissipate them; through warfare, corruption and cronyism (e.g. conflict diamonds).[1] These countries also often seek to protect their fragile economies by excluding foreign products, which further dampens the prospect that mobile resources (capital, technology) will be sent there.

I find it hard to imagine that a people would willingly suffer instability, disease, starvation, and even death due to a lack of resources and their own immobility, without attempting escape. One would expect that at least more able or ambitious persons would migrate instead; and many do.[2] This presents economic problems for both the abandoned and the receiving state. But we are learning that developed countries can use economic migrants to fill low-wage jobs and compensate for a low birth rate. So, rigid immigration policies may eventually become a thing of the past.[3]

However, many persons are too uneducated, too unskilled or too immobile, to escape their fate. And a lack of prospects can be terribly enervating.[4] Persistent inequality and a lack of opportunity and resources—or even the presence of resources, badly managed—can hamper economic growth, and prevent the least developed countries from meaningful participation in the global economy.[5] This is so despite international efforts such as the UN's Millennium Project, or national legislation (e.g. the U.S. African Growth and Opportunity Act)[6] that try to promote the inclusion of less-developed countries in the global marketplace.

So if people cannot be transported to places where resources and opportunities can be found, can resources be brought to them? To a certain extent, this already happens. Crisis aid is most common (e.g. the Afghan earthquake or Indonesian tsunami). But this is not *development* aid, it is restoration aid. Foreign aid that will, at best, leave the affected county as well off as (but no better off than) it was before the crisis.

As regards development aid, the wealth gap, and therefore inequality, between rich and poor countries is said to be increasing.[7] And developed countries' promises to help developing countries (e.g. the Doha Development Round of GATT) have not been fulfilled and/or their impact on overcoming poverty was overestimated.[8] Indeed, it is probably well beyond the resources of international organizations like the UN, and possibly even the collaborative efforts of the wealthy nations of the world—unless they were to short-change their own populations—to close this gap. But, properly managed, the growth of international trade may help reduce it.

Actually, the wealth gap between developed and developing nations is narrowing; chiefly because the economies of the two most populous developing countries in the world—China and India—are growing very rapidly. Rapid economic growth is not limited to these two nations, however.[9] So we can expect that improved trade relations could advance other developing countries as well.

If labor is relatively immobile and natural resources are scarce, mobile resources like capital and technology can help fill the gap. However, maldistribution is exacerbated by market exclusion; quotas and high tariff barriers placed on developing country exports by developed nations[10], and developing countries' protection of their own markets.[11] These "export only" economies won't grow much if they do not, or cannot, participate in the world economy. But because they are so export dependent, they are acutely sensitive to economic downturns in developed economies.[12]

Consequently, many less developed countries are held back, not just because they lack resources and have restricted access to post-industrial countries' markets, but because they have not adjusted to globalization. Those that have are growing their economies rapidly.[13]

So, in the absence of natural resources, it may be possible to help emerging economies modernize by exploiting highly-mobile resources. The rapid development of e-commerce in India and China did not require vast natural resources. But it does require political stability, and an able and committed workforce. The adoption of other modern technologies—such as genetically-modified seed to increase crop hardiness and yield—has also helped economies in Asia, Latin America, and Africa to grow.[14] These seem to be within the reach of almost any developing economy, particularly with the help of developed economies and international organizations. Without these, however, technically inert economies are likely to be left far behind.[15]

What is necessary to turn this resource disparity around? Obviously, developed countries need to do their share by opening their markets to less developed countries and by assisting in their technological development. But developing countries must do their share too; chiefly by becoming more open to bilateral trade and by developing institutions that allow capitalism to work.[16] Finally, there is the prospect that some poor countries, rich in biological resources (South America) or underdeveloped mineral resources (Africa), will find constructive ways to develop these resources.[17]

As the gap closes between developed and developing nations, tensions are reduced.[18] Everyone benefits from efficient use of resources, and suffers from their dissipation and misuse. Inequalities will continue to exist, of course. After all, arithmetically, no more than one-half of anything can be "above average." And, as long as nation states are the principal decision makers, their leaders will be under constituent pressure to favor national over international interests.[19] But as we have seen, inequalities will gradually be reduced thanks to global trade.

Chapter V

Differences in Political and Market Structure

Another huge difference between and among trading nations lies in their economic philosophies and market structures. The growth of transnational business has illuminated as never before the problems created by discordant state policies and regulatory schemes. Evolving as independent economies, it was only natural that each nation would adopt a market philosophy and regulatory system that would advance domestic goals and possibly deter foreign competitors. (For example, Article 82 of the European Community Treaty makes actionable an "abuse" by a company in a "dominant position" within its industry. This may not threaten many European companies, since most are small and possibly meant to stay that way. But it could threaten large U.S. corporations such as Microsoft).

The fact that these differences exist should surprise no one. They merely codify local views, often historically or culturally based, about the appropriate relationship between government, business, and the citizen/consumer. But in a global market local practices can seriously distort, consciously or unconsciously, marketplace efficiency.

Local policies and standards may reflect legitimate social and economic concerns, of course, such as consumer protection or the need to raise government resources. But they can be used as devices to protect local markets from foreign competition as well. (The European Union moratorium on genetically-modified organisms[1] would seem to have a foot in both camps.) If such constraints are brief and objectively justified—for example to allow an economy to adjust to an unexpected, external shock—then little harm is done and some good may come of it. But if foreign products are routinely excluded simply because they are different, then the consumer is denied access to alternative products and domestic products are not tested competitively. Neither producer nor consumer wins. The market goal of offering the best product at the lowest price is frustrated. To be certain, there are other objectives to be taken into consideration, such as environmental protection and taking care of the less-able. But these are objectively-supportable and, if applied to foreign and domestic goods alike, are reasonable restraints on the marketplace.

Of course, not every world economy could survive being instantly opened to foreign competition. Some are too fragile; too isolated. The shock would be too great. But for healthy developing economies to insulate themselves from foreign competition, except for short periods and for compelling reasons, virtually assures that their economy will not grow and remain competitive. For developing economies to unnecessarily protect themselves from market forces simply perpetuates their weakness and does nothing to accelerate their transition to healthy market economies. It has been shown time and again that countries that are slowest to adjust to market conditions, or reject them altogether, grow most slowly; whereas those that liberalize their economies grow more quickly.[2]

There is no completely free market, of course. Even the freest (possibly the United States) has numerous regulations; covering consumer and environmental protection, product safety, and so forth. It isn't the total lack of regulation that determines an efficient market, but limiting regulations to an optimal level.[3] There are degrees of openness (market liberalization) and consequences that flow from each. For example, suffocating state labor regulations and the incompletion of the common market have prevented the European Union from realizing its ambitious Lisbon growth initiative.[4]

In a previous book, I suggested four different economic models: capitalism; macro-socialism; micro-socialism; and communism.[5] I observed that each reflected a different relationship between the state, business and the citizen/consumer,[6] based to an extent on historical and cultural traits.

Of course, there are many more variations than just these four. And the differences are probably less stark than I portrayed them to be (for analytical purposes). Indeed, there is some doubt the latter two exist today, at least to the same degree that they did when that book was published in 2000.

The type of capitalism the United States practices, which I sometimes call "cowboy capitalism," thrived from the late 1980s until at least late 2007. During that period, the U.S. gross domestic product (GDP) grew 72 percent, a "rate [that] out-stripped ... virtually every other advanced country." Payroll jobs increased 31 percent, and business productivity rose 50 percent. But American capitalism has its downside as well. There were two recessions, albeit brief, and we are now facing a third. There was a dot-com collapse. Americans' personal-savings rate has fallen from 11 percent of disposable income to zero; trade deficits have ballooned; and sub-prime lending burst the housing bubble.[7] Although the U.S. outpaced most other developed nation's growth in 2005,[8] its *laissez-faire* style of capitalism encourages entrepreneurship that can lead to serious excesses such as junk bonds and the Enron debacle.[9] Cowboy capitalism can boom; but it can also bust. It is not for everyone.[10]

An alternative to the American approach is what I call the macro-socialistic approach of the European Union (EU). It is typified by generally slower growth,[11] but with a much wider social safety net. The problem is that slow economic growth may not support the social programs, so a shift toward capitalism and entrepreneurship is needed. The EU's Lisbon Agenda, aimed at making the EU the world's most competitive "knowledge-based economy" by 2010, is not only likely to miss its target, it is virtually impossible without a substantial shift toward capitalism, away from its overburdened social system.[12] The EU also suffers from the fact that its common Market is still incomplete, and is hostage to residual nationalism.[13]

Another aspect of the EU that bears watching is its enlargement. The ten new Member States that joined in 2004 are much more inclined to capitalism than the EU's prior (Western European) fifteen states, and other new entrants are likely to feel likewise.[14] Thus, while it is true to say that the U.S. is becoming more socialistic; the EU is gradually becoming more capitalistic. Nonetheless, I think the inclination toward market protection in the EU, the so called "fortress Europe," will die hard.[15]

Then there is Japan and its Asian look-alikes. I call these micro-managed export economies, in which government and business often collaborate to produce maximum economic outcomes. It wasn't long ago that Japan was lionized as a highly-efficient economy.[16] Many smaller Asian economies, including the so-called "little tigers" — Hong Kong, Singapore, South Korea, and Taiwan — profited from Japan's import-resistant, export-oriented model. But, of course, with increasing globalization, these economies could no longer sustain their high level of domestic control, and they suffered severe downturns.[17] As I put it: For lack of periodic adjustments to a competitive marketplace, they suffered one *big* adjustment. Their economies have emerged from that experience stronger, albeit less micro-managed. Japan, after more than a decade of recession or near-recession, is more privatized and competitive. It is less bureaucratic and more open, with better growth prospects. Its Asian look-alikes turned the corner even sooner.[18] So, reclusive, hierarchical, Asian economies also seem to be moving towards a capitalistic model, albeit cautiously.[19]

The last broadly-described economic model is communism, although it can hardly be considered a factor in today's globalized world. Communism (with a capital "C"), as practiced in Russia and China, has proved an abject failure.

Commune-ism (with a small "c") never was successful on a national scale, although it prospers in some communities (the Amish).

The collapse of Russian Communism ushered in a chaotic form of "instant capitalism," that may have been (except for its liberalizing effect) worse economically than Communism. There was no infrastructure to support a capitalistic model so millions of dollars were wasted, and many Russian citizens were less well off. Whereas Communism may be enervating, the excesses of unrestrained capitalism may be worse. Hence Russia has pulled back from its early post-communist economic euphoria to try to get its economy in order.[20]

The other large communist state of consequence is China. It took note of Russia's problems, and opted to put itself on a more gradual, albeit capitalistic, trajectory in 1997.[21] In that respect, China is no longer truly Communist. But the shift has led to an overheated economic boom and economic reports that are too rosy.[22] For China has substantial domestic problems to deal with.[23]

For one thing, the new prosperity is realized primarily in costal cities, and not in western rural regions where two-thirds of Chinese still live on the land. In these regions, there are daily protests against the government; some of them violent.[24] Given China's robust economic growth, the rich/poor gap will almost certainly grow, putting even greater pressure on the Communist system and its leadership.[25] Second, the economy is dominated by state-owned companies, some 300,000 of them in 1997, with the majority losing money. In 2002, the state still accounted for one-half of industrial output, although it had reduced its work force by one-quarter, and it will take time to privatize these dinosaurs.[26]

China's four largest state-owned banks make 61 percent of the country's loans and hold 67 percent of deposits, but are effectively insolvent. This is because they have lent to failing state industries rather than promising private enterprises. Thus, they have starved the latter of capital, while building up a non-performing loan portfolio equal to one-quarter of China's gross domestic product.[27]

Last, but not least, there is the military (the People's Liberation Army or PLA). It controls an estimated 50,000 factories, producing everything from ammunitions to cosmetics. Although some PLA companies depend on the state for orders, their profits average around 15 percent annually, making them a substantial counterweight to the civilian government.[28]

Whereas the Chinese are used to government corruption—high and low—the turn towards capitalism brings new opportunities for exploitation and moral decay.[29] Nonetheless, Chinese leadership seems convinced that the way to a better future is to become more entrepreneurial. But, private entrepreneurs find it difficult to compete in what is still largely a state-run economy.[30]

It is just as difficult, if not more so, for western corporations to profit from the perceived "gold rush" in China. Things aren't always what they seem in a non-transparent, state-managed economy. Foreign multinationals find that doing business is not easy, and often not lucrative. "[N]ot all the dream deals that are signed materialize [and] there is evidence [that] an increasing number turn sour."[31] This risk is reflected in the fact that, of $60.6 billion in foreign direct investment (FDI) in China in 2004, three-quarters came from other Asian states that presumably knew the risks and/or how to deal the "Asian way." Only $8 billion of that amount came from the U.S. and Europe.[32] On the other hand, now that western firms have been allowed to enter a previously closed market, and after a period of adjustment on both sides, a mutually-beneficial economic and political relationship with formerly-communist China should emerge.[33] Indeed, there is already evidence of greater openness and transparency on the part of what was once a very isolated, secretive government.[34] Put differently, China's central government is trying to strike an appropriate balance between capitalism and a state-managed economy; and accepting the fact that the central government no longer has total control.[35] But, whereas Asia's chief advantage is cheap labor, America's is efficiency.[36] So, there is increasingly little left of the Russia/China Communist economic model.

Technically, India is a democracy. But its economy is centrally-managed. However, it is gradually liberalizing and expanding its domestic economy to compete with China and participate in the expansion of global trade. It has more global talent than China, but a government and infrastructure nearly as primitive.[37] Indeed, India's government seems more ambivalent about rapid economic growth than either China or India's growing middle class.[38]

So that leaves Cuba and North Korea as they only true examples of Communism in the modern world. And hardly anyone would argue that they are good economic models, although there is evidence that they too might become more capitalistic.[39]

The truth is that repressive governments and overregulated economies distort the global market at their peril. If they don't attract resources and aren't competitive, they can't succeed in the long run, even—perhaps especially—in isolation.

Does this mean that the Western capitalist economic model has won out against all others? I don't think so. As suggested above, today's economic systems are fairly fluid, and shift to left and right from time to time in an attempt to secure greater economic advantage. Moreover, the snapshot given here does not fully factor in historical, cultural, social or political influences, as well as resistance to change.[40] Although there may be some harmonization of systems around a capitalistic model, I do not expect uniformity any time soon. Even Alexis de Tocqueville, a keen observer of government structures, said he would "regard it as a great misfortune [for governments to take the] same form ... all over the world."[41] Europe and Japan still need to liberalize their economies somewhat.[42] Whereas quasi-capitalistic emerging economies have grown to the point that they are producing about half the world's output measured by purchasing power parity, while not materially interfering with developed economies' growth.[43] Hence, there is evidence that the success of various economic models ebbs and flows with the times.

To illustrate this point, we might look to Latin America today. After years of military rule, dictatorships, and governmental chaos, many Latin American countries turned in the late 1980s and 1990s toward various forms of democratic capitalism; albeit not without some residual chaos and corruption. Significant economic growth ensued, but when it did not meet the high expectations of the working poor and recession hit, there was a reversion to populist/socialist leaders.[44] Whether they will succeed in improving their nations' economies or not, only time will tell. But outside investment is bound to be chilled by the prospect of expropriation and over-regulation.[45] And potentially-beneficial, regional trade agreements (for example, the Free Trade Association of the Americas) will be put on hold; although bilateral agreements between willing partners will continue to be pursued. In the end, I suspect that newly-elected populist leaders will realize that some of their promised social programs are economically unaffordable without the tax income that a robust economy produces. Ultimately, voters may prove more upset with government corruption and mismanagement than with capitalism *per se*, and accept the latter.[46]

In sum, there may be more than one successful form of political and market structure. History, culture, politics, and economic experience all play a role. And different approaches may be tried by the same country at different times or by different countries at the same time. I believe however that, of all these factors, economic success is the most important. That is, if a nation's historical, cultural, or political preference is not feasible economically, they will eventually give way to one that is. All of the models discussed above have proved effective at one time or another. But globalization is causing more and more countries to adopt models that have at least some attributes of capitalism.[47]

That is not to say that the American version of capitalism will triumph. It is too much of a "winner-take-all" system for most countries. Even the U.S. is moving away from it. Americans are working less, while Europeans are working more.[48] But both underregulated and overregulated economies have proved ill-suited to today's trading world. Long-term protections beget the same from one's trading partners, and trade withers. Moreover, the useful discipline of a competitive marketplace is lost. Isolation is a recipe for failure.

Likewise, involving the government as an active market participant has its downside. It opens the door to patronage and corruption, since there is no bottom line that has to be met. And it robs the private sector of incentive and capital. Today, privatizations seem to be on the rise.[49]

Private assets go where the returns are greatest and therefore reward economies that are open and stable; governed by the rule of law. The market punishes by degrees those that are not. In general, emerging economies that are most open grow fastest. This reveals itself in a sort of economic "ladder," in which economic growth increases tax revenues which the government can put to work building infrastructure, improving health and education, leading to greater productivity and yet more growth. The larger the market, the greater its potential for growth.[50]

There is also an increasing public concern about emerging and marginalized economies, and rightly so. Not that the rich/poor gap will ever be closed entirely. That would be both politically and economically implausible. But that does not mean that those at the bottom of the economic pyramid can't have enough to live comfortably.[51] Indeed, the economic success and stability of developed countries is improved if the least developed countries are stable.

Clearly, political and economic models are in a state of flux around the world. I do not want to make too much of their differences. For I believe that those differences have begun to shrink as there is more information about best practices. Although I do not foresee uniformity, I do believe various models are coalescing around forms of quasi-capitalism, with a socialist stripe.[52] That should produce greater participation, greater efficiency, and increased returns in the global marketplace.

Chapter VI

Trade in Goods and Services

A. Introduction

In simple terms, trade is often measured by the amount of goods and services imported and exported by various countries. (A third critical trade component, capital, will be dealt with in the next chapter.)

To the best of my knowledge, every nation—and certainly every developed nation—consumes the majority of the goods and services its economy produces. Nevertheless, the *rate* at which trade in goods and services grows each year far exceeds the growth rate of domestic consumption.[1] The volume of merchandise trade was nineteen times greater in 1999 than it was in 1950, while the world's total output increased only six fold. In about the same period, the proportion of the world economy attributable to exports more than doubled; from 7 to 15 percent. Worldwide, exports amounted to $12.5 trillion in 2005.[2]

Much of this growth was measured in terms of goods, not services. And the United States is predominately a service economy, whereas it is a net importer of goods.[3] Moreover, service exports are significantly harder to measure. Eventually, the U.S. economy should profit from the world's increasing demand for high-tech products and services. As U.S. consumers currently benefit from low-cost, low-tech imports.[4]

In recent years, the United States has been the principal engine of global economic growth; the "consumer of last resort." This cannot (and should not) continue. And, thanks to improving conditions in Europe and Japan, as well as the rapid growth of emerging markets, the consumption burden will be more widely shared.[5] While there is some concern that large emerging economies like China and India will shoulder America aside, they are just as likely to become fertile markets for U.S. exports. Both have huge infrastructure needs; needs that U.S. firms can supply.

Although business conditions in China are difficult for some American companies, and its trade surplus with the U.S. is huge, China's economy will eventually slow; U.S. exports to India, for example, have doubled since 2003.[6] The key is to engage these large, developing states; not to isolate or vilify them. For their own growing pains provide problems enough.[7] Besides, as the economies of these large states grow, wages will rise, domestic consumption will increase, as will respect for intellectual property and the rule of law. The playing field will eventually become more harmonious and balanced.[8]

One must not forget that, whereas the United States is a net importer, it imports chiefly goods, nearly sixty percent of them from its NAFTA partners, the EU 15, and Japan. However, the U.S. is a net exporter of services; the core of the U.S. economy, which are in demand in the aforementioned markets, and also Latin America, Asia and Africa. Although U.S. service exports are equal to only 43 percent of goods volume, they are in positive territory (particularly in the fields of businesses and financial services, education and telecommunications), and are growing considerably faster.[9] Moreover, growth of U.S. service exports could spike if the agricultural logjam in the Doha GATT talks was broken and market access was increased for services.[10]

Even if some U.S. service jobs are offshored, the "impact ... is far [greater] in popular perception than on actual ... employment ... patterns." If "the U.S. [lost] up to 3.5 million jobs due to offshoring by 2015 ... the number of jobs affected [would still be] small...." Isn't it better to compete in a global marketplace than to try to protect one's market, burdening consumers and making that market inefficient and perhaps uncompetitive?[11] In my view, the sooner artificial barriers to trade can be removed, the better it will be for everyone. But, so long as protectionism is driven by national politics and strategic relationships (not economics), there will be barriers to trade.

B. Barriers to Trade

There are millions—perhaps *many* millions—barriers to absolutely free trade. There is not space here to address them all. But the mention of a few of the most important ones will reveal their numerous vices (and occasional virtues).

For many years, tariffs on imported goods were the primary way local economies protected themselves from foreign competition. But this denied all traders the comparative advantage of specialization and raised prices for consumers.[12] Over some eight negotiating rounds through 1993, the General Agreement on Tariffs and Trade (GATT) substantially reduced tariff barriers on manufactured goods from around 40 percent worldwide to less than four percent today. (U.S. tariffs average less than two percent). But they remain high for consumer goods such as clothing and shoes, and are especially high on agricultural products.

Agriculture is by far the most protected and highly-subsidized market sector, still averaging around 40 percent world wide. This is especially devastating for developing economies that specialize in agricultural products and face "effective tariff rates" as much as 30 times higher than those applied to higher-tech exports from wealthy economies such as Japan and the European Union.[13] In 2007, American farm subsidies ran about $17 billion (versus $130 billion in the EU and $50 billion in Japan, in 2005). Most of these subsidies don't go to small farmers, but they place developing agricultural economies at a severe disadvantage in the world market.[14]

The EU grants duty and quota-free access to many agricultural products raised in former member-state colonies (the so-called African, Caribbean and Pacific [APC] countries), while similar products from other developing states face high tariffs and quotas. The Uruguay round of trade negotiations added agriculture to the GATT agenda, but reduction of agricultural tariffs and support has been grudging, wasting tax dollars and costing consumers (especially poor consumers) millions, for they have to pay support prices in an artificially-constrained market.[15] Nonetheless, due to other advantages, some nation's farmers (Brazil) are learning to compete with agri-America.[16]

In addition to setting high tariffs, developed countries pay farm support to supplement farm income and subsidize exports, flooding the market with under-priced farm produce. Not only do less developed agricultural economies have trouble gaining access to developed countries' markets, they must compete with those countries' subsidized agricultural goods in the open market.[17] Leading agricultural exporters, such as Australia, Brazil, and the United States, profess to want all agricultural markets opened. But the European Union and Japan are resistant to such liberalization.[18] Eventually the barriers and supports must end, of course, for Brazil has won a battle to eliminate cotton export barriers by 2007, and the EU has pledged to end farm supports in 2013. Other barriers may experience the same fate.[19]

A barrier-free agricultural landscape may not be altogether fair, however. Developed country farms are huge and efficient. Whereas developing country farms tend to be just the opposite. In a head-to-head competition, the latter's lack of irrigation, lower yield, and transport problems may make them uncompetitive.[20] Cross-border agricultural trade has increased three fold since the late 1970s, however, so an open competitive market may be in sight.

Even if all tariffs, farm supports, and export subsidies are eliminated, there would still be residual barriers to agricultural exports. The most obvious are sanitary standards, regarding the use of pesticides for example.

Then there is the European Union's antipathy toward genetically-modified organisms (GMO's), hormone-fed beef for example. The EU's standard for exclusion—the so called "precautionary principle"—stands traditional food and drug security on its head. It requires that there be scientific proof that the product will do no harm, rather than the usual approach that it is likely to cause harm. The WTO recently rejected the EU logic, and opened the door to safe GMO products.[21]

Finally, there is the concept of multi-functionality: the belief in Europe and Japan that farms and farmers are not just producers of agricultural foodstuffs, but perform social and ecological functions as well, as husbands of the soil. According to their reasoning, these functions need to be protected and subsidized.[22] I agree with the concept, but it can be used to perpetuate unwarranted protection for local farmers.

All this runs contrary to the theory of the Doha Development round of GATT negotiations, which were supposed to improve the economic fortunes of developing countries by giving them special and differential (S & D) treatment in the marketplace. Unfortunately, there has been little progress toward that end, and that has held up progress in other important market-access sectors (non-agricultural market access/NAMA). Although it now appears that developing countries are unwilling to increase market access for non-agricultural goods in return for lower barriers on their agricultural exports.[23]

C. Non-Tariff Barriers to Trade

With many former tariff barriers now being substantially reduced or eliminated, attention has shifted to non-tariff barriers to trade, or NTBs. Several were mentioned in the previous section, including quotas, purity standards, support payments, and export subsidies. There are many more, however. The mention below of just a few of the most common ones will give the reader some sense of the problem.

1. Standards in General

Food and drug standards were mentioned above, but there are many other product standards that govern what goods and services can be imported and marketed within a state. Examples would include automotive parts, electric appliances, medical devices, and the doctors who implant them. Some standards are clearly necessary to protect consumers, human and animal health, and safety. But, where the standard lacks a reasonable basis or scientific justification, it is more likely than not that it was designed to exclude foreign goods simply because they differ from domestic goods or is a capitulation to political pressure to protect a local industry.[24] In doing so, these standards distort the marketplace and inhibit free trade. One possible solution is to negotiate "mutual-recognition agreements" (that is, we will accept your product to be safe if your certify it to be so, and vice versa).[25] Inconsistent norms, whatever their rationale, mean smaller markets.

2. State Aid

I have mentioned state aid for farmers and farm exports, but many governments in Europe, Asia and much of the rest of the world pump public money into failing private enterprises—"national heroes"—to prevent them from going bankrupt. If this is done on a short-term basis, allowing the industry to restructure and survive, preserving jobs, it might be defensible. But, where support continues over a long term, it wastes public funds and perpetuates a loss-making enterprise that contributes nothing to the marketplace. Something similar might be said about state monopolies that compete with private sector companies (energy, telephones, railroads), but which do not have to break even or show a profit. There is no market incentive to perform, for they can rely on infusions of public money.[26]

3. Dumping

Dumping is described as exporting a good for sale in a distant market at less than its cost of production or sale price in its domestic market. In some cases, it may be nothing more than offloading surplus merchandise at "bargain-basement" prices. But that can't go on forever, or the firm will go bankrupt. So *predatory* dumping has to be a situation in which a competitor gains market advantage through something other than best business practices (e.g. state subsidy; prison or child labor). When a market is threatened with a sudden influx of inexpensive foreign goods, it often alleges "dumping" and imposes a retaliatory tariff. But the comparative advantages of various producers are terribly difficult to quantify. So the claim of market disturbance due to illegal dumping can be nothing more than a veiled non-tariff barrier. Thankfully, dumping claims are diminishing as global markets harmonize.[27]

4. Restricting Market Entry; Quotas, Regulations, and "Red Tape"

Yet another way to burden free trade is to restrict market entry, set quotas, impose regulations on foreign competitors, or encumber imports with customs procedures (red tape). All are common practices in developing economies, particularly to protect local producers and generate government jobs. The problem is that these practices perpetuate inefficiencies (closed markets) and raise transaction costs (red tape).[28]

5. Anti-Trust Rules

Many less-developed countries don't think much about competition rules. This is particularly true when the state runs enterprises (energy, transport, telephone, postal) with which the private sector cannot compete.[29]

Developed countries have adopted competition rules to ensure fair competition within individual markets. But what constitutes "fair" differs markedly from state to state. How large must a corporation's share of the market be before it is "dominant"? If it is dominant, what act constitutes an "abuse" of that dominance? What behavior constitutes an attempt to monopolize? The United States and Europe alone have very different perspectives on these matters.[30]

Eventually, competition rules will be adopted and enforced by the WTO[31], since competition regulation is one of the Singapore issues (trade facilitation; public procurement; financial services; and competition). None are truly on the "front burner" of GATT negotiations at present and only trade facilitations is on the agenda.

6. Taxation

Taxation is yet another way to burden foreign goods, as for example, levying a tax on a good which has no local equivalent (oranges in Great Britain); thereby raising revenue by taxing the foreign product, but without burdening local producers and possibly diverting consumers to their products.

Another approach is to levy a tax on transactions that have some connection with your territory, even though the tax conflicts with the tax system where the provider resides and burdens the sale.[32]

7. *Intellectual Property Piracy; Transshipment*

Intellectual property (IP) is becoming ever more important to both developed economies (where it is generally produced) and developing economies (where it is licensed and used to promote development). There is concern about a "digital gap" developing between first and third world countries. But, if IP owners fear that their property will be pirated by developing countries, compromising their rights and income, they will not send it there, slowing development.[33] Hence, intellectual property theft can pose a barrier to trade and development.

So does the practice of "transshipment." That is the practice of shipping locally-produced goods through a third-country, labeled as theirs, in order to avoid import restrictions on the producing country.[34]

It should be obvious from the foregoing that there are many barriers to free trade in goods and services. However, they are gradually being whittled away through international agreements and the process of globalization.[35] In times of slow economic growth or robust foreign competition, there will always be political pressure to protect domestic industries and jobs. But will that strengthen or weaken America's hand? We are not likely to grow stronger in a noncompetitive environment, or by denying trade opportunities to other countries.[36] Trade barriers erected by one nation only beget reciprocal barriers by others. Moreover, trade barriers rarely work, and they often hurt the very state that employs them. A far better approach is to engage all traders and facilitate trade by removing inequities.[37]

D. How to Stimulate Trade in Goods and Services

As suggested above, there are numerous ways to give less-developed nations a stake in global trade. But first we must admit that their economic growth increases competition for raw materials and market share. That is the consequence of "globalization" and, to some extent, it *does* threaten developed countries with slower growth and potential job losses.

We must remember, however, that the United States is not for the most part in competition with developing economies. Principally, we export high-tech goods and services to the developed world. Canada, the EU 15, Mexico and Japan, in that order, account for about two-thirds of our exports, and nearly 60 percent of our imports come from them, although China slips into third position at just over 12 percent of imports.[38] Our balance of trade in products remains negative (over $665 billion in 2004), while trade in services still favors us. U.S.

services trade surplus reached $100 billion in 2006, while exports to India doubled between 2003 and 2005.[39] However, low-cost foreign goods help consumers and keep inflation in check. So there is both a benefit as well as a burden in trade with developing nations. One would hope (indeed, expect) that, as these economies mature, they will generate increased demand for the high-tech goods and services that America supplies; for huge trade deficits are not economically or politically sustainable.[40]

Neither should we assume that globalization and economic growth benefit the rich but not the poor. Economists (who don't agree about much) do agree "that free trade is almost always better than protection."[41] Indeed, a massive World Bank study of 92 countries concluded that the incomes of the poorest fifth of society rise proportionately with average income overall, where conditions for economic growth prevail (the rule of law, openness to international trade, macroeconomic stability, and developed financial markets).[42]

Since developing economies' growth should increase demand for developed countries goods and services, the U.S. and the European Union took a leading role in launching the Doha Development Round of GATT trade negotiations in Doha, Qatar in November 2001. Among many provisions meant to help developing economies were: an agreement to discuss phasing out agricultural export subsidies; to give those countries more leeway in meeting their GATT obligations (implementation issues); and to adjust intellectual property protection to address their urgent need for medicines.[43] Of course, it is easier to agree to negotiate than it is to conclude negotiations, and so the talks had to be re-launched again with U.S. and EU help after a period of near sclerosis.[44]

The talks, still not concluded and unlikely to conclude any time soon, have predominately dealt with increasing market access; trade facilitation (removing "red tape"); and special and differential (S & D) treatment for emerging economies. Quite recently, some progress was made in both the agricultural and services sectors. But promising mini-ministerial talks on agriculture, non-agricultural market access, and services abruptly collapsed when developing countries could not get the concessions they wanted on special safeguards for farmers and infant industries.[45]

Of course, concessions to developing economies must end at some point. Otherwise there is no incentive for them to take on the full burden of WTO membership. Moreover, not all developing economies are alike, nor need the same concessions. Otherwise, large emerging economies like China and India could become virtually free riders.[46]

What has been manifest in this latest round of trade negotiations is that emerging economies have organized themselves and participated aggressively in the process.[47] When they used their muscle to scuttle the WTO mini-ministerial in Cancun, Mexico in October 2003, a new balance was struck between developed and developing nations.[48] For a period there was concern that the failure of global trade talks would result in bilateral or regional trade arrangements that would undermine the WTO. And to some extent that happened. But concessions to the developing-country group (the so-called G-20) at Geneva in July 2004 and at the Hong Kong ministerial in December 2005 put the GATT process back on track.[49] Not everyone was pleased with the concessions made, especially in the agricultural, manufacturing and services sectors. But they may have been prerequisite to any deal.

During periods when the Doha round negotiations seemed to languish, or in parallel with them, regional trading groups continued to grow. The largest, of course, is the European Union, which continues to expand its membership.[50] NAFTA merely codified an existing Western Hemispheric trade relationship. The Asian Pacific Economic Cooperation (APEC) forum has some influence; representing as it does over twenty diverse nations in the Pacific Rim.[51] But I am most concerned about the efforts in Asia, and even South America and Africa, to develop influential trade associations that *exclude* the United States and other developed nations.[52]

With the exception of the European Union, none of these regional initiatives has the sweep of the GATT/Doha agenda; nor do they regulate nearly as much trade. (The Doha agenda covers 96 percent of world trade, while U.S. free trade agreements (FTAs) cover only 12 percent).[53] For their part, developed traders like the EU and the U.S. have passed legislation to encourage and assist less-developed nations to join in the global trade boom.[54] This is because their involvement, every bit as much as that of developed economies, will result in a steadily expanding market for western goods and services.

Quite aside from GATT treaties or regional or bilateral trade agreements, competition and trade are facilitated if multiple producers can agree on a common standard (particularly in rapidly-evolving fields like telecommunications) or accept one another's standard as sufficient (mutual-recognition agreements, or MRAs).[55] Global intercourse cannot flourish under a potpourri of local regulations, and protected markets are inherently wasteful and inefficient.

Of course, neither developing nor developed countries live in a perfect world. Foreigners invest in one country rather than another for economic, and not political, reasons. The money may be well or poorly spent. External events can impact one economy more than another.[56] Hence, the process of stimulating positive international trade is more art than science.

E. Conclusion

Market opening is always difficult, both politically and economically. This is particularly so when economic conditions are uncertain; which has been the case of late. And yet market opening is a one-off event, which although it may precipitate some short-term hardship, should result in long-term gains via a larger market and best practices. "Despite the [contrary] claims of [its] opponents, all credible evidence supports the fact that globalization and free trade have resulted in enormous benefits to both the developing world and highly industrialized countries." An Australian-commissioned study in 1999 estimated that trade reform could raise world GDP by at least $400 billion. But the increase could be much larger. Despite the sharp rhetoric of its opponents, globalization actually works. The world economy would be much poorer without it.[57] The ultimate key, of course, is enforceability. There is not much virtue in trade liberalization if it can easily be evaded. Hence, a dispassionate arbiter such as the WTO is needed to resolve disputes.[58] This opens the door for more small and medium-sized enterprises (SMEs) to participate, and for consumers to cast their vote.[59]

Assessing all the evidence, it seems undeniable that global trade has been a net contributor to the growth of world GDP, and particularly the growth of less-developed countries. And that the WTO, which has been called the world's "most powerful international body" and "hugely beneficial" for Americans, is the best forum to advance trade's benefits, rather than a patchwork of bilateral or regional agreements. Much of the anxiety about globalization simply seems misplaced.[60] But this is just the economic side of the equation.

For some years, Americans have been the buyers of last resort, spurring growth in an otherwise sluggish world economy. This has led to mounting foreign debt, and an overextended economy. Meanwhile, emerging economies are cutting into American's trade share as south-south trade grows.[61] Some economies have reacted by adopting protectionist measures. This is unfortunate. Economies don't grow in isolation. Nevertheless, there will always be political pressure to protect markets, even from the growth of developing economies.[62]

Eventually, there will be market consolidation and harmonization. We might as well adjust to it. Foreign investors will buy American businesses, and vice versa. What is needed is for each major economy to cooperate and pull its own weight, so that one country isn't perceived to be getting ahead at the expense of another. Gradually that coordination seems to be evolving through a combination of high-level meetings and market adjustments to competitive pressures.[63]

What is needed most is political and business leadership. Instead of bowing to constituent pressures, someone needs to explain to an ill-informed and skeptical public the virtues (as well as the unavoidable vices) of global trade.[64] In sum, the United States has profited from trade in goods and services (particularly services), and they represent a growing proportion of our gross domestic product.

Chapter VII

Capital and Investment

Capital is another essential resource critical to comprehensive economic development. It comes from many sources, both public and private. But the consensus seems to be that the majority of economy-building capital is private, not public.[1]

One astute social commentator estimated in 1990 that "200 billion dollars' worth of currencies [were] traded *every day* in London, New York, and Tokyo alone"; more than one trillion dollars weekly. Of this, an estimated ten percent went to support trade while ninety percent was pure speculation. A more recent estimate set this figure at $3 trillion daily; or about 7.5 percent of world GDP every day.[2] Obviously, not all of this money is invested in trade, far less in global trade. But it does afford some perspective regarding the importance of capital to globalization. And, according to one authority, the next great globalization will be financial. Given its fungibility and global reach, that may be so. Simply put, capital flows dwarf trade flows.[3]

A. Public Capital

First, what about public capital? In stable, developed economies where tax revenues are reliable and substantial, there is public money to invest in economy-building. But, generally speaking, developed countries like the United States spend most of their tax revenue on services, entitlements, and security and very little on economic infrastructure.[4] Of course, these countries have the resources to make special, short-term investments to stimulate a sluggish economy (tax breaks; infrastructure projects). But if these continue long-term, they starve the private sector of capital and substantially increase the national debt. (Both happened to Japan in the 1990s and its economy went flat.)[5] Public spending on economic growth must be judicious.

Large public capital expenditures are also possible where tax rates are high and public spending is a large component of GDP (for example, Sweden, at 26.9 percent),[6] or where the economy is state-run (China). But this drains capital away from the private sector too, and the public money may not be used efficiently, since there is no bottom line (profitability), and there is a virtually inexhaustible supply of capital without regard to performance.

Similar circumstances obtain where there is a high national savings rate (Japan) and/or the state runs all major banks (China). In these situations, money may be borrowed to advance "political" purposes, without regard to risk assessment.[7]

Another way for countries to raise public capital is to issue state securities. Until quite recently, this practice was limited mostly to developed economies that were deemed credit-worthy. But, with the rapid growth of some emerging economies, with more-stable governments and improved regulatory systems—and capitalists' zeal to participate in these booming markets—it is becoming more common for developing economies, even some of the less developed, to raise public capital by issuing securities.[8]

Of course, developed countries like the U.S. have long engaged in deficit spending. This is not particularly good even for strong economies, for it mortgages their future to foreign creditors. And there may eventually be a limit on the latter's willingness to lend (at least on favorable terms).[9] On the other hand, borrowing engages foreign investors in the success of the debtor economy, including emerging economies. But the latter at least could prove risky; making it prudent for emerging economies not to borrow—or investors not to invest—too heavily.[10] Indeed, some emerging economies have felt it desirable to pay off their foreign debt, if possible.[11]

The other principal forms of public capital funding are foreign aid and lending through international institutions like the International Monetary Fund (IMF) and World Bank. U.S. foreign economic aid peaked in 1993 at just over $24 billion and has been shrinking in relative terms ever since, excepting a spike in 2003 due to Afghanistan and Iraq. This excludes disaster aid, however. The same is true for most other developed nations in the world. The message is simple; capacity-building (see chapter IX), both public and private, will in the future be a substitute for the foreign aid of old (often called Overseas Development Aid, or ODA). And, if it is restored, it needs to be better coordinated so that there are not surpluses and gaps.[12]

That leaves only the IMF and World Bank as dispensers of public funds to weak or weakened economies. But even their roles are changing. Both are Bretton Woods institutions, with the IMF designed to provide emergency loans to countries experiencing short-term liquidity problems. Beginning in the 1990s, as a result of several regional crises, the IMF made large loans to Mexico, Thailand, Argentina, South Korea, Russia, Brazil and Turkey. Although most of these adventures ended successfully, the fund has only around $220 billion to lend; a drop in the bucket by global capital standards.[13] Furthermore, it is alleged that bailouts of this sort encourage reckless financial behavior, and that outright debt forgiveness, even for the world's poorest countries, sends the wrong message about capital management and debt.[14]

The World Bank, on the other hand, gives grants and soft loans to aid 81 of the world's poorest countries with capacity building, hoping to make them more stable, more democratic, and more effective economies. In that process, the Bank, that once eschewed involvement in the beneficiary country's political process, realized that weak governments, profligacy, and outright corruption, threatened to dissipate the largesse without material gain. Accordingly, the Bank's President cancelled, suspended, or refused loans to poor countries that are likely to waste its money. Whether this carrot-and-stick approach will work, only time will tell.[15] Meanwhile, it seems obvious that the Bank needs to continue its work, draconian or otherwise, because the very least-developed economies are not likely to get capital infusions elsewhere and, as a consequence, will remain poor and a potential drain on the global economy.

The same cannot be said for the IMF. Its primary borrowers have been developing economies that, thanks to today's global capital liquidity, some developing countries' high savings rate, and increased access to private capital, have less and less need for crisis capital. Perhaps the Fund should not be disbanded entirely (there is always a crisis lurking somewhere), but maybe its role should be changed.[16] Suffice it that the global financial world has changed dramatically in the past twenty years, and the Bank and Fund need to keep pace.

Recently concerns have been raised about the impact of sovereign wealth funds (public capital resulting from unbalanced trade flows). Obviously this money can be used for political as well as economic gain although public investors have foresworn the former aim.[17]

B. Private Capital

The discussion of public capital availability and distribution would be more relevant if it formed a larger proportion of global capital and investment flows. But almost all authorities agree that most capital is private. And private capital availability, distribution, and redistribution are somewhat at the whim of multinational corporations, banks, and speculators whose actions can stimulate or depress global markets and economies, particularly in developing countries.[18] We have seen this happen recently in both Asia and Latin America. Since private capital favors well-run countries and companies, it tends to reward prudence and punish profligacy, unlike some public funding.[19]

No one seems to know exactly how much private capital is invested at any given time in the global economy, but the amount of foreign direct investment (FDI) in the U.S., and U.S. FDI abroad, gives some idea of the magnitude. In 2004, FDI in the U.S. was over $1.5 trillion (up from $395 billion in 1990) and U.S. investment abroad was nearly $2.1 trillion ($431 billion in 1990) and flows keep increasing.[20] Summed, these amounts would be equal to our annual federal budget, or about one-quarter of U.S GDP. And FDI does not include all capital and investment in play.

The flow of global capital and investment has been described as a "gigantic circulatory system," but one that does not serve all areas of the globe optimally.[21] For example, the bulk of U.S. FDI goes to Europe (53 percent) and inward FDI comes from Europe (71 percent). This is called north-north investment.[22] Far lower amounts of U.S. FDI go to (or come from) Asia (19 percent), Latin and South America (16 percent), the Middle East or Africa (around one percent each). Conversely, nearly three-quarters of FDI in Asia's hottest market, China, comes from Asian economies (versus just $8 billion from the U.S. and Europe).[23]

Of course this situation is not static. Various crises, or just a loss of business confidence, can cause sharp drops in the flow of capital. And, when this happens, capital often flees to secure markets like the U.S.[24] What is happening, however, is a sharp rise in investment in developing countries (many of them "southern"), and therefore more north-south and even south-south investment.[25] This certainly widens the global playing field. And the effort to attract more foreign (particularly western) FDI stimulates reform.

In general, FDI inflow is good for growth.[26] However, foreign capital (at least that not invested in green fields, factories and the like) can ebb and flow quite rapidly. (What I call "hot" money). This certainly contributed to the Asian financial crisis of 1997–1998. And capital does not always go to those countries that need it most. Even when it does it can be difficult to absorb.[27] For example, India has a government and business climate that is probably preferable to China's, but it attracts only one-twelfth China's FDI. Despite reform efforts in some African nations, they attract virtually no FDI. However, too much liquidity fuels speculation and inflation.[28]

If attracting and holding domestic and foreign capital and investment is so important to all nations, but particularly developing economies, what is necessary to do so? This is a complicated question. The answer depends somewhat upon whether the investment is relatively fixed (plant, licensed production, joint venture) or highly fluid (cash and securities). Whichever it is, however, it should surprise no one that the key to attracting capital is to have a stable government, a good regulatory system and business environment, low corruption, transparency, and the rule of law.[29] In the absence of these conditions, investment will be limited. A capital crisis can lead to substantial reforms, but subsequent slow growth can result in backsliding and retrenchment.[30] On balance, however, emerging markets are reforming and liberalizing, and this makes them better candidates for foreign capital and investment. The more they reform, the less volatile they are.[31]

C. Mergers and Acquisitions; Private Equity

The public and private investments discussed above are not the only ways in which business is becoming more globalized. Although the number and value of cross-border mergers and acquisitions ebb and flow, they are clearly harmonizing the business world. The same is true of the widening-role of private and public equity.

1. Mergers and Acquisitions

The history of mergers and acquisitions (M & A) from 2000 to 2006 has been an interesting one; most particularly because an increasing number are interstate or international. During the 1990s, an era of booming economic growth and low inflation in the U.S., corporate M & A soared. In 1999, their value approached $1.5 trillion; netting over $5 trillion since 1994. Once, policy-makers were concerned that "too many mergers would stifle innovation and raise prices." But government and the public have grown used to ever larger companies and more foreign investment. Many have relaxed policies that might deter or discourage mega-mergers. Hence, cross-border business consolidation, once rare, totaled $720 billion in 1999.[32]

A slowing global economy, the dot-com bust, and the events of 9/11 cooled this practice. But not for long. By 2005–2006, businesses had restructured, economic growth had begun again, and mergers were once more in vogue; this time aided by large private equity firms. In the first quarter of 2006, the value of global M & A activity averaged $10 billion daily, only this time Europe accounted for more activity than the U.S.[33] But, having learned something from past M & A failures, today's deals, although bigger, also appear to be better.[34] Just what one would expect from a maturing global market.

M&A activity reached new highs in 2007, before being slowed by the credit crunch. But it is expected to revive again once the banking shakeout stabilizes. Furthermore, it has spread to new sectors (European banking) and to emerging economies.[35]

Naturally, all this growth and consolidation doesn't appeal to everyone. In Europe especially, corporate size is a concern, hostile takeovers are considered ungentlemanly, and governments are protective of domestic industries. Eventually these concerns will wane, for the pressures on the EU market to grow and consolidate seem inexorable. In just five months between October 2005 and March 2006, in five EU member states, the largest transactions totaled $268.4 billion.[36]

Of course, some very sensitive industries could be protected from foreign investment or takeovers (for example, a Dubai company's bid to operate at several U.S. ports.) But if this exclusion is too broad it will provoke retorsion, harming U.S. businesses and jobs.[37]

2. Private Equity

A lot of M & A activity has been made possible by the rapid growth of private equity firms. In general, private equity firms buy out undervalued companies, restructure or break them up, and then sell them on, or they provide venture capital for promising start-ups or mergers. Once derided as "corporate raiders" and "asset strippers," today venture capitalists are viewed more positively, providing capital liquidity in a rapidly-changing market. In 2004, "private equity funds world-wide invested $302 billion, up by two-thirds from 2003 ... America saw the fastest rise, with the total value of deals more than doubling ..." In Europe, investments grew by 37 percent.[38] Like M & A, venture capital ebbs and flows. Although many deals go sour, over the past 20 years venture capital investments have returned 15.7 percent per year on average. Consequently, improving economic conditions and global consolidation peaks venture capitalists' interest, especially in booming industries like technology and telecoms. In Europe, however, possibly excepting Britain, the much needed private-equity industry is just catching on.[39]

Another way to raise capital is through an initial public offering (of stock), or IPO. Key emerging-economies' companies—particularly in China and India—have been hugely successful in raising assets to expand their business and global reach.[40]

3. Financial Services Consolidation

All this domestic and international activity has led, as you might expect, to increased globalization of financial services themselves (banking, securities, and insurance). It is estimated that the face value of contracts in interest-rate and currency derivatives now exceeds $200 trillion; fifteen times America's annual GDP. Banking, once almost entirely domestic, has become a national and international business. Europe, which hoped to consolidate its financial services industry around the euro, is finally observing progress.[41] Meanwhile, there is increasing consolidation in financial markets generally, promising greater efficiencies, but diminishing America's dominance.[42] Small wonder, for the industry is one of the most dynamic and fungible worldwide, and it is appropriate for Europe and Asia to play a larger role.[43]

To take just bank consolidation as an example, in China, banks are escaping state control, in Japan, three new mega-banks have swallowed eleven old banks, and in the U.S., the ten largest commercial banks control 49 percent of America's banking assets; up from 29 percent just a decade ago. The EU has proceeded more slowly, but since the introduction of the euro in 1999, financial-industry mergers have been roughly equal to those in the U.S.[44] Technology makes much of this integration possible. But uneven regulation and local protectionism have slowed the development of a truly international financial service market. We are also a long way from agreement on an international banking discipline, although, given the trends described, and financial services' global impact, one is almost certain to emerge.[45]

D. Problems with Global Capital Markets

1. Reserve Currencies

The increased concentration and globalization of capital markets presents some unique problems; so far unaddressed. The first of these involves world reserve currencies. Whereas many nations hold vast quantities of U.S. dollars "in reserve", they do not participate in any meaningful way in setting U.S. monetary policy. Although the impact of monetary policy is often global, with few exceptions (like the European Central Bank), that policy is set at national level. A weak U.S. dollar makes American exports cheaper, but foreign imports dearer.[46] But it also makes the U.S. dollar less attractive as a reserve currency. Indeed, Japan and China, the largest holders of foreign-exchange reserves, have trimmed their purchases of U.S. Treasury bonds. Hence, the dollar's share of foreign reserves has fallen from about eighty percent in the mid-1970s to around sixty-five percent today, due largely to the advent of the euro and rise of Asian economies.

There have been and will be doomsday predictions about the dollar's demise. But, as long as it remains the world's primary reserve currency, it is in everyone's interest to keep global capital flows fluid and stable. This may require some sort of international monitoring system such as that adopted at Bretton Woods after World War II, to deal with post-war turmoil. The Bretton Woods fixed-exchange-rate system began to break down in the 1970s, as developed countries began removing capital controls and in the late 1980s and 1990s as developing countries began to participate in capital markets. Meanwhile, the quantity of global capital has ballooned. So we have a much larger and more robust capital market today, but less control over it. Control, still exercised at local level, is exercised by fewer global players.[47] Greater equilibrium might be achieved if major currency managers (chiefly the U.S., EU, the Japanese and possibly the Chinese) act in concert. That failing, there are always clubs like the G7 or OECD that might broker a deal. But whether they have the stomach, or cohesion, or capital market influence to do so is uncertain.[48]

The euro is clearly the world's second reserve currency, and has given other currency traders an alternative to the U.S. dollar.[49] That said, the euro has plenty of problems of its own. For it is obliged to serve sixteen rather different economies, and the European Central Bank (ECB) seems to stress low inflation over economic growth.[50] On the other hand, currency harmonization within the European Community is definitely increasing. Shoehorning diverse national currencies into the euro was no easy task, but it brought a degree of commercial discipline (the convergence criteria), and widened the base of participating currencies, so that shocks and speculations (which ended the first European Rate Mechanism) are less likely.[51]

In a number of ways, the euro has achieved its intended goals. In a few short years it has become a stable, reserve currency; aided comparison shopping; reduced transaction costs; and encouraged financial market consolidation. But, with only about half of twenty-seven EU member states as subscribers, and with some of those in default on their commitments, it has not yet produced the market convergence, alignment of economic cycles, and economic growth envisioned. Until there is greater harmonization in Europe's single market, the euro's one-size-fits-all monetary policy may be too loose for booming economies and too tight for sluggish ones. Nevertheless, the euro is a net success, and has improved its performance over time. Despite an early, sharp drop against the U.S. dollar, the euro has proved remarkably strong.[52]

The world's third reserve currency is the Japanese yen, although it is not nearly as widely held as the dollar or the euro, and most yen holdings are in Asia.[53] Because Asian economies are so export-oriented (not just Japan, but South Korea, Hong Kong, Singapore, Taiwan and, of course, China), they routinely intervene in money markets to hold down their currency's value against the U.S. dollar (and by implication the euro). This cannot go on forever. But it is likely to continue as long as domestic consumption in these economies remains weak. That may be changing. Recently, Chinese officials loosened the peg of their currency, the yuan, to the U.S. dollar, and have indicated that they will be more flexible about its exchange rate in the future. That will give other Asian countries more flexibility as well, but it will also give China more influence over Asian monetary policy. Indeed, the basket of currencies that replaced China's dollar peg favored the dollar, Asian currencies (chiefly the yen), and the euro, in that order.[54]

Although China's growing economic influence makes it less likely that it would abandon its currency in favor of a "regional Asian currency" (based on the yen and yuan), China has promoted regional economic solutions in the past (for example, an "Asian [monetary] fund" to address the monetary crisis of 1997/98).[55] But that was ten years ago. Today China may feel that the yuan, not the yen, will be the new Asian reserve currency. I do not expect this matter to be worked out *de jure*, in the near term. But *de facto* solutions to monetary instability and competitive devaluation might be agreed; for example, in an expanded G-7.

2. Sovereign Wealth Funds

I have mentioned sovereign wealth funds before. They are vast amounts of foreign capital amassed by sovereign exporters due to a favorable balance of trade. That capital could be used to fund social programs, or to build infrastructure to improve economic competitiveness. Or it could be invested in foreign securities to turn a profit. But it also can be used for geopolitical purposes, for example to insulate a ruling hierarchy or to undermine a competitor's position. That is, the funds can be used for social and political ends, as well as economic ones. The former uses turn capitalism somewhat on its head. The targeted market is likely to react by raising protections; thereby skewing ordinary market functions.[56]

Although some sovereign wealth fund operators have foresworn such intentions, and others have actually agreed not to do so, the opportunity is there, and the risk remains.[57]

3. The Sub-Prime Mess

The world's most recent problem involving the scale, integration, and yet under-regulation of global financial markets, is the sub-prime loan mess. In order to perpetuate growth in a highly-liquid, extended bull market, brokers began lending at sub-prime levels to home buyers who could scarcely afford the loans. When rates adjusted or credit got tighter, defaults occurred and foreclosures followed. But the sub-prime loans had been packaged with better-quality securities to obtain an AAA rating, and were then sold on as quality paper to unsuspecting buyers.[58]

Once the problem was exposed, with little ability to assess the extent of risk, panic set in and financial institutions of all stripes (some with little exposure) suffered sharp devaluations. By one estimate, world stock values declined by $3 trillion in just one week.[59] The extent of the damage is unknown—scary in itself. But some experts think the "crisis" is overblown; certainly a serious regulatory failure, but exacerbated by a loss of confidence in market function. It is, to date at least, nowhere nearly as severe as the Great Depression of 1929–33, to which it is often compared. Furthermore, the U.S. and foreign response to this economic downturn has been as constructive as governments' responses to the 1929 stock market crash(isolation) which actually deepened the crisis. But heightened public anxiety can easily lead to prolonged regulation and mission creep.[60]

In time the full extent of the harm will be known, and capital markets will return to a degree of normalcy.[61] But rebuilding confidence in them may take longer. The whole mess might have been avoided through better regulation and more transparency. But regulatory schemes are chiefly national, whereas capital markets are now clearly international.

E. Problems of Coordination and Cooperation

1. U.S. Trade and Budget Deficits

As mentioned before, there are serious problems with U.S. trade and budget deficits. Will the post-"baby boom" generation save more and consume less (especially foreign goods)? If so, will foreign consumers pick up the slack? Will Congress and state governments live within their means, or will they blame trade imbalances on foreign trade practices and raise barriers; including denying the U.S. President trade promotion authority (to expedite trade agreements by disallowing Congressional amendments)? Unless this happens, won't foreign governments refuse to negotiate with the U.S. and/or raise reciprocal barriers, resulting in trade wars? Will foreign governments continue to buy American debt, and at what premium? Or will they eventually dump American assets, with what financial repercussions?

Efforts by individual nations to protect their economic positions without considering the impact on other states (for example, the EU's posture on agri-

cultural supports) may be politically advantageous and produce short-term economic advantages, but a "beggar-thy-neighbor" policy is generally counter-productive.[62]

2. Accounting and Taxation

One need look no further than the Enron and WorldCom scandals to realize
that accounting standards may be suspect, even in a reasonably-well-regulated
business environment such as ours. Similar problems have arisen in Europe and
Asia. What is needed, of course, is a consistent, transparent, and enforceable set
of international accounting standards that allow comparisons of companies' balance sheets, and reveal enough information to permit sound business judgments.

The European Commission has taken the lead in pushing for international
standards devised by the International Accounting Standards Committee, a
London-based body backed by the accounting profession. Indeed, the Commission passed a regulation (No. 1725/2003 of September 29, 2003) to advance the process. Even China agreed to work with IASC. But a similar American
group, the Financial Accounting Standards Board, felt the IASC's standards
were too weak, and threatened a dual system. Eventually the differences between the two systems were narrowed so that a uniform international system
is now in prospect.[63] But even that won't prevent some "creative accounting"
or outright fraud.[64]

There is also a problem with national tax systems insofar as they are not
uniform throughout the world. Under different systems, businesses run the
risk of being taxed twice or, with luck, not at all. Internet sales might be an example of the latter, since they are not conventional commercial transactions and
are consummated between the seller and buyer outside the public view. The mind-
boggling complexity, disparate incentives and disincentives, and targets and
rates of taxation are also barriers to consistency.[65]

Another complication is between the income tax system used in the U.S.
and the value-added tax (VAT) system common in Europe and elsewhere. If income isn't earned in America, then no tax may be owed. But, if it is, then a tax
may apply. Needless to say, multinational corporations are becoming quite
adept at transferring income and expense between and among different countries so that more income and expense is shifted to countries with the lowest
taxes. Since tax policy is set at national rather than international level, countries can lower taxes to attract or keep business (for example, Ireland). But
even in a VAT system, it is not always easy to say exactly where value was added
and, since each nation depends on its tax system for public revenues, there are
bound to be disputes about who should tax what.

One prospect is to harmonize tax systems and rates regionally, or worldwide. But this strikes deeply at national sovereignty. Another alternative is a flat tax (everyone pays the same rate), which is popular in Central Europe. It is easy to assess and collect, but quite regressive. Eventually, some equitable international tax system will be worked out, because revenues from corporate taxes have been shrinking. But it isn't likely to happen soon.[66]

3. Fiscal "Crises"

Another problem that plagues the global capital system is various fiscal crises. In recent memory we have experienced them in Mexico (the 1994 peso crisis), Southeast Asia (the 1997–1998 "Asian contagion"), Russia, and large developing economies in South America. Most recently, it was the sub-prime loan crisis, discussed above. But, unlike the others, that one befell what was thought to be a well-regulated capital system. Whether due to America's slowing economy, its vast current-account deficit, the weak dollar, or the banking crisis itself, it is acting to rebalance the global economy.[67]

Many people consider periodic capital crises endemic to a globalized financial world, and that they are often cathartic in that, once resolved, they leave behind better-balanced economies and stronger regulatory systems.[68] Because the global stock of financial assets is so large, however (a recent article estimated that between 1980 and 2000 they grew at more than twice the rate of wealthy countries' economies; from $12 trillion to $80 trillion), one must worry about the impact of abrupt changes on the world economy. Obviously, there are going to be some surprises, some disappointments, and some irrational capital flight.[69] But the real story, I think, is not that these crises happen, and continue to happen despite efforts to avoid them, but that they generally are brief and localized, rather then lengthy and global.[70] And, since various crises affect different economies differently, international solutions are elusive.[71] Which is not to say that international coordination won't eventually evolve.

Certainly there are risks when a huge amount of investment capital enters and leaves emerging markets every year in search of the best returns. That figure was put at $472 billion in 2006. But the rapid inflow of this so-called "hot" money can cause inflation and speculation, whereas rapid outflow can result in destabilization and economic collapse. Indeed, unwarranted panic and herd behavior often exacerbate fiscal "crises,"[72] although they are often shallow and short-lived.[73] These almost-unavoidable events in the evolution of global capital markets should teach valuable lessons that gradually improve regulatory and legal systems, and dampen enthusiasm for excessive short-term debt. Eventually, capital will flow back to effected markets, but speculation takes its toll and will not end any time soon.[74]

4. Capital Controls

Given the boom/bust scenarios described above, it is not surprising that some parties have urged renewed capital controls.[75] With the breakdown of the Bretton Woods exchange mechanism in the 1970s, capital controls became national, whereas finance became global. Local controls can be imposed, of course, but at the risk that they will deepen the crisis. But, if more control is needed — and it probably is — what form would it take, and who will provide it?[76]

One suggestion is that the IMF increase its surveillance of global monetary developments, and focus more on regions and less on nations, particularly those with developed economies. But the sub-prime crisis indicates that developed economies can cause problems too. Perhaps the best suggestion is to study how one country's economic policies affect the nations with which they trade, and to weigh more heavily the impact of large emerging economies such as China, Mexico, and South Korea.[77]

Another suggestion is that the Group of Seven industrialized nations (G-7), should set economic policy, as it has in times past. But that is unlikely, because rapidly emerging groupings of developed or developing nations (the G-10, G-20, or G-99) want a say in how financial markets are structured and regulated. Therefore, while the G-7 sill has clout, its members speak more for themselves than global capital markets generally.[78] G-7 membership could be expanded, of course (Russia was recently added). But it is not evident that Russia has more influence on global economics than China or India, and if the G-7 becomes too large or diverse it will have difficulty agreeing on any one policy.

It is also possible that an expert international group — similar to the World Intellectual Property Organization (WIPO) in the field of IP, or the Basel (Switzerland) Group that promotes global banking standards — could agree on a system to regulate global money flows. But, like the Basel II standards, they may be too strong for some economies and too weak for others. And even the new Basel standards were inadequate for the sub-prime crisis.[79]

Another approach, proposed by Professor James Tobin, a Nobel laureate in economics, is to tax currency conversions in international business transactions ("Tobin tax"). This would cover a lot more than speculative currency exchanges, since much of this activity involves routine interbank settlements. While this may dampen abrupt money outflow, it will also reduce inflow to developing economies, because capital would be less mobile. And developing economies frequently need foreign capital to grow. Furthermore, the tax would have to be uniformly adopted and enforced at national level, which is unlikely. In the end, temporary controls maybe preferable to permanent ones.[80]

Certainly the most promising proposal concerning the regulation of global capital flows is the Multilateral Agreement on Investment (MAI), originally proposed by the OECD, but just as likely to be taken up by the WTO as one of the "Singapore issues." Should either group (especially the WTO) adopt such a plan, it would have a very broad reach. That might dilute its terms, but it would also embrace more financially-fragile economies. It would take time to work out the details, but when (not if) such a system comes into force; it will solve some of the cyclical problems described above. However, it must be a reasonably-comprehensive system, and fair to less-developed economies.[81]

Two problems remain with respect to global financial crises. The first is whether more regulation would help avoid them. And the second is whether regulation should be at national or international level.

If better regulations, more oversight, and greater transparency would avert a financial crisis, then it should be pursued. But an occasional crisis may be unavoidable, and overregulation can dampen business growth. The sub-prime crisis seems to have turned more on a lack of trust than a lack of regulation; although both played a role.[82]

If more regulation is warranted, will a patchwork of potentially inconsistent national systems do the job? Financial services regulation is traditionally national. But financial markets are clearly global; with more players, fewer rules, and limited oversight. The sub-prime crisis has spurred nations to improve their own regulatory systems, and to look beyond their borders.[83] But it has also spawned discussions about international regulation.[84]

Whatever the final outcome, some good seems to have resulted from the various capital crises described. One is that the parties talking about developing a global financial architecture are listening more to the most affected economies. And the U.S. has signed bilateral investment treaties with a number of small economies to protect both them and American investors.[85]

Naturally, competition among emerging economies for foreign direct investment creates problems. Does the recipient country or business concede too much to the investor? Will investors stay the course if things look shaky, or will they bolt, making matters worse than they really are? Does enough FDI go where it is most needed? If too much flows to one country (a function of herd instinct), will it be used wisely or create profligacy and inflation?

Witness the competition for FDI between China and India—two of the world's largest emerging economies. India, the more transparent and "Westernized" of the two, attracted only one-twelfth of the $60 billion in FDI that was invested in China in 2004, even though China's economy is less transparent and may be overheating. The quest for FDI may cause rivals to do things they otherwise would not. And there is the possibility that FDI rivals will partner. Even individually their growing influence on global capital flows is evident. Finally, the growth of the private sector in previously state-run economies will also increase the uncertainly of capital flows.[86]

Last among the problems mentioned here regarding capital movements, is related criminal activities such as Ponzi schemes, international money-laundering, and counterfeiting. Along with capital itself, these underworld practices have gone global, and will require more than national efforts to curb them.[87]

F. Conclusion

Following the Asian financial crisis of 1997–1998, a serious financial market meltdown seemed remote. The crisis was brief, the recession shallow, and the reforms salutary, if incomplete. Economies that were most open and flexible recovered quickly. International concern about the regulation of global capital markets increased dramatically, although no solution was found. Obviously, serious capital imbalances need to be corrected. That means the U.S. needs to put its financial house in order, and emerging economies need to reform and better regulate their capital markets. Although some progress was made on this front, the sub-prime crisis indicates how much more needs to be done.

Eventually, I think that multilateral negotiations and treaties will help to stabilize world currencies and capital flow. In fact, I expect that someday there may be just three major currencies in the world. This will lead to stronger, better coordinated global financial architecture, leveling booms and busts. It will also lead to a larger, more harmonized, and more competitive market; with better balanced domestic consumption and export/import trade.[88]

Chapter VIII

Labor, Health, and the Environment

This chapter examines the effects of globalization on labor markets, world health, and the environment. One might wonder why these three seemingly-disparate subjects would be addressed in a single chapter. The answer lies in their interconnectivity and synergy. A nation cannot change policy in any one of these areas without affecting another, and it does not matter where one begins; although labor is the logical first choice. Indeed, as an economy matures; moving from agrarian, to industrial, to a service base, all three sectors are affected in many ways.

Agrarian economies are typically regional. Labor, and its effect on the environment, is localized, as are environmental changes that affect health. Has overproduction in years past lowered yield today? Has the use of pesticides caused health problems? Problems in all three areas can be addressed locally. In an industrial stage, work becomes more centralized. Some individuals migrate to industrial sites while others remain on the land to provide food for the city dwellers. Environmental problems that stem from industrialization are felt both in the centers of labor (overpopulation, air pollution), but also downstream or downwind of industrial centers (air and water pollution, soil erosion due to monoculture farming, industrial waste). Health problems accompany industrialization. Rivers and lakes contaminated by industrial effluent and urban sewage can infect millions, and population density and poor heath care lay the foundation for the rapid spread of disease. With industrialization, however, come scientific and medical discoveries that combat many of these effects.

Finally, as an economy becomes service based, labor markets can be more diffuse, health care improves, and some environmental impacts are outsourced along with industrial production. Generally, service-based economies have higher wages and lower population, because there is less agriculture and industry.

This represents the usual economic progression (or "ladder") of emerging economies, including America's during the 19th and 20th centuries. In their struggle to survive, poor populations frequently degrade the environment.

With better jobs and higher wages the equation is reversed; health care and education improve and environmental degradation is reduced.[1] Many developing economies are presently on the bottom rung of this ladder.

This chapter is meant to show how the process of globalization affects labor, health, and the environment in both positive and negative ways. It brings jobs and capital to developing countries, but also westernizes native cultures. It can lead to the destruction of rainforests, but can also provide alternative employment options for slash-and-burn farmers. It can facilitate transmission of diseases of possibly pandemic proportions, but can also produce vaccines to cure those diseases.

A. Labor

1. Introduction

The electronic age, modern transportation, and the rise of multinational businesses (some to the size of nation-states), have transformed the world's labor markets. In the past, labor markets extended only as far as laborers were willing or able to travel. Laborers lived near their work. This led to the rise of the modern industrial city, as work became increasingly centralized in urban hubs. Farm productivity improved with mechanization, so unemployed farm workers migrated to cities in search of employment. Factory owners reaped the benefits of a centralized, growing work force and the ability to move their products to market at increased speeds. The newly industrialized labor force was poorly-paid, lacked heath care, and tended to live in overcrowded housing. Employers had little incentive to look after their workers' well being, because laborers were readily available.

In the West, factors as diverse as unionization, education, improved medical services, and mass transit helped bring about better labor practices. However, the 40-hour workweek, safety regulations, and heath benefits for workers drove up employers' costs. These changes prompted employers to look elsewhere for inexpensive labor to meet the demand for inexpensive consumer goods.

The process described above accepts that a nation's economy and labor market will evolve. America today, is chiefly a service-based economy. This has given rise to concerns that American jobs will be outsourced overseas. Conversely, protectionist laws designed to keep jobs in America would hinder our ability to profit from less expensive foreign products, probably violate free-trade treaties, and ultimately might harm America's economy. Like it or not, the number of "globalized" workers—both inside and outside the United States—has quadrupled since 1980.[2]

2. Outsourcing and Offshoring

Although often used interchangeably, "outsourcing" and "offshoring" have somewhat different meanings. "Outsourcing" is defined as the transfer of non-essential jobs to an external entity that specializes in that operation. It is based on economic efficiency. "Offshoring," means creating foreign jobs by setting up operations abroad, possibly because labor is less-expensive and regulations less-strict, but also to avoid import tariffs and to serve foreign markets, allowing American business to grow.[3] There are many opportunities in emerging economies around the world. We should not ignore them for they help grow our economy and create jobs.

The rationale behind outsourcing is founded on the economic theory of comparative advantage, attributed to the 19th Century English economist David Ricardo. In his book, THE PRINCIPLES OF POLITICAL ECONOMY AND TAXATION, Ricardo compared the cloth and wine trade between England and Portugal. In England, cloth could be produced inexpensively while wine production was costly. In Portugal, both cloth and wine could be produced cheaply. While it was cheaper to produce cloth in Portugal than England, it was cheaper still for Portugal to produce excess wine, and trade that for English cloth. England benefited from this trade because its cost for producing cloth was not changed, but it could get less expensive wine in return.

Today it is less costly for post-industrial economies to move labor-intensive jobs to sites with inexpensive labor. Although the complexities of the transaction are greater than the example given, the result is that the West essentially trades what its highly-skilled workforce is best at producing (medicine, computer programs) for the labor-intensive products of inexpensive labor. Westerners then can buy certain products (toaster ovens, clothing, and shoes) for less than they could if they were produced locally. Then, the producers of toaster ovens can purchase high-tech Western goods with the money they earned by assembling toaster ovens.[4]

Despite the sound economic principles and common sense logic behind this, there are political repercussions. Goldman Sachs estimates that half a million Americans were laid off during the past three years due to outsourcing. Forrester, an information technology consulting firm, estimates that the total number of outsourced U.S. jobs will grow from 400,000 in 2004 to 3.3 million by 2015; an average of a quarter-million job losses per year over the next decade.[5]

This process has been criticized as a "race to the bottom," in which Americans lose good jobs while multinational corporations exploit poorly-educated and poorly-paid foreign workers (many of them women and children) and take advantage of lax environmental and safety standards. Its critics say it amounts to "neo-colonialism." The main problem, however, is that it is largely untrue.[6]

First, foreign workers in emerging economies want and need jobs in order to grow their economies and improve their quality of life.[7] Second, there are 137 million jobs in America today, which means that jobs lost to outsourcing account for less than two tenths of one percent of total employment in America. Moreover, the 250,000 outsourced jobs lost each year accounts for less than two percent of the 15 million Americans who lose jobs annually; many to take another job.[8] The fact is, most American jobs simply cannot be performed in other countries. Doctors, waiters, hotel managers, and taxi drivers all have jobs that require them to be in physical contact with their clients. In a service based economy, most of these jobs cannot be outsourced.[9]

Throughout history jobs have been created, lost, and migrated in the U.S. and around the world. They are not static. Remember that the shoe and furniture industries of New England migrated to the South; and its heavy manufacturing to the mid-west. We long ago accepted that certain industrial jobs were migrating overseas; automobiles, shoes, apparel, steel. And some jobs disappear almost entirely. Where is the hearty blacksmith or barrel maker of yesteryear? Labor markets must remain flexible to be competitive. This is why America is more and more a high-tech, service economy today. Job "churning" is endemic to a thriving economy.

Moreover, concern about outsourcing ignores the fact that it often is not successful and those jobs return to the U.S. or, that foreign businesses, in order to serve American consumers, establish themselves here, creating (insourcing) jobs in our economy.[10] There is but a small difference between the number of outsourced and insourced jobs.

Aside from this "backlash," there are "natural limits" to shifting service jobs overseas. The government estimates that "well under" one percent of unemployment is due to outsourcing. Moreover, during the past decade, U.S. multinationals created about five American jobs for every three foreign jobs.[11] Job migration is not a one-way street. Jobs may migrate *from* America, but also *to* America. It is the *net* loss or gain that counts. Indeed, a recent study by the World Trade Organization and International Labor Organization concluded that trade liberalization had a "positive overall" effect on employment. And whereas it tended to increase income inequality in developed countries, it reduced it in developing countries.[12]

Despite these seemingly reassuring figures, Americans who work in the manufacturing and service sectors naturally feel a degree of job insecurity. The former also is traditionally a union stronghold. Hence, those with the greatest chance of losing their jobs have political clout.[13] But, as noted economist, Paul Krugman, reminds us: the "whole idea of counting jobs gained and lost ... [is] a misunderstanding of the way the U.S. economy works."[14]

Multinationals that engage in outsourcing and offshoring have been criticized by anti-globalists and politicians as "Benedict Arnold" corporations. Nothing is said about "Benedict Arnold" consumers; whose thirst for a wide variety of lost-cost goods contributes heavily to the process. As said, the job loss is relatively small. And there is not a great deal that laborers, consumers, voters, or governments can do about it. Labor-intense jobs will naturally migrate to places where labor is plentiful and inexpensive.[15] That boosts market efficiency and competitiveness.

But it is wrong to think that the Chinese and other Asian nations are stealing "American" jobs. If China is stealing anyone's jobs, it is those of its Asian neighbors. For the jobs that the Chinese perform are labor intense, low-skill, low-paying jobs—not the type that America should be highly-motivated to save. Inexpensive labor is China's comparative advantage. If any country might be stealing American jobs, it would be India; through its IT centers.

In general, Indians are better educated than the Chinese and speak English. But this applies only to a small percentage of India's workforce, so that finding and retaining qualified employees has become a real problem for India's IT startups. Moreover, many Indian technicians are ill equipped to handle complex queries, and are prone to linear (learned) responses, rather than creative thinking.[16] So there is clearly a limit to outsourcing or offshoring. Besides, even Japan outsources to China; and China itself sheds jobs due to the restructuring of loss-making state-owned enterprises (SOEs).[17] Moreover, China's contribution to globalization lies mainly in the area of assemblage, not design or high-tech manufacture. When a sophisticated electronic device is labeled "made in China," it is more likely to have been assembled there than to have been designed or have its technical components fabricated there.[18]

What Americans do best, and the jobs they ought to pursue, are the high-tech, high value, and high-paying positions in the global economy. This is the "skills premium" that we are used to enjoying. If certain jobs inevitably go offshore, we should focus on creating, and attracting, better jobs; as for example those created by foreign direct investment in the U.S.[19] This is America's comparative advantage.

With shrinkage of the U.S. labor force due to the retirement of "baby boomers," and given the fact that America is not producing enough technicians to deal with the growing workload, offshoring of some jobs may actually *help* the economy. But we need to stay at the technological forefront to continue to prosper.

"Job hopping" in Indian high-tech firms is already epidemic. Salaries for well-trained engineers in India rose 15 percent in 2005, and salaries represent 70 percent of business overhead. Rents are rising too.[20] Eventually, the wage gap between offshore and onshore jobs will close, and offshoring will slow down.

Concurrently, economic growth in emerging economies produces new consumers and stimulates demand for imports; particularly high-tech imports. Today, China spends almost all of its export earnings on imports; albeit not yet enough on imports from the United States.[21] Moreover, as developing economies mature they will have more need of the types of goods and services that post-industrial economies provide. The consumption of their growing middle class will increase trade, and raise wages. Even now, joint ventures in the developing world create jobs in developed economies.[22]

Given that economic forces will eventually resolve the alleged inequities associated with globalization, as they have in the past, it seems pointless for an ironic amalgam of liberal anti-globalists and conservative politicians and labor unions to oppose outsourcing and offshoring. In the latter case it smacks of protectionism thinly disguised as concern for the health and safety of foreign workers. Even the former underappreciate the zeal of developing countries to move forward economically. Besides, ring fencing the American economy simply won't work. And if it did, our trading partners would surely retaliate. Then we would be worse off, given our dependence on trade.[23]

Finally, protecting the American workforce from foreign competition distorts the market; something we have traditionally condemned. A protected market can lead to worker lethargy, higher prices, and less innovation and efficiency. Rather it is the spur of competition that makes markets efficient, productive, and innovative. Protection can never succeed as more than a stop-gap, short-term measure.

For example, when Toyota decided to build a new RAV-4 factory in Ontario, Canada, passing over the southern U.S., where it already had plants, it cited Canada's national health system, which saves auto manufacturers large sums compared with U.S. costs, the high quality of Ontario's work force, and the fact that Japanese auto companies with plants in southern US have been disappointed by laborers' poor level of training.[24]

So compete Americans must; not just against low-wage Asian workers, but against high-tech workers in developed countries as well. But why should we be afraid to compete? Recall the hand-wringing that accompanied the "right-sizing" of American corporations in the late '80s and early '90s? That process led to a decade of rapid economic growth. Now we are confronted with another labor/production shift. Why shouldn't we succeed again? Would protectionism help us do so? I think not.[25]

Of course, some American workers will be displaced by global competition. Their plight can be addressed through retraining programs, wage-loss insurance, and portable health and pension benefits. It is this safety net that can protect workers' morale and keep them abreast of economic changes; not abortive attempts to save "American" jobs. In fact, the federal government offers assistance to workers displaced by foreign trade; the Trade Adjustment Assistance (TAA). But only about 2 million workers have qualified, and many have found new jobs.[26] The challenge is to create new and better jobs, and to train workers to do them, not to grasp after jobs that will inevitably move offshore.

Besides, where is it written that any jobs are "American" jobs? Are there German jobs, and British jobs? Don't we have to compete for them against other willing laborers? Isn't this what makes markets resilient and efficient? Surely a highly-skilled and efficient workforce can compete with a low-skill, labor-intensive one.

3. Labor Standards

Another complaint against offshoring is that it allows companies to escape Western labor standards. Anecdotes abound about the working conditions in foreign "sweatshops," and many are true. Indeed, most economists agree that the existence of sweatshops in America and Europe during the Industrial Revolution enabled those economies to grow rapidly during that period.

Inexpensive labor is the comparative advantage of many developing countries. Consequently, they argue that they are put at a competitive disadvantage when developed nations and international organizations try to impose higher Western labor standards on them; labor standards those economies cannot afford, they argue, until they too become developed economies.[27]

But the truth is, when multinational corporations offshore production, they also export higher labor standards. In general, multinationals run safer and more humane factories and pay higher wages (albeit lower than the U.S.) than local producers. The investment is probably rewarded with better quality and higher production; making it less likely that the foreign venture will fail. That is, a free market approach provides a type of solution to the "sweatshop" problem. Indeed, some foreign workers complain that U.S. companies do not allow them to work enough.[28]

Perhaps most remarkable is the fact that Congress has succeeded in passing a law that requires labor standards to be part of any U.S. trade agreement;

China has boosted worker's rights; and U.S. labor unions (generally opposed to globalization) have begun to work with a state-sanctioned Chinese union to raise labor standards (at least at foreign and private companies).[29]

While some corporations probably do engage in a "race to the bottom," consumer aversion to "sweatshop" conditions has helped to improve labor standards in the developing world. According to a recent FORTUNE magazine article, the bad press and reduced sales American companies like Nike experienced as a result of revelations about horrid conditions in their overseas factories, induced many Western companies to improve and monitor overseas production. Hence, Western companies are likely to elevate developing countries' health and safety standards when they open factories in the developing world. Other businesses compel foreign suppliers to raise standards in order to avoid having a sweatshop label attached to their brand. This process reflects globalization's potential to actually improve labor conditions.[30]

Improvement is not entirely consumer driven, however. Reports show that the poor quality of overseas labor has led to outsourcing retrenchment, with American companies bringing jobs back to the U.S. (the "boomerang "effect") after a brief and unsuccessful venture in India or Taiwan. These reports by no means signal an end to offshoring. Rather, they signal that there is a limit to its viability.

The concern now gripping the U.S. services sector has affected the industrial sector for well over thirty years. Since 1970, manufacturing jobs in the U.S. have dropped by more than one-half, but without any huge impact on the economy. For all the concern about the erosion of the America's manufacturing base, and the shifting of production overseas, real manufacturing output in the U.S. has been growing almost four percent annually since 1991; faster than GDP. America remains the world's largest manufacturer. China, with six times America's workforce, is far less productive. Indeed, America produces about twice as much as China, measured by value.[31]

Nevertheless, outsourcing and offshoring help to compensate for shrinkage in the U.S. labor force. As "baby boomers" retire, the American labor force will shrink. We also seem not to be training enough engineers. Finally, there are those labor-intensive, unskilled jobs (crop-picking, for example) for which we have often turned to immigrant labor. But with a slowing economy and wage gaps shrinking, migrants (at all levels) may not come, or go home.[32]

It is also worth observing that emerging countries experience monumental growth problems; problems that an expanding economy might help them to address. It is common for less-developed economies to have major health and pollution problems, and to waste resources through inefficiency; particularly subsistence agriculture. China, for example, is home to five of the ten most-polluted cities in the world in terms of air quality. You can imagine the health problem this creates. And China's pollution is exported as far as Oregon. Moreover, China's industry is wasteful; requiring three to ten times more energy per unit of output that of the U.S., Europe, or Japan. The plight of the rural poor threatens social unrest. Conversely, a robustly growing economy gives China and other emerging nations more resources to address their problems than they would have if denied economic opportunities.[33]

4. What Is Lost, or Gained?

Globalization has dramatically changed the structure of world labor markets. Technology has allowed tasks to be allocated around the globe. Clearly there are virtues and vices involved in the process. There is no unalloyed upside or downside.

On the upside we could list the greater variety of less-expensive goods available to consumers; increased foreign investment in the U.S.; innovation; and keeping inflation in check. Increased trade also tends to raise developing countries' living standards; making them less dependent on developed countries' largesse, and better able to address their own problems. On the downside, there is anxiety about job losses and dislocation occasioned by work being shifted offshore and by companies moving part or all of their operations abroad. Social and political problems arise from rising unemployment and ballooning trade imbalances.[34] Pressure to resolve or reverse these negative aspects of globalization is generally brought at national level, whereas the problems themselves are international.

If labor mobility creates problems, it also offers solutions. The rapid economic growth of India, China, South Korea, and even Vietnam, equips these countries to better address their own social and political problems. And it creates a consuming middle class with a passion for western goods.[35] Even booming economies like China have to adjust their workforces in order to remain competitive.

Is the world better off as a result of globalization? The results are understandably mixed. Millions have been lifted out of poverty; health and education are improving in developing economies; as are peace and security. There are many reasons for this, but economic growth, through trade, is one of the foremost. Without the opportunities provided by trade, the developing world would be far less able to deal with its multitude of problems and be an even greater drag on developed economies.[36]

I believe that modest, but uniform, labor standards will eventually be adopted. For the moment, the World Trade Organization (WTO) has chosen not to add this political "hot potato" to its agenda. (After all, more than one-half of WTO members are developing countries, and cheap labor is their chief comparative advantage.) As a consequence, the International Labor Organization (ILO) has taken the lead in attempting to promote minimum labor standards. But its efforts are hampered by uneven ratification of its conventions and the lack of a credible enforcement mechanism. However, some bilateral tree trade agreements (for example that between the U.S. and Jordan) include labor and environmental standards. This almost certainly is a precursor to regional and global standards.[37] Multinational corporations also are improving and harmonizing foreign labor standards.

Globalizing labor markets also may exacerbate social problems. The economic boom in China has lifted millions out of poverty, but it also has led to moral decay and unrest between rich and poor. Reports indicate that class tension has been increasing steadily along with China's GNP.[38] Most people pursue work that will enable them to climb the economic ladder. In overpopulated developing nations where demand for non-farm employment is high, this increases the opportunity for factory owners to exploit workers.

Statistical and anecdotal evidence indicate that foreign-owned corporations tend to treat workers better.[39] But they may also slow economic growth, since much of the profit is sent abroad, where the corporation is headquartered. Hence, although FDI tends to improve working conditions and build infrastructure in developing countries, it can also interfere with well-planned economic development.[40] Like so many things related to globalization, outsourcing and offshoring have both an upside and a downside.

B. Health

1. Introduction

World health may be the area most affected, both positively and negatively, by globalization. The speed with which products and people transit the globe increases the potential to spread disease and the prospect of a pandemic. But, globalization can also spread knowledge and access to medicine required to fight disease.

Traditionally, public health has been a national concern. With increased mobility, however, disease has become a global concern; but one without a global plan. When populations were largely agrarian, diseases and immunities were localized. A cholera outbreak might debilitate a town, but the survivors would thereafter be resistant to that strain of the disease. Because travel was rare and difficult, the spread of disease was limited. With population concentrated in cities, and trade among cities and regions increased, the prospect of disease and its spread increased as well. One early example is referred to as the "Columbian exchange."

When Europeans landed in the new world in 1492, they brought diseases (small pox, typhus, and measles) against which the natives had no immunity. Anthropologists estimate that, in one generation, the Native American population had been reduced by 90 percent, largely due to smallpox alone. Isolated island populations, such as the Caribs and Arawaks were entirely destroyed. In return, European explorers brought syphilis back to the Old World, completing the exchange. Today, the rapid spread of HIV/AIDS, and the threats posed by avian flu, BSE/CJD, and SARs are the modern-day equivalent.

In addition to concern about the rapid spread of disease and pandemics, today's global health concerns include the deplorable conditions that exist in much of the developing world, and their demands on world resources and growth; and how to address these twin problems. The answers given will impact heavily on human welfare; if not survival itself.

2. Health Problems in the Developing World

The health problems of the developing world are often ignored and unaddressed until they are projected in all their horror on the evening news, or threaten to spill over into the developed world.[41] Nearly one-half of the nations in the world are, to some degree, impoverished, overpopulated, and/or diseased. They constitute a drag on the global economy and are seedbeds of instability and illegal migration.

Different statistics come from a multitude of sources, but their magnitude provides perspective concerning the seriousness of the problem, particularly in developing countries. The World Health Organization calls the growth of preventable, treatable, infectious disease a "global crisis." The loss of life and acute illness caused by HIV/AIDS, malaria, tuberculosis, and diarrhea alone extract a "terrible toll." It is estimated that between 6 and 9 million people die annually from these diseases, chiefly in Sub-Saharan Africa, and over 17 million die from all infectious diseases; 9 million of them babies and young children.[42] The economic effect on these populations is obvious. There is little time for anything but survival.

Malaria alone kills three thousand persons a day; two-thirds of them children. However, pneumonia, a treatable disease prevalent in poor countries, is the "leading killer of children world wide, taking a life every 30 seconds ... [It is] a world-wide killer on a par with AIDS, malaria and tuberculosis ..." As a consequence, "child morbidity and mortality [is] rising in many countries." Apparently, the optimism that treatable diseases could be controlled worldwide led to compliancy and allowed their resurgence. Old diseases like tuberculosis, malaria, and cholera are making a comeback in many parts of the world[43].

In addition to disease there is malnutrition; which of course contributes to disease, dying, and unproductivity. An estimated one billion of the world's 6.4 billion people are malnourished. (Six hundred million, chiefly in Europe and America, are overnourished). As many as 86 countries worldwide cannot grow or buy enough food to sustain their populations. As a result, 6 million children die annually due to malnutrition. And 2 billion more persons are exposed to disease because they have access only to contaminated water; 1.5 billion suffer from diarrhea.[44]

The reason for all this disease and death has much to do with the nature of the economies the victims inhabit. Most are subsistence farmers, on small over-worked and unproductive plots. They have no irrigation, and so depend entirely on rainfall at the right time. But parts of Africa have suffered from years of drought. In Malawi, for example, nearly one-half of its population desperately needs food aid. In southern Africa nearly 12 million do.[45]

Due to extremely high levels of disease and dying, adults are often too sick to work, or work productively, or they must care for the ill and dying. Less developed countries and their populations are caught in a "self-perpetuating cycle of disease-induced poverty." Death from malaria alone has doubled in the past twenty years.[46]

Overpopulation is also a chronic problem for the developing world. Generally, developing economies are agrarian and agrarian societies historically have high birthrates because farming is labor intensive. Since agrarian societies also have high infant mortality rates, a woman might need ten pregnancies to raise five mature children. As an agrarian society slowly becomes industrialized, health care tends to improve, reducing infant mortality. If pregnancy rates do not decline correspondingly, more children are born than the economy requires. The result is profound overpopulation, which can severely tax economic growth. World population of 6.4 billion is growing by about 74 million a year, and could reach 9 billion by 2050; almost all of it in the poorest countries.[47] With overpopulation come the slums and shantytowns that surround major cities throughout the developing world. In these shantytowns, poverty and disease are endemic.

For the governments of these countries, these problems are notoriously difficult to tackle. Increased health education is an obvious solution. But, despite the change in social conditions, making large families unnecessary, when social status increases with every birth, education struggles against longstand-ing social norms.[48]

If access to potable water, adequate nutrition, sanitation and health care are improved, a short-term population explosion could occur; putting even greater stress on regional and global resources until reproductive restraint (typ-ical in developed economies) eventually kicks in. Ultimately, population con-trol must be a key component of overall economic growth. For, once a shantytown is born, it quickly increases the spread of disease and despair, since the disease bred there is never contained and national productivity can be se-riously reduced by its spread. It is estimated, for example that the HIV/AIDS pandemic currently ravaging southern Africa could reduce its economic growth rate by one-half over the next 15 years.[49]

Conversely, a growing economy can increase the resources necessary to fight disease. It is well-established that prosperous nations are more likely to ad-dress health and unemployment problems than poor ones. But this assumes that increased government revenues due to economic growth do not fall vic-tim to corruption (common in less-developed economies), and will be applied to drugs and food aid and not to other purposes.[50] Improvements in health care in developing countries are often unequally distributed. Wealthier, urban dwellers frequently get a disproportionate amount of benefit versus the agrar-ian population; creating class tensions.[51]

Additional barriers to food and drug distribution are raised by concerns about food safety, intellectual property protection, and the threat of pandemics. Regulations that seek to guarantee food safety and wholesomeness are merely prudent. But when they reach the level of excluding all genetically-modified or-ganisms (GMOs), they can seriously disrupt the free flow of much-needed foodstuffs to needy populations worldwide. I cannot quite suppress the suspicion that some safety regulations are purely reactionary or veiled attempts to pro-tect local markets from competition; particularly when no threat to health has been established. But, then, some are clearly warranted.[52]

Of course, even developed countries have difficulty affording and deliver-ing the health-care expected of them. And wealth discrimination exists there as well. But it is not as often a matter of life and death, or economic stagna-tion, as in poor nations.[53]

Then there is the conflict between the protection of intellectual property rights, assured by the WTO's trade related intellectual property agreement (TRIPs), and the plight of less developed countries that can neither afford to buy needed drugs at market prices or to manufacture them. It should surprise no one that large pharmaceutical companies (big pharma) patent their drugs in order to protect and recoup their investment in research, and that developed countries cannot afford the high prices charged. Neither have many of these countries the capacity to invent and/or produce needed drugs on their own. If the TRIPs agreement is to be followed to the letter, big pharma could enforce its patents against these needy populations. Then the drugs would either be unavailable or a huge amount of money would have to be committed to their acquisition. So a compromise was worked out. It allowed poor countries to override the TRIPs agreement and import generic equivalents of essential medicines needed to address major health crises.[54] The United States, looking to protect big pharma, objected to a liberal interpretation of the diseases covered and the nature of the "crisis" embraced by certain developing countries and the World Health Organization. There was a natural concern that the latitude would be used to address not just acute but also chronic diseases, and that excess production or importation would be sold-on for profit, or that patented formulas would be pirated. But, in the end, big pharma was wise to cooperate with developing countries that threatened to invoke a "compulsory license" to produce needed drugs. To do otherwise would have gotten very little support in the WTO, and might compromise the whole patent process in the third world.[55]

Another drug-related problem for disease-ridden developing countries is that the strain of the disease plaguing them may not be the strain for which a drug was designed and marketed in the developed world. In such cases, big pharma cannot justify the research and development expense to serve a potentially small and impoverished market. Some non-market inducement must be found. One suggestion is an "advanced purchasing commitment" (APC), whereby wealthy economies would agree to buy a vaccine, if one is found and proves viable, to protect against a third-world disease.[56]

The main problem with global health has been to get wealthy nations and persons to concentrate on it for the long haul. It is different with national disasters; acute famine, prolonged drought, floods, earthquakes, hurricanes and tsunamis. They dominate the news, and there is an immediate—albeit quite brief—outpouring of concern and largesse. These are self-conscious quick-fixes, soon forgotten. They are mere band-aids; not a solution to the global health problem. The threat of a global pandemic (discussed below), is a different matter. Unlike disease in chiefly poor countries, the threat of a global pandemic concentrates the mind.

On the public side, the emergence of more stable, semi-democratic governments in Central Africa, and the creation of the African Union, has given the region a profile and voice. Previously, Africa was caught in a "Catch 22." It couldn't attract money because it was not stable, and it couldn't improve its stability without outside assistance. But that may be is changing.

Second were the Millennium Development Goals of the UN, meant to cut extreme poverty and hunger (and its collateral effects) by one-half between 1990 and 2015. In 2000, rich countries pledged 0.7 percent of GDP to the project. But a 2005 progress report suggested that these "pledges [were] so debased by non-delivery that [they were] widely perceived as worthless." That does not mean that no progress is being made, however. The U.S. contributed $200 million to the Global Fund to Fight AIDS, Tuberculosis and Malaria, and the EU is struggling to reach a goal of 0.5 percent of GDP. If goals are not always met, the multinational dialogue and capital transfers are important. The Johannesburg World Summit on Sustainable Development in 2002 reiterated the Millennium promises and added a few more concerning poor country market access, rich country farm subsidies, and the Kyoto emissions goals. If the goals are ambitious and the results modest, at least the issue remains on the front burner.[57]

The European Union, already the largest provider of overseas development aid (ODA) in the world, is gradually turning its development efforts into a Community-level policy, and hopes to double its aid by 2010. The EU donated euro 58 million in 2005 to fight AIDS, malaria and tuberculosis. And pledged an additional euro 197 million for global food aid as part of its 2006 work programme. Together with its constituent member states, the Community has allocated more than euro 1.1 billion toward fighting disease. And it has joined the U.S. in "establishing, resourcing and promoting" the Global Fund to Fight AIDS, Tuberculosis, and Malaria, which has mobilized $3.5 billion to support 300 programs in 127 countries.[58] Of course, many other nations, and international organizations such as the World Health Organization (WHO), also contribute to the public effort to eliminate poverty, hunger, and disease.

The more remarkable story may be on the private side, however. Private philanthropy is flourishing due to rapid wealth-creation and its uneven distribution between rich and poor. According to FORBES magazine, there were 691 billionaires in 2005, up from 423 in 1996 (63 percent increase); about one-half living outside the U.S. And no private donor presently has a higher profile, or more influence on the philanthropic process, than the Bill and Melinda Gates Foundation. It spends well over a billion dollars a year on various poverty and health projects; nearly as much as the WTO. That amount is likely to balloon considerably now that Warren Buffett has pledged a large part of his wealth to the Gates Foundation. Moreover, the Gates have inspired other wealthy individuals to open their pocketbooks. In 2004, charitable giving in America rose five percent to a record $249 billion; over two percent of GDP. This is more than any other large country, both in absolute terms and as a percentage of GDP. Gradually Europeans, Asians, and even Latin Americans are increasing philanthropic giving, although they are held back by the fact that so-cialist governments control more capital and are expected to deliver more pub-lic services.[59]

    What may be more exceptional, however, is the type of projects that these foundations have elected to fund. Rather than making short-term, generic contributions to individual donees that are often quickly exhausted with little impact, Mr. Gates gave up his job as head of Microsoft in June 2008 to focus full-time on philanthropy. Meanwhile, the foundation has spent billions of dollars on education and global health issues. But it has done so in a more fo-cused and entrepreneurial way. It encourages partnerships among researchers who would normally seek funds competitively. It builds performance meas-ures into all projects, so that money is not wasted if no progress is realized. It convenes panels of experts rather than hiring them in-house. Finally it is di-viding its health funding between treatment and prevention; including a search for new vaccines and better delivery systems, particularly for diseases that chiefly affect the third world. Research funding for cardiovascular diseases and diabetes currently exceeds funding for the "Big Three" diseases (HIV/AIDS, malaria, and tuberculosis; chiefly third-world diseases), by at factor of four. The Gates' half-billion dollar "Grand Challenges in Global Health" alone sug-gests how adventuresome and yet focused the foundation can be. Conversely, the business-like approach taken by the Gates Foundation has its critics.[60]

3. Pandemics

    In the developed world, there is probably no greater health concern than the pandemic. Originally, pandemics had a limited reach. The Justinian Plague, which originated in Egypt in 541, is said to have killed up to one-quarter of the population of the Eastern Mediterranean, but was confined to that region. The Bubonic Plague, brought from Asia by Italian merchants, was confined mostly to Western Europe. But, with increased travel of persons and goods, pandemics are more wide-spread and more threatening. For example, the Spanish Flu in the early 20th Century, now believed to have been a strain of bird flu, broke out in three far-removed locations and killed an estimated 20–40 million peo-ple around the world.[61]

    A pandemic, from the Greek *pan* all + *demos* people, is an outbreak of an infectious disease that affects people or animals over an extensive geographi-cal area. Although, cancer affects persons in every country of the world, is not a pandemic because it is not infectious. In order for a particular disease or virus to reach pandemic proportions, it must have certain characteristics. First, it must be highly contagious, and it must have a gestation period long enough for those infected to spread it to many others. As a general rule, the developed world has no vaccines against, or treatments for, pandemic diseases that spring suddenly to life. But global actors are far better able to respond to a global pandemic than a patchwork of national actors; some of whom are chiefly concerned with local matters.[62]

4. HIV/AIDS

The HIV/AIDS virus is believed to have originated in Africa some time before it made its first appearance in the U.S. in the early 1980s. Originally confined to a small group of at-risk individuals; homosexuals, intravenous drug users, and prostitutes, it quickly spread to a wider population and suggested pandemic proportions; an incurable, deadly disease that infected the psyche of the Western world as much as it did the immune systems of those who contracted it. By the early 1990s, Western governments had begun intense campaigns to educate people about avoiding infection and devoted millions of dollars to the search for a cure. Roughly twenty years after AIDS first started making headlines in America, infection rates are down and an expensive cocktail of anti-retroviral drugs have tremendously increased the lifespan of those infected. AIDS, in the developed world, has ceased to frighten us.[63]

In the developing world, however, AIDS has become the unmitigated disaster that Westerners once feared. Most developing countries do not have the resources, the infrastructure, or in some cases the inclination for such a campaign. In some countries, such as South Africa and China, government leaders simply denied the problem existed. When the problem appeared in the former, less than two percent of the population was infected. But, after fifteen years of neglect (2003), South Africa had more HIV positive citizens than any other country; 5.3 million in a population of 45 million. In Thailand, where an outbreak of the disease was addressed head on, infection levels were as low as one percent, and have remained so. In China and India, the world's two most populous countries, there is a high concentration of HIV in some populations, and the disease is spreading faster than government efforts to contain it. In Russia too, government efforts are modest compared to the threat. For a lack of testing, or other "risky" behaviors such as unprotected sex, and peasants selling their blood in China, many of those infected with HIV do not even know it. Hence, numerous experts predict the worst is yet to come. For AIDS continues to spread.

Presently over 40 million people are infected with HIV. Five million more are infected with HIV and three million die every year.[64] Although anti-retroviral drugs have extended lives in the developed world, citizens of developing nations cannot afford these drugs. Drug companies in Brazil and India are finally producing affordable, generic versions of the anti-retroviral drug cocktails. However, to do so, they had to threaten to violate the TRIPs international patent law agreement and incur the anger, and often economic retribution, of the Western nations protecting their patent holders.[65] Denial and neglect may yet allow HIV/AIDS to develop into the "perfect storm."[66]

In Africa, slow economic development and lack of education may be the greatest contributing factors to the ongoing epidemic.[67] Political instability throughout much of the African continent has deterred foreign investment. This, in turn, has slowed economic development, which increases political instability. In many African nations, warlords and intertribal wars wreak havoc on the nation's crops and water supply. Under such conditions, primary education takes a back seat to day-to-day survival. Unfortunately, these conditions are also prime breeding grounds for the spread of AIDS. Many Africans do not know how AIDS is spread, or even what a condom is. Lack of knowledge, combined with roving bands of soldiers, traveling throughout the country raping those they don't murder, increases the spread of AIDS exponentially.

That does not mean that everything is doom and gloom. Governments and other agencies are beginning to acknowledge and address the problem. Anti-AIDS programs are becoming larger and more coherent. Public knowledge has increased, as has HIV/AIDS research, and more money is being effectively spent on treatment and prevention. In 2003, about $4.7 billion was spent to fight AIDS in low and middle-income countries, up from just $200 million in 1996, but well below the $10 billion that is needed each year to keep AIDS in check. The cost of the drug "cocktail" necessary to contain the disease and prolong life has fallen from $10,000 per patient annually to as little as $140. Drug delivery systems have improved and, thanks to the WTO agreement concerning "compulsory licensing," poor countries without the capacity to manufacture their own drugs can import generic versions at low cost. But the need for these drugs continues throughout the AIDS suffers' life, and compulsory licensing dampens drug-makers' enthusiasm to search for new drugs. Likewise, the percentage of infected persons receiving anti-retroviral therapy varies widely; from 62 percent in Latin America to just eleven percent in Sub-Saharan Africa to five percent in North Africa and the Middle East.[68] In some areas (India), AIDS is less prevalent than once feared. And the number of persons infected, though still high, is falling.[69]

If containment measures continue and are successful, HIV/AIDS may never turn into a pandemic. But it surely is an epidemic with vast social and economic implications. Many farmers and teachers are expected to die from the disease, affecting food production and education. The number of AIDS orphans is growing rapidly. Babies are born with AIDS; health care workers contract it from unsterilized needles; patients from tainted blood. Malnourished persons can not fight off sickness; sick persons cannot farm, or provide for their children. In some impoverished African countries, more than one-half of the population may die from AIDS. In southern Africa, it is expected to cut economic growth by one-half; in a region that is already well behind economically. The disease is so enervating that, along with drought, all of Africa's famines are attributed to it. It is such a threat to productivity that large companies are providing anti-retroviral to their workers.[70] Eventually, HIV/AIDS will probably be brought under control; epidemics usually are. It bodes well that governmental inertia has been largely overcome; more money is available to fight the disease and for research. Nevertheless, the impact of HIV/AIDS on the global economy has been, and will be, enormous and continuing.[71]

5. The Cost of Disease to the Developed World

In the abstract, it is easy to discount or ignore the effect that disease in developing countries has on the developed world. In the end, however, disease in remote places can profoundly affect post-industrial countries in two ways: one obvious and one less so.

The obvious way is that diseases arising in developing civilizations can affect the developed world by person-to-person transmission and mutation. Although the developed world has more immunity to disease due to greater access to antibiotics, better health education, and more sanitary conditions, disease is adverse to stasis. Although Western medicine has discovered a small pox vaccine, widespread transmission of small pox in the developing world may produce a strain that our vaccine does not prevent and which eventually may reach Western shores. A new vaccine probably will be discovered, but many lives could be lost before this happens.

The less obvious way that disease in emerging economies affects the developed world is through economic drag. Many of the goods and services consumed in the developed world are produced or performed by inexpensive labor in the developing world. If widespread disease prevents those workers from performing these tasks, the cost of goods and services would be affected. In the short-run, the cost to the developed world of preventing or treating disease in the developing world may seem exorbitant. However, the global harm that third-world diseases can cause grows steadily greater.

Progress continues on the global health front; the result of greater awareness, better treatment, increased research and funding. Major diseases eventually may be subdued worldwide, if not entirely eliminated. But that requires early detection (especially in less-developed countries where new and epidemic diseases tend to arise), transparency, and the commitment of wealthy country resources (money and know-how) to contain diseases before they spread. It may seem counterintuitive to spend public money on an outbreak of disease a world away. But health problems are increasingly global. They require a global response.

6. Avian (Bird) Flu

Dominating the headlines during 2005–2006, the strain of bird flu known as H5N1 was touted as the next great pandemic. H5N1 is especially deadly (over one-half of those infected died) because it is a strain of flu that humans have never encountered. Our immune systems are ill equipped to fight it. Moreover, there were three flu pandemics during the last century, and experts think another is overdue. Although this particular virus has not yet mutated so that it can be transmitted from one human to another, epidemiologists believe that when it does, it could kill as few as 1.4 (mild scenario) or as many as 142 million persons (worst case) around the world. Hence, a possible bird flu pandemic provides an interesting globalization case study.[72]

Because fowl are easy and inexpensive to raise and have high nutritional value, they are a staple food. The problem with this is that, in less developed countries, people live in close contact with their livestock, often sleeping in the same house or same room. So it is no surprise that bird flu surfaced first in Hong Kong (in 1997), although it was seemingly expunged through a massive bird cull. It resurfaced again in Indonesia and Viet Nam in 2003 and quickly spread through Eastern Asia, the Middle East, and eventually to Europe.[73]

Until recently, it was common for developing countries to suppress news about the outbreak of potentially-epidemic diseases. One reason may be a loss of face or stigma, for such things are most likely to happen in those nations. This may have prompted China's secrecy in the early days of the SARs epidemic. Just as likely, it is the wish to avoid panic and to contain the disease quickly, preventing serious economic impact, such as a loss of tourism or a ban on exports. (When Thailand's flu troubles became known, its poultry exports plummeted by over one billion dollars.)[74] Secrecy was Britain's initial reaction to the BSE crisis. Once these problems are known, however, they move from national to regional or even international issues. That is the case with bird flu today. SARs was the pandemic that did not happen. BSE was largely contained in Europe. As a result of international action, perhaps bird flu will be quelled as well.

After all, there is no conclusive evidence of human to human transmission yet. And, although viral infections are known to mutate rapidly, it is conceivable that prophylactic measures will contain the disease. However, there are many persons who smuggle banned poultry or hide birds to naively avoid an export ban or culling. Transmission by wild bird migration also thwarts international efforts to control transmission.[75]

There is even the remote possibility that human-to-human transmission may prove difficult.[76] But this prospect does not excuse a lack of preparedness on the part of both developed and less-developed nations. And so President Bush proposed in the United Nations an "international effort" to address a possible flu pandemic by pooling resources, boosting surveillance, and improving governments' capacity to respond to outbreaks. This is certainly a better international response than those in past flu pandemics. But the only effective method of containment is an anti-viral vaccine and that is time-consuming to produce and in short supply. No vaccine currently available specifically targets the H5N1 strain.

The best vaccine available (Tami flu) was quickly purchased and stockpiled by wealthy nations under pressure from their citizens. But this left less-developed countries to fend for themselves. Moreover, most of the world's flu vaccine is produced in just nine countries; including five in Europe, Canada, and the United States. This raises a practical and an ethical question. Should developed countries protect themselves, and hope the flu is contained in less-developed nations? Or should vaccine be rushed to places where the flu breaks out, hoping to stem it at its source, before it spreads? (No more than a one-month buffer, considering global interconnectedness).[77]

Doing nothing is risky and short sighted, if not immoral. Particularly since third world diseases often spill over into the developed world; witness AIDS. Hence, the developed world needs to address the cycle of poverty and disease in developing countries, or suffer the consequences. Indeed, there is some evidence to suggest that, as developing economies advance, they become more prone to rich-country maladies like heart disease, cancer, and diabetes.[78] In the end it is probably far less expensive to anticipate and inoculate against disease, than it is to treat it once it begins to spread.

Whatever happens, increased transparency, and cooperation among the world's governments and scientific communities is surely a good thing. And the fact that an epidemic — if one does come — did not arrive sooner, gives scientists extra time to research effective vaccines, and streamline their production and distribution.[79] Whether the epidemic comes or not, the pan-global mobilization it provoked bodes well for future international health efforts to save lives, and billions in trade, especially for the most-vulnerable economies.

C. Environment

1. Introduction

Often compromised in the quest for economic progress, the environment may be the world's primary loser in the globalization game. For increased pollution is a natural—and seemingly inevitable—by-product of increased production. Additional pollution is generated by the transport of goods and services to consumers that steadily increase with population growth. On the other hand, experts have found that economic growth improves efficiency, which generally is "environmentally beneficial"; and that greater wealth increases the demand for and affordability of environmental protection.[80]

Unfortunately, some multinational corporations ignore the polluting effects of globalization, while some anti-global environmentalists condemn globalization as if it had no benefits whatever. All economic growth cannot be bad, or the world economy would have to stop dead. That is not going to happen. What is urgently needed is some workable trade-off between economic growth and environmental protection. A balance needs to be struck. For Buckminster Fuller warned us decades ago that environmental sustainability was the key to humankind's future.[81]

That said, protecting the environment in a global economy in which individuals, companies, and nations act individually, presents a real problem. The economic incentive for production and development are high, and the environmental impact of one farmer failing to rotate his crops, or one factory emitting pollutants, is negligible. However, when millions of acres are sowed with wheat or rice year after year and when millions of factories around the world spew out pollutants, the collective environmental harm is enormous. Today the global fishing fleet consists of 24 thousand factory ships and two million commercial craft. They pull eighty million tons of fish from the sea each year; four times the 1950 total. And the Grand Banks have been fished out. Obviously something must be done to save this precious resource.[82]

Unfortunately, individual incentives to engage in less-harmful practices are few. Land and crop rotation can be expensive, pollutants are an unavoidable byproduct of most production, and demand for fish keeps growing. Often, environmentally-friendly production is expensive or more complex. Because economic incentives rarely favor environmentalism and the environmental impact of individual acts is negligible, few individuals choose the healthy alternative. This, despite the fact that social benefits would be great, and profit loss could be limited. In the absence of consensus, environmental protection becomes a collective action problem.[83] The environment has become an issue that requires national and international governmental oversight and regulation, which, properly managed, will in time overcome the objections of those industry and business leaders around the world who regard "environmentalism" as contrary to economic growth.[84]

Consider just one example of the conflict between globalization and the environment, and the role that government could play in addressing it. The U.S.'s NAFTA agreement with Mexico allowed U.S. companies to ship components to Mexico for assemblage in border factories. The Mexicans wanted the work, and their less-expensive labor made the completed products more competitive in the marketplace. However, Mexican factories were not subject to U.S. environmental standards. As a result, they released industrial pollutants, reducing water and air quality in communities both in the U.S. and Mexico. Although the U.S. government has attempted to raise Mexico's environmental standards, the results are mixed.[85]

Whichever side of the environmental divide one is on, it is clear the world's environment is being degraded. Pollution cannot be contained within the polluting state. It travels downwind and downstream, affecting others. Likewise, an inevitable side effect of globalization is pollution and population growth. Both threaten the globe's future.[86] But globalization also raises awareness of the problem, promotes collective responses, and provides some tools to deal with the threat. This section explores the effects of globalization on environmental degradation, the prospect of governmental regulation, and the possibility that free market economics help to mitigate environmental harm.

To give just a small picture of the environmental problems facing future generations, consider that the world population now stands at 6.4 billion; four times the number in 1900. At current growth rates, it could reach nine billion by the year 2050, with most of the growth in the poorest countries. Poor agricultural practices cause the loss of over twenty billion tons of topsoil every year. And two billion people have no access to clean water.[87] Fortunately, the environmental movement is beginning to gain traction in developed nations; for the third world cannot tackle this problem alone.[88]

There is not room here to address the manifold environmental issues of concern, but we consider the major ones; for example, pollution/global warming, energy, resource depletion, endangered species, and waste disposal.

2. Pollution

Inextricably linked with development are the problems caused by pollution; development's unfortunate byproduct. Nearly everything produced is a source of pollution when manufactured. And most continue to be so when used.

Something as integral to development as a factory cannot be built without concrete and steel, yet the production of those materials creates harmful emissions. Once built, the machines must run on gasoline, diesel, or electricity, all of which emit pollutants, when burned or in their production. Finally, whatever a factory owner decides to produce, will create effluent, or difficult-to-dispose-of byproducts.

In a world without governments, economic growth would likely progress, untroubled by its environmental impacts, until environmental degradation began to impact growth, profit, human health, or all three. Few actors would change practices in order to market themselves as "environmentally friendly" before this point. Since costs would likely be higher and profits lower, the incentive would insufficient. This is essentially what free-market advocates preach; their tipping point is continuously postponed by marginal profitability. However, before environmental degradation became severe in Europe and America, governments stepped in to regulate the worst polluters. That has had some effect on slowing environmental damage. However, it was resisted by businesspersons who argue that regulation raises costs, reduces profits, and forces job cuts.

What the opponents of environmental regulation choose to ignore, especially when those regulations affect their business, is that environmental damage is harmful to the economy as a whole. China's environmental track record provides an interesting example.

During the late 1980s and 1990s, China experienced unprecedented economic growth and industrialization. Its economic planners at that time believed that unfettered development was the most efficient way for China to modernize. The government quickly realized, however, that unregulated development hurt the economy more than it helped it. By the year 2000, problems caused by China's environmental degradation cost it an annual 8 to 12 percent of its $1.4 trillion GDP in direct damage, such as the impact of acid rain on crops, medical expenses, work lost due to illness, and money spent on natural disaster relief. As a result, China implemented ambitious emission-reduction targets, and boosted environmental spending to 700 billion yuan ($85 billion) for 2001–2005; equivalent to 1.3% of GDP. These reforms were only marginally successful, however, because a 2007 World Health Organization report estimated that three-quarter million Chinese still die prematurely every year due to air and water pollution. Some of the reports findings were so "sensitive" that they were suppressed by the Chinese government.[89]

Environmental damage in China came from more than just factory emissions, however. Inefficient farming caused desertification that has resulted in repeated, debilitating dust storms in Beijing. In 1998, after deforestation caused the Yangtze River to burst its banks, killing 2,500 people and costing billions of dollars in damage, China issued orders to protect, rehabilitate, and replant its forests.[90]

Populous, rapidly-developing emerging economies are the most polluted. So it is no surprise that the top five most polluted cities in the world are in India (2), China (2), and Egypt. Their residents inhale about five times more smoke and dust than residents of America's two most-polluted cities, Los Angeles and New York. Indeed, 14 of the 20 cities with the highest concentrations of sulfur dioxide (precursor to acid-rain) are in China. Much of the reason for this pollution is the need for energy to drive booming economies; and in China this means high-sulfur coal. China mines produce nearly one billion tons of coal every year. Coal provides three-quarters of China's energy. But it is dangerous for the miners and those who breathe the polluted air. And China's neighbors, Japan and South Korea, complain of acid rain "made in China." Worldwide, between 800,000 and 1.6 million premature deaths are attributed to pollution and the climate change it fosters; most of them in emerging countries. But even emerging economies like India, which is making an earnest effort to address pollution, do not have the infrastructure to control the problem.[91]

Transportation-related pollution also increases rapidly in emerging economies, due to the need to move raw materials, people and finished goods. Food production, population growth, and industrial processes also increase demand for water. In China, some 400 cities suffer acute water shortages and one-half of its rivers are polluted.[92] As far back as 2004, President Hu committed China to a more sensitive "green" policy, if for no other reason to impress the world of China's first-world status by the time of the 2008 Beijing Olympic Games. But, given China's decades-long emphasis on growth and the low value it places on ecological projects, this may be a hard ship to turn around. Nevertheless, China is making progress with solar and wind energy, and getting help from others; notably the EU. For FDI and technology transfer seem necessary to achieve any slowdown in Asia's pollution output. On the other hand, as wages rise, pollution seems likely to decline; probably a combination of moving up the economic ladder, efficiencies, and consumer concern.[93]

This brings us naturally to the UN's Kyoto Protocol on climate change, launched in 1997 and meant to reduce greenhouse gas emissions below 1990 levels by 2012. While solid in principle, the negotiations were contentious in terms of each countries' obligations and whether reduction goals could or would be met. In the end, China, the second-largest contributor to global warming (with 14 percent of greenhouse gas emissions) and other major Asian polluters like India and South Korea were excused because they were developing economies. The U.S., responsible for 22 percent of global greenhouse gases, never ratified the treaty, which languished for many years before Russia (in return for EU support for its WTO membership bid) agreed to sign and brought the treaty into force. Technically the U.S. was left out, but it continues to participate in negotiations aimed at pollution and climate control, for they continue to be a major global threat.[94]

3. Climate Change

The Kyoto Protocol is a principal example of international regulation meant to address environmental harm. It is actually an amendment to the United Nations Framework Convention on Climate Change (UNFCCC). Countries that joined Kyoto agreed to reduce emissions of carbon dioxide and five other greenhouse gasses below 1990 levels by 2012, or to engage in emissions trading if they could not. The objective was the "stabilization of greenhouse gas concentrations in the atmosphere at a level that would prevent dangerous anthropogenic interference with the climate system." The proposed cuts were quite modest, however. Despite this, many of the world's largest polluters declined to join the protocol.

Although once a signatory, the U.S. never ratified the protocol. The reasons for this are varied. President Clinton never submitted the treaty to Congress. President George W. Bush objected to the free ride given developing countries, and the strain Kyoto would place on the American economy.[95]

Developing countries such as China and India, insisted they should be exempt because the bulk of greenhouse gasses currently contributing to global warming were produced by developed nations.[96] This argument makes sense if conditions were static. However, global warming was unknown during the years of western industrialization. Today we know that global warming affects the entire globe. Hence, the climate-changing effect of greenhouse gases should be the concern of every nation.

The question remains whether Kyoto signatories will meet their reduction targets. If they do, a lot will be due to emissions trading, which is more likely to limit the growth of emissions than to reduce them. The EU scheme, eventually meant to expand world-wide, allocates emission allowances that conservators can sell to polluters. But, if the allocations are too generous, there is little reduction and little market demand.[97] And this is before Russia (a seller) and Japan (a buyer) join the EU to create a global system. So whether a trading scheme will reduce emissions on a global scale is open to question.

Environmentalists claim that Kyoto's allocations were too generous, while businessmen worry that the extra cost of emission purchases or control will make them uncompetitive. Neither seems to be true. British Petroleum was able to reduce emission below 1990 levels in just five years at no net cost. Hence, a successor to Kyoto seemed possible.

A December 2005 conference in Montreal tried to envision a post-Kyoto world (after 2012). The U.S. and China would have to be involved and a compliance mechanism would be necessary, as would the transfer of clean technologies to large developing-country polluters.[98] By the time of the G-8 summit at Gleneagles in mid-2005, which included the U.S., political positions had begun to soften. Some states had enacted emissions standards, and U.S. voters and businessmen had become more concerned about global warming. Although the summit did not set definite standards, it did agree that climate change was a "serious long-term challenge" that must be addressed with urgency and resolve.[99]

American businesses such as GE, Ford, DuPont and IBM were adopting more environmentally-friendly practices for both economic, and public-relations reasons. After all, the cost gap between renewable and conventional energy is shrinking, and one day may favor the former. Beyond business incentives, however, it is difficult for me to accept that multinational corporations are born polluters with a callous disregard for human health. Businesses also see opportunities in green technologies.[100]

Thanks to the leadership of the European Union, a breakthrough of sorts was achieved at the Bali climate conference (December 2007). An agreement was reached among 187 nations, including the U.S., China and India, to develop a global climate change policy by the end of 2009, to replace Kyoto (which expires in 2012). The U.S. government and businesses had gradually accepted the proposition that climate change was a serious global problem that must be addressed. But the government still refused to accept binding and legally-enforceable emissions targets. And businesses for their part saw public relations and business opportunities.[101]

In addition, China and the "Group of 77" developing countries—heretofore free riders under the Kyoto agreement—agreed at Bali to adopt "mitigation plans." And China, India and other developing economies in Asia and Central and Eastern Europe are among the world's largest polluters today.[102]

The biggest questions unresolved at Bali are what exactly is to be done, by whom, and at what cost. It is clear that the poorest nations will be hit hardest by climate change; severe storms, floods, droughts, malnutrition and starvation. But it is the rich countries that have the capital and technology to arrest environmental degradation. Will they commit so much when the danger seems so remote?

On the other hand, the estimated cost at present is a relatively affordable 3 percent of global GDP; expensive, but not outrageous.[103] Much of the answer turns on just how urgent the situation is perceived to be. And, unfortunately, opinions differ among the primary stakeholders; scientists, economists, business persons, politicians, and the general public about just how urgent the problem is. Nonetheless, international consensus to confront climate change does seem to be building. Indeed, a further step of sorts was taken at the G8 summit in mid-2008 (with major developing-country polluters present) when the G8 leaders agreed to "adopt" 50 percent cuts in greenhouse gas emissions by 2050. But no details were agreed to, and the target date is a long way off.[104]

Both public and private leadership is necessary to accomplish this goal. And for the moment the European Union seems to have assumed the mantle of environmental superpower. Because population density in Europe is about five times that in the U.S., the Europeans are more concerned about the environment than Americans, or most of the rest of the world. But they must be careful about setting regional standards concerning genetically-modified organisms (GMOs) or chemicals that exceed what other global players are willing to accept, and that could upset the delicate balance between trade and environmental protection.[105]

The problem is that the potentially-irreversible damage done by pollution and environmental degradation is gradual and subtle. Before we reach the "tipping point" of irreversibility, mankind as a whole must agree upon a sustainable solution. I doubt that will happen before 2010, but it might by 2012.

4. Energy

The main reason for the increase in greenhouse gas emissions and environmental pollution is the production of energy. Developing economies, and today's technological advances: air travel; robots; the internet; cell phones, to name but a few, all require energy. Indeed, energy demand may increase by as much as 50 percent by the year 2030. But the main sources of energy today, oil and coal, are notorious polluters. So greenhouse gas emissions are expected to rise by a similar amount. Yet a reliable supply of energy is essential to economic growth. Where will tomorrow's energy come from; will its rising cost influence the global economy; will it further pollute the environment?

Americans consume almost 21 million barrels of oil a day, about one-quarter of the world total. China, now second at 6.4 million barrels a day, could double its demand by 2020. But both countries produce only about one-half of the oil they consume, so they must import the rest. Global production, however, is near capacity, so prices rise. And, with over seventy percent of oil reserves controlled by state-owned companies, oil security could become a problem; as the Europeans discovered when Russia sharply reduced its supply of natural gas.[106] Many of these national oil companies are poorly run, and have failed to invest sufficiently in infrastructure, so production is not likely to increase. Moreover, new resources are most likely to be found in these countries, since exploration of other areas has been relatively thorough, although some new fields may yet be discovered. Of course, offshore oil exploration in U.S. waters could, and probably will, be increased. But this will satisfy America's energy needs for only a few more years, and there are serious environmental hazards involved.

A tight market is prone to disruption; whether through armed conflict, natural disasters (Gulf hurricanes), or political maneuvering.[107] And nations rich in oil and gas are likely to try to leverage their position in the marketplace. But since energy sales are the principal source of state income for most producers, and consumers have some flexibility in supply, the room for maneuver may be less than it appears. Thus, while "energy security" is important to global growth, it does not seem to be a serious threat at present.

If demand for energy in both the developed and developing world (China/India) is rising steadily relative to supply, then it also raises the specter of energy competition. But, rather than spawning hostilities, shortage could lead to greater cooperation and emphasis on efficient use of energy. For there is much wastage. For example, China's iron and steel industries consume 16 percent of China's energy versus 2 percent for the same industries in the U.S. (albeit smaller). Whereas America's least-efficient user is residential housing.[108]

A greater concern would seem to be the cost of energy. There have been four prior occasions on which it was thought the world was "running out of oil." And yet output has increased by sixty percent in the past three decades, and we are not sure we have reached the "peak"; the "age of permanent shortage." But if developing-country demand keeps rising and new resources or efficiencies are not found, energy costs will continue to rise rapidly for both businesses and consumers, with the potential to seriously dampen economic growth. Energy, as a percentage of U.S. goods imports, more than doubled between 1997 and 2007.[109]

All this anxiety about energy shortages marginalizes an equally great concern. And that is the harm to the environment done by burning such vast quantities of fossil fuels. Pollution of every sort is increasing rapidly in both developed and developing countries. There is no longer any serious doubt that something must be done about out-of-control energy consumption and global warming. But, when it comes to what should be done, there is no consensus. That America should reduce its dependence on foreign oil seems indisputable. That we could ever become energy independent seems far fetched. Yet no plan has emerged. And we should not have to cobble one together rapidly in the face of a real energy crisis. Nor should it pit nations against one another due to scarcity.[110]

One of America's foremost futurists likened the earth's energy resources to an "automobile's storage battery which must be conserved to turn over our main engine...." He felt that mankind could not afford to expend the world's fossil fuels faster than they were being replenished. But it seems that we are doing so. For it takes many, many years for coal and oil deposits to be formed. He felt the need to "convert man's spin-dive toward [energy] oblivion into an intellectually mastered power pull-out into safe and level flight"; in other words, "sustainability."[111]

That lesson is gradually beginning to sink in. Large multinational corporations are exploring renewable energy sources (solar and wind) and trying to reduce fossil fuel consumption and emissions in order to become at least "carbon neutral." Governments are helping them by devising carbon trading systems. Some Swedish companies have even pledged not to use fossil fuels faster than their rate of regeneration. That is a pleasant thought, but hardly a globe-encircling one.[112]

More reasonable by far is to tap into the rich store of the earth's renewable energy; solar, wind, wave, geothermal, nuclear and so forth. These are quite feasible methods of producing energy; indeed, the first is the ultimate source of fossil fuel in the first place. What is needed is a greater investment (capital and research) in bringing these technologies to market. And certainly western economies have the resources to do that. But developing economies cannot expect to get a permanent bye either. Indeed, two (China and South Korea) have joined the U.S., EU, Japan and Russia to build a reactor to test fusion as a sustainable source of energy.[113] These are both short-term and long-term projects. But if we do not begin now, we will pay far more later.

5. Other Sources of Environmental Degradation

There are so many other environmental problems that there is room here to address only some of the largest and most-obvious; notably, farming, fishing, deforestation, and waste.

a. Farming and Deforestation

As mentioned earlier, comparative advantage drives the process of globalization. Food production, on its face, may seem to have similar economic advantages; tropical countries are well situated to grow crops that require lots of sun and heat, and countries with abundant space are well situated to grow staples like wheat and corn. While monoculture farming may be profitable for those growing bananas in the Caribbean or wheat in Kansas, it can have dire environmental consequences; crop specialization can make countries overly dependent on export trade. Monoculture farming also degrades soil quality and, ultimately, the environmental and economic health of the region. Single-crop countries lose their independence, because they must import foods that might be grown locally, and because of the harm monoculture can do to the environment.

In a particularly perverse example of how the developed world can exploit emerging economies in the name of free trade, the WTO's Trade Related Intellectual Property (TRIPs) agreement permits corporations to patent life forms such as seeds. Once patented, indigenous farmers, who sowed these crops for generations, must pay a fee to the patent holders in order to grow native crops. Generally, the only way these farmers can afford the seeds is to buy them in bulk. But sowing so many seeds with the same genetic make-up reduces biodiversity, further degrades soils, and increases the likelihood of famine due to crop failure.[114]

Consider also the plight of a Brazilian dirt farmer. In order to feed his large family, he must level some rain forest; a resource important to everyone. But, because his farming methods are poor and his yield is low, he quickly degrades the soil, much of which is lost to erosion. So he levels more rainforest. He will not stop, however, until he is given a better alternative. Environmental protection is rarely a concern of an unemployed, impoverished, starving population.

As a result, about thirty percent of the earth's tropical forests have disappeared since 1960, most due to logging, with about 100 thousand square miles lost every year, and only a small amount replanted. Twenty-two thousand square miles of arable land turns to desert every year and, thanks to poor agricultural practices, 20 billion tons of topsoil is lost. Or consider Afghan farmers who plant poppies that are used to create 6,100 tons of opium, not because they support the Taliban or wish to fuel drug addiction, but because it is the most valuable crop they can grow.[115] Given alternatives, better farming methods, and irrigation, not only could we curb much environmental damage, but starving populations might be saved. Indeed, it has been established that as poor rural economies develop they take better care of the environment. This might particularly be the case if hearty, pest-resistant biotech (GMO) crops were planted in inhospitable regions. GMO crops have been opposed by the EU, and viewed with suspicion by some agricultural populations, but they are gradually catching on outside the U.S.

b. Fishing

Over-fishing is also an environmental concern. Fish stock is a renewable resource, but only if allowed to restore itself regularly. As with all other environmental extractions, sustainability is the key. And yet, there is no adequate international control to prevent over-fishing. Moreover, the fishing process causes collateral damage to other species, just as deforestation results in specie and habitat loss. But specie protection adds to the expense. The damage that globalization is doing to our oceans threatens the marine habitat fish stocks need to recover.[116]

c. Waste

There was a time when human waste was biodegradable, or at least did not pose any serious, long-term threat to the planet. But today's dependence on fossil fuels and high-tech electronic devices pose a whole new threat. The latter account for about 20 to 50 million tons of waste a year. Only about ten percent is recycled and half of that is done in developing countries, where the process may be environmentally unsound. Large quantities of e-waste end up in U.S. landfills, where its synthetic chemicals, lead, and other metals leech into the soil and groundwater; eventually turning up in food and animals, including humans. This new form of long-lived waste is one of the "most complex and non-biodegradable forms of trash ever." But, excepting the EU and Japan, there are no standards concerning its control. Waste reduction and recycling need to be priorities before we poison our atmosphere and ourselves.[117]

Whereas environmental regulations slow the process and increase the cost of globalization, they are a necessary restraint on productivity and consumption run amok. If some extreme environmentalists seem to favor a return to the Stone Age, which is improbable at best, ecological balance is necessary; and ultimately unavoidable if life on earth is to be sustained.[118]

D. Conclusion

While globalization has contributed to labor unease, the spread of disease, and various environmental ills, it also has raised global awareness about these problems and contributed to their solution. Clearly, it is the developed nations of the world that have the primary responsibility for addressing the problems, for they contribute heavily to them and have technology and resources that developing economies do not. But the latter have a role as well. The problems won't be solved if developing-country polluters are given a free ride; which they often claim is their due. Conversely, higher labor and environmental standards should not be employed to rob developing nations of their comparative advantages; as they often believe they are. Sadly, intransigence on both sides has made a final solution difficult.

Setting international labor, health, and environmental standards assumes that the world's economies are homogenous enough to agree on a common standard. I do not believe that this is the case at present. But I do see progress toward that goal. There is no great mystery about what needs to be done. The United Nations' Millennium Goals, the Johannesburg Summit on Sustainable Development, and the Copenhagen Consensus all give ample testimony of this. Moreover labor, health, and environmental standards are already finding their way into bilateral trade agreements; a probable precursor to broader agreements. The International Labor Organization is working on minimum labor standards. There is a U.S./EU joint declaration on HIV/AIDS, malaria, and tuberculosis and the Kyoto protocol. Eventually, these issues will make it onto the negotiating agenda of the WTO. If globalization has created these problems, it also can contribute to their solution. If the problems are global in scope, why should the solutions be otherwise? And, if we can arrest growth of the polar ozone hole, why should these problems be beyond our reach?[119]

Chapter IX

Capacity Building

A. Introduction

Generally speaking, less-well-developed and least-developed nations (as opposed to emerging economies) have domestic problems so severe and systemic that for the most part they are unattractive to global traders. Hence they are marginalized in the globalization process, and will not profit from it without substantial help; often called "capacity building."

The causes for their not reaching a greater level of development are numerous, involving both political and economic factors. Less and least-developed economies are characterized by unstable governments, isolated and under-developed economies with weak regulatory regimes and poor infrastructure. In some of the worst cases, dictatorial and/or corrupt governments operate by whim and cronyism (as apposed to market-driven decision making.)[1] Resources are scarce, and those that exist are often squandered, which discourages internal and external investment. In other cases, civil conflict so destabilizes the country that economic planning is impossible. Or the country is so poor that mere subsistence takes priority over planning.

There is little or no rule of law or it cannot be reliably enforced, so property and capital are at risk.[2] A lack of economic regulation makes investment too speculative. Due to poverty and a lack of potable water and adequate sanitation, famine and disease are widespread. And the resources needed to address these problems are siphoned away from long-term development goals by persistent crises.[3] Small wonder that these countries have poor labor, environmental, and safety standards, and high unemployment.

The domestic problems of each developing country are somewhat different, of course, but the list above, while not exhaustive, suggests some of the more common challenges these economies face and which hold them back.

Without the basic ingredients of life, and the infrastructure to deliver them, economic growth is stifled. With poor prospects for return on domestic investment and financial insecurity at home, much of the country's wealth, if any, is invested abroad.[4] Poor governance is common in developing countries. That fosters economic waste and corruption that further deters growth.

Developing countries' economies are generally export dependent. But they often are unable to exploit export opportunities due to weak infrastructure and external constraints, like import tariffs and non-tariff barriers such as agricultural subsidies and sanitary standards. It is not uncommon for post-industrial countries to protect their agricultural sector (a small—and shrink-ing—proportion of national GDP) through a combination of tariffs, quotas, supports, and export subsidies. Unsubsidized and inefficient farmers in less-developed countries simply cannot compete.[5] This prevents the latter from gaining a foothold on even the lowest rung of the economic ladder. Sanitary standards, while important, generally have an exclusionary effect as well.

In developing countries, overpopulation, mixed with generally poor levels of health and education, also frustrate economic development. The core of the work force is low-skilled, earning relatively low wages. Many are unem-ployed.[6] Some developing countries must cope with civil unrest and even armed conflict.

Globalization has improved the living standards in numerous developing countries, so that significantly fewer persons in the world are living in extreme poverty today than there were fifty years ago, when an estimated 55 percent lived on less than a dollar a day.[7] The substantial decrease in world poverty over that period owes a lot to the development of a robust world economy.

However, the gap between the developed and developing world has widened. This leads to tension, anger, and even backlash (especially against the U.S.; the wealthiest large nation on earth). The events of 9/11 and thereafter bring into sharp focus the potentially-explosive friction between developed and unde-veloped economies; leading directly to the so-called "development" trade round of GATT negotiations (the Doha Development Agenda).

The efforts of developed states to build economic capacity in less-developed countries are one way to close the development gap and assuage their anger. However, this implies a transfer of capital and know-how to those states, and perhaps some leniency toward them with regard trade rules and their en-forcement.[8] But these transfers are not always supported by the public in the donor state and can be misused by the donee state. Without capacity build-ing, however, the isolation, hostility, and plight of less developed economies will increase. Their problems will spill over into the developed world. That would be disadvantageous to both. For, if developing states cannot export goods to developed states, they will export violence, drugs, disease, environ-mental problems and refugees.[9]

It is clear that these states cannot profit from the global economy without substantial help. Indeed, it is widely accepted by the international community that capacity building is anchored in economic development and poverty reduction.[10] But, to attract that help, less developed countries must put their own houses in order, as members of the African Union have lately realized. As long as they remain isolated and unwilling to reform, less developed economies will benefit very little from globalization.

Whatever the reasons, the failure of developing countries to meaningfully participate in the globalization process has left 1.1 billion people—21 percent of the world's population in 2001—isolated in extreme poverty (living on less than $1 per day).[11] By providing appropriately focused foreign aid and trade opportunities conditioned on sound governance standards, developing economies can build capacity and profit from the global marketplace.

B. Foreign Aid

Foreign aid comes from many sources, both public and private, and has a variety of objectives. Some aid is humanitarian in nature; meant to address man-made or natural crises. Some involves cross border investment. And some is what we think of as public foreign aid, although that has shrunk considerably in amount. Indeed the reader may be surprised to learn that sixty percent of U.S. foreign aid today comes from private rather than public sources.[12] Nevertheless, government aid, or Overseas Development Aid (ODA), remains significant.

1. Humanitarian Aid

Humanitarian aid is extended to all countries in time of crisis, including developed countries, which by definition should not need it. It is meant to deal with a variety of catastrophes, including civil war, earthquake, tsunami, floods, drought, malnutrition and disease. This type of public and private aid provides for the feeding, sheltering, and medical treatment of refugees and maintenance of services and order during a time of crisis. One example followed Hurricane Katrina, when countries that normally receive U.S. aid offered aid to us instead.[13]

This form of aid helps all countries, and especially developing countries, avoid social instability during unexpected crises. It is a complement to development aid. However, emergency aid differs starkly from development assistance, since it is temporary; in response to an acute problem. It merely restores, or attempts to restore, the affected nation to normality. Thus, humanitarian aid does little or nothing to aid build capacity.

Development aid, on the other hand, is meant to have a lasting impact. Some forms of development aid can take longer to have that impact than others, however. Late-impact aid includes that aimed at education, human health, environmental protection, and other social services and infrastructure development; including state-building.

2. Public Assistance

While some academics still debate whether it was necessary for the U.S. to give billions of dollars in aid to Europe under the Marshall Plan,[14] Congress seems to have generally accepted the value of foreign assistance in a post-9/11 world. Since 1960, U.S. ODA has quadrupled. As a percentage of GDP, however, ODA has declined; falling to 0.1 percent in 1998 from about 0.5 percent in the mid-1960s. Since 1990 U.S. ODA has not surpassed 0.21 percent of GDP.[15]

Although the U.S. has never reached the UN-recommended ODA target of .7 percent of GDP, the U.S. gives more in ODA than any other individual country save Japan, and gives more in *total* development assistance (public and private) than any single nation. However, the European Union and its constituent member states lead in total aid.[16] Much of the EU aid is earmarked for 79 underdeveloped African, Caribbean, and Pacific (ACP) countries, most of them former colonies of EU member states. Indeed, the EU expects to double ODA by 2010 and to reach the U.N Millennium development goal of .7 percent of GDP by 2015. But that raises the spectre of "welfare colonialism."[17]

While the amount each donor offers and the programs they support will vary, governments typically offer foreign aid for purposes that are strategic, political, and/or economic in nature. Humanitarian aid in a crisis is fairly apolitical, although not entirely so.

The initial context for foreign aid was the Cold War, during which nations on each side offered development and military aid to those they perceived to be their allies. While foreign aid continues to be strategically distributed, the focus changed with the end of the Cold War. U.S. aid presently favors allies in the War on Terror, the War on Drugs, and opponents of nuclear proliferation. Preferential treatment in aid distribution is also given to countries that engage in democratic reforms.[18]

Like humanitarian relief, late-impact aid is meant to help developing countries improve governmental and social stability. If social inequalities are ignored and critical public services underfunded, it may prompt excluded groups to civil disorder.[19] Hence, foreign aid (ODA) is essential not just to improve developing countries' ability to compete in the global marketplace, but also to maintain peace and stability; a precondition for growth.

ODA that leads to job creation and technology transfer is especially important to capacity building. Projects of this sort tend to have a much earlier impact on a country's economy and can aid political stability. Early impact aid encompasses most construction projects, including expanding transport infrastructure, improving communications networks, and developing other physical infrastructure. Programs that offer debt relief or temporary budget support to developing countries also have immediate effects on their capacity for development. But, as Professor Krugman has observed, huge inflows of capital make success immediate, but illusory, if the developing economy isn't succeeding in its own right.[20]

Of course, public financial assistance to troubled economies is not just bilateral, as is the case with most ODA. Multilateral agencies like the World Bank and International Monetary Fund (IMF) also seek to build capacity and stability. And the United Nations has recently weighed in with its own ambitious program to halve extreme poverty in the world by 2015.[21] Each of these organizations depends upon the largesse of its members, of course, but otherwise they operate largely free of national influence.

The World Bank is a long-term lender to poor countries that need capital to build their economies. The IMF makes emergency loans to troubled member economies in order to stabilize them during a fiscal crisis. It has been relatively successful in that role, although its clients are chiefly marginal or emerging economies that need substantial fiscal reform.[22] During the Asian fiscal crisis of 1997–98, the IMF was accused of setting insensitive, draconian reform standards as a pre-condition for loans. But, partly as a result, Asian economies have grown larger and stronger, so there is less need for them to borrow. Indeed, forty percent of emerging-market debt is now rated "investment grade," and IMF disbursements have dropped from over $39 billion in 2002 to just $1.9 billion in 2006. Emerging markets have grown stronger, more open and learned lessons from their excesses of the 1980s and 1990s. They also have been aided by a surge of private direct investment.[23]

Those borrowers that are strong enough to do so are keen to pay off their debt to the Fund, in order to save interest payments and to escape its discipline. But this assumes that those countries will impose sufficient fiscal discipline on themselves.[24]

Meanwhile the Fund and Bank are reforming themselves; making their practices more flexible and increasing the influence of emerging economies such as China, South Korea, Turkey and Mexico, in order to reflect the global economy as it is today, rather than as it was in the late 1940s, when these institutions were created.

The World Bank has cracked down on corruption and poor governance; primary reasons for the waste of borrowed funds.[25] Indeed, when emerging economies grow strong enough, they are able to issue their own debt.[26] And debt relief has been granted to some of the world's poorest countries. This could chill the willingness of lenders to lend and encourage the profligacy of borrowers, but it is the only way to relieve crippling debt burdens and allow these countries to focus on development rather than repayment.[27]

Regional banks have been set up (for example, the European Investment Bank, EIB) to make development funds available in various regions. This probably will further diminish the role of the World Bank and IMF. But perhaps the time for that has come.

3. Foreign Direct Investment (FDI)

The rise in FDI—although technically not foreign aid—has also done much to assist developing countries, and reduce their need for ODA; at least those countries that can attract FDI. FDI rose to $916 billion in 2005, 29 percent higher than 2004. Much of the growth was attributable to increased investment in developing countries. While most developed-nation FDI flows to other developed states, FDI to developing countries reached a high of $334 billion in 2005; most of it going to Asia. Moreover, FDI flows between developing countries themselves has increased over fourteen times (to $61 billion) in the past twenty years. Indeed, three-quarters of FDI in China is Asian. Only thirteen percent comes from the U.S. and Europe.[28]

The latest (perhaps last great) challenge is to draw Sub-Saharan Africa into the global trading system. This is no easy task, for the countries of this region have few prospects and have been marginalized by the globalization process for many years. Nonetheless, their resuscitation could relieve a persistent drag on global trade (ongoing civil wars, disease, and starvation). Indeed, Africans themselves are collaborating to improve economic integration; for they are tired of being viewed as the world's economic basket case.[29]

C. Virtues and Vices of Aid

Most donors no longer dole out foreign aid in the perfunctory manner that developing countries came to expect. In the past, great sums of money were spent on development assistance with paltry results. Often, corrupt officials siphoned off money or channeled it into inefficient state-owned industries. Hence, the aid did not reach its intended beneficiaries. In other cases, the financing was insufficient in amount or duration to achieve its intended goals, or planning and implementation was poor.

To be effective, foreign aid and the recipient country's corresponding development efforts must lead eventually to self sustainability. Continuing dependency is dangerous, since funding is not always available, or sufficient, or may not go to the neediest parties. But aid that is pledged must be timely and consistently delivered, otherwise the donor himself contributes to the failure of the enterprise. Indeed, the long-term reliability of aid can be more important than the amount. But giving is fickle, and at present around a dozen African countries are dependent on aid for a fifth or more of their national income.[30]

Hence, foreign aid needs be allocated in a way that creates incentives for countries to develop economically and politically and avoids creating further obstacles to this process. Aid is often conditioned on continued monitoring of projects during and after their implementation. This requires that programs be well-designed and transparent and that accurate data be collected at various stages to permit objective assessment. If the project ceases to be productive, it needs to be revised or terminated. But the conditions and assessment that accompany the aid shouldn't overwhelm the project itself. Some "policy space" is needed if capacity is to be built. Since public financial aid may never be adequate to meet all needs, attention has increasingly turned to multilateral coordination, cooperation, focus and oversight. Rather than simply more aid, the target is better (more productive) aid.[31]

D. Private Development Assistance

As noted previously, private (as opposed to public) development assistance represents about two-thirds of the total amount; about $33.6 billion in 2000. It has grown rapidly in recent years, and comes from a variety of sources, including foundations, universities, religious groups, corporations, private organizations, and individual remittances. Of these, the latter three are especially important. While corporate assistance to developing countries was only $2.8 billion in 2000,[32] corporate contributions to economic development skyrocket if one includes FDI. Admittedly, FDI is not technically foreign aid, but it can be a huge factor in capacity building.

Since developing countries generally have limited capital resources, FDI can be vital to their development.[33] It frequently leads to improvements in infrastructure, such as factories and communications, and generally involves the transfer of technology, and modern management methods.[34] It also creates jobs. In addition, increases in foreign investment tend to stimulate domestic investment.[35] Conversely, developing countries often invest abroad, so that the outflow of FDI can exceed the inflow.[36] And, where the investment climate is marred by corruption, macroeconomic instability and weak and uncertain government regulation, the risk to investment can chill the incentive to do so.[37]

As previously said, most developed-countries' FDI goes to other developed countries; those that have wealthy consumer markets, transparent and predictable regulatory systems, and a reliable rule of law. Hence, of the estimated $916 billion of inward FDI in 2005, $422 billion went to the European Union. Of the $334 billion that went to developing countries, most went to emerging economies like China, Taiwan, South Korea and India. Unlike ODA, very little goes to the least developed countries. Nonetheless, global FDI exceeds U.S. ODA by 90 times and all U.S. foreign aid by 40 times. In less attractive Asian nations, Latin America, and Africa, so-called "third-world multinationals" tend to invest more heavily than first-world investors, due perhaps to their experience operating in regions where politics and the economy are volatile. It is estimated that more than one-third of the FDI that developing countries receive comes from other developing countries.[38]

Countries with stifling bureaucracies and poor infrastructure, such as India, have a relatively difficult time attracting investment. Government red-tape and public opposition to privatization and foreign investment has not helped India attract large quantities of FDI to build its economy.[39] Conversely, China has begun to allow foreigners greater control of local companies. These changes have given China access to foreign technologies, which help its enterprises become more efficient and competitive in a global market.[40]

Growth opportunities in China take investors only so far, however. China's investment climate, while showing signs of improvement, still suffers from an "opaque bureaucracy and maze of ever-changing rules," which accounts for the significant gap between the foreign investment that is contracted annually and the amount that actually materializes. The opaqueness of the Chinese market and uncertainty of returns may explain why most investment in China is Asian.[41]

According to USAID, private organizations ($6.6 billion), religious groups ($3.4 billion), and foundations ($1.5 billion) constitute the next largest proportion of private development aid. But this does not begin to account for the resurgence of targeted foreign aid from such sources as the Gates Foundation and others. According to one source, charitable giving in the U.S. was $249 billion in 2004—about two percent of GDP—and is on the rise. Admittedly, not all of this philanthropy is aimed at developing nations, but some of it is narrowly focused on their most endemic problems and could prove an enormous boost to developing nations.[42]

To me, the most unexpected source of private financial aid to developing economies is individual remittances; money sent by immigrant wage-earners back to their native country. This amount reached about $276 billion in 2006 according to the World Bank. In some cases (Haiti), it was a full one-quarter of GDP. Obviously, it underscores the virtues of—and need for—enlightened migrant-worker programs. But, like all offshore aid, remits (and migration) decline when economies tighten.[43]

Of course, capital transfer—public or private—has both virtues and vices. One does not want it to become a new form of colonialism, creating dependency and a permanent underclass. The aid must be temporary, with the eventual goal being donee self-sufficiency. Neither should aid be exposed to corruption and waste. Finally aid is no substitute for domestic consumption in a healthy, growing economy. Without cooperation, coordination and focus, none of these things are likely to happen.

E. Expanded Trade Can Fuel Economic Growth for Developing Countries

Although domestic consumption forms the largest part of most nations' GDP, foreign trade can be a powerful stimulant to economic growth. For example, an estimated twenty percent of the growth in U.S. per capita GDP between 1950 and 2003 has been credited to trade.[44] For developing countries, trade can be even more important.[45] Poverty and illness often reduce domestic consumption, making developing economies even more dependent upon export trade. This should not be resisted, but accommodated, by developed nations. Indeed, the lesson of September 11, 2001 should not be for developed nations to close their borders and protect their wealth. Rather it is to allow developing economies to participate fully in economic growth. For there is good evidence that increased trade, fairly conducted, aids both rich and poor; and it is isolation that cripples them.[46] So it is no wonder that, shortly after the attacks on the World Trade Center and Pentagon, an ambitious "development round" of trade negotiations was launched by WTO members in Doha, Qatar; the so-called "Doha Development Round" of GATT.

Given the title of the round, and the anxiety at the time about isolated, underdeveloped countries, one might have expected rapid progress in the negotiations. (The round was scheduled to end in 2006). Unfortunately, the inclusive vision that launched the Doha Round evaporated quickly, when groupings of less-developed countries (the so-called G20, G33, and G99) aggressively sought greater market access and lower trade barriers, particularly for agricultural products, while conceding very little themselves. Developed economies meanwhile balked at abolishing agricultural supports without being given greater access for and lower tariffs on their manufactured goods and services. Both sides seriously overplayed their hand. So, by the time of the 2003 WTO ministerial in Cancun, Mexico, the position of the two camps had ossified to the point that any rapid conclusion of the talks was unlikely. Thus, despite five more years of talks, developed and developing country negotiators remain far apart.[47]

Oftentimes, developing countries have a comparative advantage in agriculture, although it may be limited to only a few goods, such as coffee, bananas, or cotton. Unfortunately for those countries, agriculture remains a bastion of trade protectionism. Agricultural products are almost universally subject to high tariffs and other import restrictions. While the average American import tariff has fallen from 40 to 4 percent since World War II, the average applied tariff on agricultural products is still eleven percent. For processed agricultural products, the tariff is even higher. And agricultural import tariffs in developing countries can be five to ten times higher still, due to the special and differential treatment given them under the GATT Agreement on agriculture.

While high tariffs protect developing countries and their domestic industries from foreign competition, widespread protectionism limits trade, which can foreclose growth opportunities.[48] The competitive advantage of developing countries in agriculture is also diluted by developed countries' subsidization of agricultural production and exportation. Therefore, countries that lack a diversified agricultural sector are not likely to realize economic gains from multilateral trade reforms unless those reforms are comprehensive.

The Uruguay Round of GATT negotiations made progress in the agricultural sector by adding it to the treaty. The Agreement provides "a framework for the long-term reform of agricultural trade and domestic policies," with "a decisive move towards … increased market orientation in agricultural trade."[49] It requires countries to convert all non-tariff border measures concerning agricultural goods into tariffs, which are then scheduled to be cut an average of 36 percent for developed countries and 24 percent for developing countries. Least developed countries were not required to make any tariff reductions under the Agreement, however.

Consequently, if current Doha agricultural negotiations are unproductive and more multilateral concessions are not made, the potential gains from freer trade in agriculture will not benefit developing economies that are particularly dependent upon agricultural exports for income.[50]

While there are many barriers to accomplishing these goals, there are also many incentives for countries, developing and developed alike, to press forward. Reforms in agricultural trade may produce two-thirds of all gains expected to come from the Doha round.[51] And terminating domestic support for agriculture in the developed world would save billions of tax dollars now spent on farm subsidies, which are often paid to highly-efficient corporate farmers.[52] In Europe, domestic support causes residents to pay more than twice the world market price for protected goods, including lamb, butter, and sugar. Japanese families are even worse off, paying five times more for rice imports than they would if rice imports were duty-free. The economic growth potential in liberalizing agricultural trade would chiefly benefit the poor, whose incomes generally rise during times of significant economic growth.[53] In low and middle-income countries, an increase in agricultural trade could mean more work (and income) for the rural poor.

If the benefits of agricultural trade reforms are potentially so great, why have WTO negotiations in this sector struggled to advance? The problem is largely political. The failure of the Seattle and Cancun ministerial meetings encouraged developing countries to push developed countries for greater trade concessions; particularly in the field of agriculture. The issue is also complicated by a variety of 'non-trade' concerns: aspects of agriculture that relate to the environment, food security, rural development, national culture and other peripheral issues.[54]

The reluctance of developed countries to liberalize agricultural trade can result in paradoxical inconsistencies between their trade and foreign policies. For example, poorer countries receiving public and private development aid frequently have the growth of their agriculture trade frustrated by farm supports in the donor nations. Indeed, in March, 2005 the WTO Appellate Body affirmed that U.S. cotton support programs violated trade rules. But eighteen months later the U.S. had not compensated Brazil for its cotton sector losses.[55]

Cotton perfectly illustrates the paradox. Contrast two families who farm the crop. One lives in the U.S., where the government spends over $3 billion a year to support its 25,000 cotton farmers (many of whom receive half of their income from the government). These farmers get about 70 cents per pound for cotton, compared with a world price of about 40 cents per pound. The second family is farming in Mali, a West African country where cotton is the main export. Mali receives more than $40 million a year from the U.S. in development assistance. However, U.S. cotton subsides limit export opportunities for Mali cotton producers because they encourage U.S. cotton farmers to overproduce, and seventy percent of that production is exported. This floods the world market, so the price of the cotton for unsupported growers falls below their break-even point. U.S. tax revenue is wasted, and low-cost producers have no market. The process helps neither developed nor developing countries.

Market access restrictions also appear under the guise of sanitary or environmental standards; so-called "non-tariff barriers" (NTB's) to trade.[56]

Draconian tariffs levied against developing-country goods don't make much sense either. Nearly 45 percent of U.S. tariff income derives from levies on shoes and clothes produced in low-income countries like Bangladesh and Cambodia (both assessed average U.S. tariff rates between 15 and 17 percent). Meanwhile, Britain and France—with far greater export volume—pay average U.S. tariffs of one percent or less. The European Union is no better. In fact, its agricultural import barriers are higher than America's; although lower than Japan's and South Korea's. And the EU's "Everything But Arms" program (purportedly allowing the world's 50 poorest nations to export all non-military goods tariff-free) in fact excludes many of those goods due to "stringent hygiene and product standards."[57]

Small wonder that the great majority of WTO members hope the Doha negotiations will be concluded soon. But that seems unlikely. For one thing, the Democrats, now in control of the U.S. Congress, are generally less partial to trade treaties than the Republicans who have driven America's trade agenda for the past twelve years. For another, the President's trade-promotion authority expired in mid-2007. New U.S. trade initiatives will have to await a new President and Congress. Moreover, the EU's agricultural trade adjustments (see Chapter V) will not take effect until 2013. It will take time for both groups of negotiators to grasp where they miscalculated, and what to do next. But someone must begin that process, and no one seems ready to do so at present.[58]

Neither does there seem to be much interest in negotiating a "development package" outside Doha's broad agenda. This is because it is easier to grant and get concessions when more issues are on the table.[59] Even though the Doha negotiations are stalemated, a broadly-supported WTO "Aid4Trade" program will proceed separately from the Doha talks.[60]

Developed-country agricultural producers must realize by now that the production supports and export subsides they have enjoyed over the years will eventually be phased out. Market access for developing-country goods is gradually being advanced, if not multilaterally then regionally and bilaterally.[61] The "special and differential (S & D) treatment" that less-developed economies were promised as part of the Doha agenda (to allow them to grow strong enough to compete with mature economies) is still being pursued. But S & D treatment need not extend to large emerging economies like China, India, or Brazil.

The same is true for so-called "implementation" issues; a voluntary restraint on challenging in the WTO's dispute settlement system less-developed countries' failure to meet their WTO obligations until they are strong enough economically to comply.[62] So, while there have been and will continue to be trade concessions to less-developed nations as they mature, those concessions need not go to all underdeveloped economies or continue forever. Otherwise it will create dependencies and discourage domestic capacity building.[63]

Of course it is also possible for emerging economies to flood the marketplace with under-priced goods, as China did when textile quotas ended in 2004. As a precondition to China's accession to the WTO, the U.S. and EU were allowed to impose temporary quotas on textile imports, so as not to destabilize their markets and give them time to adjust.[64]

Because emerging economies are increasingly obliged to play by WTO rules, and complaints are brought against them when they do not, their trade behavior has improved; and trade disputes and dumping cases (the selling of under-priced goods in foreign markets) have sharply declined.[65] Indeed, economies that were previously considered "basket cases," like Vietnam, have revived their economies and some have joined the WTO.[66] Developing economies are using the WTO to make certain mature economies meet their trade obligations as well.[67]

Finally, trade facilitation (for example, simplifying customs procedures) is being advanced because almost all traders consider inconsistent and/or burdensome customs regulations a barrier to trade for nations large and small. However, harmonizing customs procedures will require a great deal of cooperation and coordination; and technical assistance to less-developed nations.[68]

Of course, none of these external stimuli and concessions will be sufficient to improve trade if developing countries do not reform their own markets and increase domestic consumption. There will never be robust global trade if it remains unbalanced. Capacity building is a temporary phase; a boost up the economic ladder.[69]

More troubling with respect to capacity building is the fact that the countries most in need of trade assistance seem least able to attract it. China, a relatively non-transparent, quasi-communist market completely outflanks India, a far more democratic one, in its ability to attract investors. Latin America has still further to go, but is way ahead of most African nations.[70] Economic conditions will never be equal in these nations, of course. But outrageous disparities need to be reduced if there is to be any equity; or, for that matter, peace and security. Otherwise, well-to-do nations are likely to be beset by migration from underdeveloped states.

Immigration has an impact on the receiving state, but it has an impact on the emigrant state as well. The former has to absorb (or otherwise deal with) the migrants. This is easier if they have skills. But many don't. Hence, they may compete with low-skill workers in the receiving state, or tax its resources. In the emigrant state there is concern about a shortage of workers and the prospect of a "brain-drain" of talented professionals. This could produce a considerable drag on capacity building. However, it opens the door to a fresh crop of willing workers who are left behind. Also, once conditions improve, many emigrants return.[71]

Without question, trade barriers (tariffs, farm support, and export subsidies) can hinder development in Africa and other developing countries. It is estimated that, if Africa could increase its exports by just one percent it would be worth five times the total amount of foreign aid it receives. Thus, the delay in agricultural trade reforms retards economic growth in Africa and other less developed countries, contributing to hunger, disease and civil strife.

F. Self Help

The foregoing two sections may make it seem that capacity-building in emerging economies is entirely dependent on external actors. Nothing could be further from the truth. Indeed, without *internal* initiatives—for example, better governance, infrastructure development, education, and economic modernization—external initiatives are not likely to establish growing, sustainable economies. But the process can be started either externally or internally, and in any developmental sector (although better governance and infrastructure suggest themselves most strongly), for all sectors act synergistically.

Despite all the negative news about the adverse impact of globalization on developing nations, progress is being made. For example, the European Union has agreed to help sub-Saharan African countries develop in three areas identified by them: governance; interconnectivity; and service delivery. The G-8 has pledged to double (to $54.5 billion) aid donations to Africa by 2010, although delivery on this promise remains uncertain. And China has offered $20 billion for infrastructure and trade financing.

But Africans deserve credit too. The economies of many countries are better run, there is less conflict, inflation is at a 40 year low, and their economies, once considered moribund, grew at nearly five percent in 2005.[72]

Latin American governments also have taken steps to reduce the chronic wealth gap in their societies, and make the poor more productive than dependent.[73] Countries in Latin America and Africa have natural resources that can be brought to market. But that requires technical skill, best business practices, and governments free enough of corruption to make certain that the increase in wealth is well invested and distributed. This is no easy task in countries with young, fragile governments and primitive infrastructure.

Developing countries also need to diversify their economies, which frequently rely on a few, or even a single export (often agricultural products). All exports of this sort tend to be low-skill, low-value products; prone to price fluctuation. But diversification requires technical skills and domestic demand, which only increases with wealth.[74] Wealth may also increase with the growth of south-south trade (between developing countries), as opposed to north-north trade (between developed economies), or north-south trade (also growing). However, promises of aid and investment may be aimed at exploiting developing countries' resources by rapidly-growing emerging economies.[75]

Following close on the heels of good governance and infrastructure are education and skills training. An educated populous generally contributes to better governance and with it better jobs and business practices, higher productivity, and increased wages. These economic improvements often result in reduced social tension, better health and a lower birthrate. Again, they act synergistically. Higher incomes and lower social costs allow sovereigns to develop infrastructure and increase trade. The opportunities once limited to a few, are gradually extended to the many;[76] the advent of a modern economy.

Of course, not all emerging economies are developing at the same pace or suffer the same problems. Some, like India and China, are well ahead of less developed economies in Sub-Saharan Africa, Latin America, and the Pacific Islands. The former have probably already reached the level of sustainability. Indeed, start-up companies in India and China have moved from competing chiefly on the basis of low wages and duplicating western technology to creating and innovating on their own, just as Japan, Taiwan and South Korea once did.[77] This is the capstone of the capacity-building process that is taking hold in more emerging economies. If it can be perpetuated through internal and external trade, it will lead eventually to competitive products, a diversified market, internal consumption, and self-sustainability.

To some extent, this evolution can be traced through a country's competitiveness rating and investment in research and development (R & D). In the former, the U.S. ranks sixth (preceded by several small countries), Japan seventh, Hong Kong eleventh, South Korea twenty-forth, China fifty-forth, and Brazil, Argentina and Venezuela, sixty-sixth, sixty-ninth and eighty-eighth, respectively.[78] With respect to R & D investment (as a percentage of GDP), Japan ranks fourth, with 3.12 percent. The U.S. is sixth, with 2.46 percent of its much larger GDP invested. South Korea is ninth (2.53%); Taiwan is eleventh (2.29%); China twenty-fifth (1.26%); Brazil twenty-ninth (1.04%); India thirty-third (.77%) and Venezuela and Mexico forty-third and forty-fourth, respectively.[79] By one estimate, the past twenty years of economic growth in China "has lifted some 400 million of its 1.3 billion people out of grinding, $1-a-day poverty." That's 20 million a year! Clearly, many emerging economies can participate profitably in the global marketplace (not to mention compete with America) *if* they can get the formula right and, in most cases, get some outside help.[80]

Nevertheless, one concern about the technical superiority of western nations and the rapid growth of some emerging economies, is that it will create an e-gap (or "digital divide") that will leave other developing nations well behind, with no realistic prospect of catching up. The failure to bridge the gap could lead to tensions similar to those created by previous rich/poor gaps both between and within countries. Fortunately, the problem has been recognized, and some actions are being taken to address it on a global scale.[81]

In 2000, the G-8 set up a "digital opportunity taskforce" (dot force) to establish goals and coordinate training to connect people, computers, and telecommunications systems around the world. Its report, "Digital Opportunities for All: Meeting the Challenge" (Genoa Action Plan), was delivered in May, 2001. In November 2005, the World Summit on the Information Society (WSIS) addressed governance of the internet. It was decided that the U.S.-based Internet Corporation for Assigned Names and Numbers (ICANN) would continue to oversee the process of assigning domain names, but that a new Internet Governance Forum (IGF) would draw together interested stakeholders to examine internet related governance and cyber-security issues. Hence, e-activity is becoming internationalized *de jure* as well as *de facto*. Indeed, a recent ECONOMIST survey concluded that technological change was improving the lives of the poor as well as the rich.[82]

G. Conclusion

By definition, developing economies—and especially less-developed economies—are "works in progress."[83] Their economies are often fragile; poised between cycles of growth and collapse. Although they and their neighbors feel their hardship most acutely, it is shared by all global traders. After all, the most-developed nations in the world fare better during periods of social stability and economic growth. Hence, the plight of less-developed countries is far better addressed through capacity-building than by direct aid (which is shrinking) or crisis management by international organizations. Economic growth is the best way to deal with the problems of overpopulation, poverty, disease, and conflict that plague less-developed nations.

These nations clearly need encouragement, opportunities, technology trans-fer, and capital investment to enter the mainstream of global trade, and to profit from it. This was the whole point of the Doha Development Round of trade negotiations, and its promised "special and differential" treatment for less-developed members. The problem with S & D treatment, however, is that it may not force the beneficiary to ever bridge the development gap, and leave it perpetually dependent. So this cannot be a one-way street. Developing economies at all levels must do what they can to put their houses in order and take the steps necessary to become self-sustaining. According to them, too many concessions—far less a trade "round for free"—would probably delay necessary changes and allow them to run a parallel course; a perpetual drag on the global trading system, and permanently dependent on outside assis-tance. Ideally, all WTO members should ultimately be subject to its rules.[84] But striking the right balance is a delicate matter.

For example, less-developed economies could plant more genetically-mod-ified crops, which are heartier and less prone to drought and disease, even though they are not welcomed everywhere. At present, many poor countries in Africa and the Middle East shun such crops. In the absence of traditional cap-ital markets, microfinance could be used to help small businesses get launched to serve local markets.[85]

Not all developing economies are equally needy, of course. Emerging economies like China and India claim developing-country status and seek con-cessions based thereon, but wield considerable clout in international trade cir-cles. Less-developed economies in Asia, Latin America, Africa and the Middle East are growing economically at vastly different rates.[86] Their contributions to world trade may be overestimated,[87] but most are not in peril. They simply manage badly. Improved access to developed-country markets will not im-prove them if they remain poor producers and export dependent.

Nonetheless, extremes of wealth and poverty contribute to social and eco-nomic polarization. And the resulting insecurity is costly to all; rich and poor alike.[88] It is well established that improved trade is good for all participants. What developed nations need to do is engage, encourage, and assist marginal economies to enter the global mainstream, rather than ignoring or compet-ing with them. Developing economies contribute to developed-country wealth as well as the obverse. And it appears that many of the former are making headway.[89]

Suggesting that the failure of developing economies to participate more fully in the global marketplace is chiefly the fault of developed economies is not ac-curate. The mobilization of resources and people behind a workable plan is the key to success.[90] Larger developing economies, emboldened by the rejection of developed-nation compromises at Seattle and Cancun, may have demanded too much while conceding to little.[91] Or local political leaders may have made ill-advised choices, contrary to sound economic judgment, in order to appease their constituents (European farmers; Latin American populism).[92] But those nations that have planned reasonably well, and embraced globalization most fully, have appeared to profit most.[93]

There remains a concern that emerging countries will push their economies too fast so that they become overheated, speculative, and risk inflationary collapse. Or, that they might use their leverage to enhance market position.[94] So developing nations must participate themselves in the capacity-building process. But this is increasingly the case, since they are more involved in, and have greater influence on, international trade negotiations.[95]

Of course, healthier and more prosperous developing countries could mean a short-term population boom, because the tragic Darwinian control of malnutrition and disease would be removed. This could strain resources and contribute to conflict and migration. However, reproductive-restraint is typical of sound economies. And some population redistribution is probably justified when one considers the quantity of workers relative to jobs in some economies. Furthermore, some highly-developed western economies have birth rates below those necessary to sustain their labor force, and are sustained by migrants who perform less-attractive and seasonal jobs.[96]

The last concern about capacity building, at least from a developing country's point of view, is the potential loss of sovereignty. Some people believe that globalization "Westernizes" and degrades developing economies, and that they would be better off without it. If these countries are content with their current economic condition, then that is a decision they have the sovereign power to make. But, without technology transfer and capacity building, many such economies would be permanently stuck in an economic rut. Indeed, most developing nations appear to welcome globalization's prospect of more and better jobs and a higher standard of living.[97] They doubtlessly resent, at least to some degree, the intrusion of Western governments and businesses. But developing countries also seek (and even compete) to attract Western capital and know-how. This inevitably comes with some oversight and reduces sovereign prerogative. However, there is no absolute independence in a globalized world. And I doubt that anyone envies the isolation of North Korea or Cuba. Perhaps not even the Cubans themselves.[98]

From a developed nation's point of view, it makes more sense to engage and assist developing economies than to ignore them. Billions, perhaps trillions of dollars might be spent trying to address their problems. But, if nothing is done, those problems will spill over into the wider world. A proactive approach is clearly the better one. And, since a complete remedy cannot always come from within developing countries themselves, developed nations need to help them stabilize their economies, give their workers something to do and the tools to do it, and start them up the ladder to self-sufficiency.[99] We must remember that all economies were emerging economies at one time or another. And that global economic growth is a fragile thing. It is in everyone's interest to keep it going.[100]

Chapter X

Peace and Security

Markets do not function efficiently in the absence of relative peace and security. And with daily reports of roadside bombs and suicide bombers in Iraq, genocide in Darfur, and ethnic cleansing in the Balkans, the last decade has seemed especially bloody. Nevertheless, exponential growth in international trade has brought a level of peace not historically seen. A 2005 study reports that, globally, wars are less frequent, great-power wars are rare, and the average annual death toll due to war has fallen substantially. Major African conflicts fell from eleven in 1998 to only three in 2005.

In the past, wars in developing countries had little impact on globalization because global trade was primarily between developed nations. With the growth of global trade however, less-developed countries have become more integrated, so their insecurity and instability have a greater impact on economic growth and trade.[1]

A diversified economy, developed infrastructure, and a productive workforce are all prerequisites to success in the global economy. However, before a nation can achieve any of these, it must have a minimal level of peace and security to encourage long term investment and technology transfer.[2] Clearly, the larger and more-robust a market, the more insecurity is forgiven by investors (China). Likewise, a country that attracts western assistance is likely to be viewed as more stable. For example, NATO security forces in northern Afghanistan have created enough security to enable record economic growth and democratic elections. Conversely, southern Afghanis are still subject to lawlessness and domination by warlords because the security forces stationed there have neglected public order to pursue Taliban and al-Qaeda insurgents.[3]

In a more peaceful part of the world, South Africa's Johannesburg Stock Exchange has reached record levels of value, suggesting a strong economy, notwithstanding the fact that violent crimes have risen over the past ten years. This trend has deterred Chinese investors, although they are used to operating in an environment of insecurity and corruption at home.[4]

Inconsistencies such as these suggest that there is no single standard to determine when a country is safe and peaceful enough to participate in the global marketplace. A healthy economy is important, but so is public perception.[5] This chapter examines the fundamental peace and security that seems necessary for an emerging nation to begin to climb the economic ladder.

Western history suggests that peace and security are based in part on democratic principles; a participatory electorate and the rule of law, rather than authoritarian order. For example, U.S. policymakers felt that direct elections in Iraq would lead to increased security and economic revival. However, deep-seated religious animosities have left the country too insecure for global investment. Instead of abstract concepts like democracy or electoral mandate, there may be more concrete and fundamental building blocks that encourage investment and trade.[6]

First, a nation must have a government that enjoys some degree of domestic and regional/international legitimacy. This does not necessarily depend on direct elections, so long as the leadership is generally respected and/or supported by most of those governed. Second, a nation must have some respect for the rule of law. That is, rules that respect contract and private property, a relatively-impartial enforcement mechanism, and a quasi-independent judiciary. Decision-making cannot be secretive or arbitrary. Finally, a reasonably equitable proportion of resources must reach the majority of the country's ethnic and sectarian groups, since many contemporary conflicts are caused by disparities between the favored and disfavored.

These elements are interdependent and variable. Although other elements may contribute to peace and security, they are less basic. Additionally, these elements are neither absolute nor automatic. Their existence does not automatically result in security and global prosperity, nor do they need to be perfect examples of the condition. Rather, they should be considered a threshold that allows a nation to participate in international trade and grow economically. Alternatively, a significant shortfall in any area could begin a downward spiral that weakens the economy and discourages foreign trade.

A. Legitimacy: Popularly and Regionally Accepted Governments

A nation becomes more attractive to foreign investors and external trade when its government achieves a level of perceived legitimacy among its population and in the international community. This legitimacy does not require popular elections and democracy, however. For example, Taiwan, one of Asia's most successful economies, has only recently transitioned to a democratic government. During much of the 20th century, Taiwan's authoritarian regime was accepted by a majority of Taiwanese and became one of the "Asian tigers," with strong trade ties to the West.[7]

Alternatively, constitutional monarchies like Jordan permit only limited public influence through a national assembly dominated by supporters of the monarchy. Saudi Arabia is a pure monarchy, excepting recent local elections. Yet most people would consider both countries responsible participants in global trade. There are a number of monarchies in the Western Hemisphere, but many, such as Britain, Spain, or the Netherlands, are constitutional in nature with a democratic electorate. However, even nations with limited or no electoral systems have been successful in international trade.[8]

This is because these governments are sufficiently secure and peaceful to allow them to trade in global markets and attract foreign investment. Persistent instability is unlikely when governments address the basic needs of most citizens.

The same was not true in Somalia under the Islamic Courts brief rule. True, life in the Somali capital, Mogadishu, improved. Seaports and airports opened, prices in local markets declined, and school attendance rose, even among girls. But the Islamic Courts achieved power through conquest so, although they enforced stability, they did not ensure peace.[9]

This forced stability did not allow Somalia to participate in international markets because its Islamist government was not accepted regionally. It did not promote relations with the outside world, threatening the borders of neighboring Kenya and Ethiopia. Somalia was more stable, but it was still dangerous, since extremist factions threatened and murdered western journalists and aid workers. Indeed, the government supported and praised jihadist violence.

Because of the government's disruptiveness, Ethiopia invaded Somalia in December 2006, ousting the Islamic Courts and reinstating the U.N. supported transitional government. It invoked martial law to restore peace and security. But, regional support pledged by the African Union did not materialize, the Ethiopians withdrew, and the jihadists regrouped. Now Somalia has neither peace nor security and is well on its way to becoming a failed state.[10] Burma's military junta has enforced peace in that country, and is wealthy due to natural gas sales, but its "ill-informed and outdated socioeconomic policies" foment instability, and the country is shunned by foreign investors.[11]

Although a country does not need to be democratic to participate in world markets, popularly elected governments are more likely to be viewed as legitimate. The Democratic Republic of the Congo is rich in minerals, water, and fertile soil, yet political illegitimacy, mismanagement, and corruption fostered economic turmoil ever since decolonization in 1964. Ongoing warfare decimated national output and increased foreign debt, preventing the government from addressing issues such as famine and disease. Consequently, the foreign investment and skills transfer needed to build infrastructure were not forthcoming and the economy languished.[12]

Another example of economic collapse brought about by political instability is Kenya. A once-prosperous African nation devolved into chaos and bloodshed after a close and flawed election. Because reconciliation has proved elusive, thousands have been killed and economic growth is at a full stop.[13]

With the withdrawal of foreign troops from Uganda and Rwanda in 2002, followed by the formation of a power-sharing government in 2003, and the introduction of some 18,000 U.N. peacekeepers, economic conditions in the Congo improved. It now has a large and growing mobile communications network and internal transport system, allowing it to harness its mineral and hydroelectric potential. The establishment of a provisional government also permitted taxation of natural resource extraction, providing revenue to further develop the nation's infrastructure and service the needs of its neglected population.[14]

These economic improvements were made possible by the United Nations' ongoing investment in the Congo's peace and security; averaging $650 million per year. Popular elections in 2006 increased legitimacy and promised lasting security in a nation that has been troubled by ethnic and tribal infighting. And increased stability brought the world's largest mining operations back to the mineral rich nation, further benefiting the country. If elected leaders had used national resources to benefit the Congolese people instead of lining their own pockets, the nation could have moved forward toward a sustainable and lasting peace. But, when a dissident ethnic militia overran weak UN peacekeepers and Congolese forces, given only "half-hearted" support by the government— that is in the absence of the peace and security—many of these gains were threatened.[15]

An example of a restoration project that is farther along is Kosovo. In 1999, NATO forces brought security to the region ending years of violence between Serbs and ethnic Albanians. Foreign direct investment, organized by the U.N., rebuilt roads, homes, schools, hospitals, and religious facilities. The U.N. installed a provisional government and NATO forces continue to provide security. But Kosovo's ambiguous international status has made it difficult to attract foreign investment. Thus, despite legitimacy and security, Kosovo still needs to stimulate economic growth. This may happen soon, since Kosovars have voted for independence from Serbia, and the U.S. and some European nations have recognized it. However, Kosovo's independence is opposed by Serbia and Russia; the latter capable of blocking UN recognition. Its status, and economy, may languish for some time due to this uncertainty.[16]

Not all attempts to rejuvenate failing economies meet with universal approval, however. President Uribe of Columbia saved an ailing economy from the "rampaging violence of drug-traffickers, left-wing guerrillas and right-wing paramilitaries." As a result of his efforts, violence has fallen sharply, and the economy is growing at 8 percent a year. But he is accused of heavy-handedness in achieving these goals, and is still suspect abroad.[17]

Perhaps the greatest success story is Vietnam, which rebuilt its institutions and economy from the shambles of the Vietnamese war to become the 150th member of the WTO in January 2007.[18]

Whether peace and security is initiated by an external body, such as the U.N. or NATO, or even by an authoritarian regime, lasting peace and security eventually require legitimate local leadership in order for a nation to participate in the global market.

B. Impartial and Reliable Rule of Law

Another critical component of economic growth is respect for the rule of law, impartially and effectively enforced. The rule of law not only maintains a nation's internal and external legitimacy, it also protects property and contract rights of natives and foreign investors. Without this security, locals remain impoverished because their jobs, land, and businesses are unprotected, whereas foreigners select alternate venues better able to protect their interests. The rule of law does not equate with democracy per se, however. Taste for the U.S. form of democracy can ebb and flow. What matters is that legitimate expectations are fulfilled.[19] Furthermore, risk is relative. Some highly attractive markets, such as China and Bangladesh, have been able to sustain strong economic growth despite weak and partial legal systems. This has largely been due to western investors' eagerness to enter booming markets, despite the risks. Nonetheless, an orderly and transparent market system must eventually emerge, since most case studies suggest that an impartial and reliable judicial system is a prerequisite to economic growth.[20]

One of the greatest threats to global trade is graft and corruption. Both the WTO and World Bank have announced major programs aimed at eliminating corrupt practices. Of course, some level of corruption is endemic in international trade. But a recent survey by the German research institute, Transparency International, found that rampant corruption existed in at least half of the 163 nations surveyed. Not coincidentally, the study found a high correlation between national poverty and corruption. Although nations are capable of succeeding economically despite a degree of corruption, a significant level chills global investment and trade, stalling the upward trend of economic growth.[21]

The most common form of corruption is bribery. Bribes are considered normal in many nations. In countries like China and Russia, civil and political officials have created a secondary market for government services, permits and licenses. Some economists argue that this promotes efficiency because state-owned resources are distributed to those who value them most. However, any market efficiency achieved through bribery is far outweighed by its inefficiencies. The purchaser pays extra, but the government generally does not reap the revenue. Further, the market is distorted because the most efficient producer may not be the successful bidder. Finally the opaqueness of the system makes it difficult for foreign competitors to compete, if indeed they legally may. Eventually emerging economies will adhere to western practices regarding the rule of law and corruption, in part because failure to do so threatens their standing in the very markets they are trying to enter, and because it doesn't make good economic sense.[22]

Chinese businesses are famous for operating under a system called *guanxi*; a term denoting personal obligations created through interpersonal connections. Guanxi is a form of social capital in countries that do not have impartial legal systems to enforce property and contractual rights. However, developing guanxi comes at considerable economic cost and is rarely enjoyed by foreigners. It often results in rampant theft of public resources for the private gain of government officials holding positions of influence. Although the Chinese have taken steps to reduce corruption, those reforms have been somewhat half hearted.[23]

In order to avoid trade retaliation, countries such as China and Russia have acknowledged that they need to improve their justice systems. China made this pledge when it entered the World Trade Organization in 2001, but bribery and corruption remain a serious problem. Consequently, many foreign companies have asked their governments to use the WTO's dispute mechanism to require that the Chinese government meet its treaty obligations. Under international pressure, China recently announced the creation of a national-level agency to guard against corruption; including the arrest and investigation of politicians accused of taking bribes and dispensing favors.[24] A thriving economy like China's can ill-afford the perception that, through laxity or corruption, it allowed tainted pet food, toxic toothpaste and seafood, and dangerous toys to enter the marketplace. Rather it must be seen as playing by the rules and being serious about doing so.[25]

Economic and legal reform in Russia has also improved. Russia restructured its legal system in the early 1990s because uncertain property rights limited foreign investment. More recent reforms focused on funding for judges and prosecutors in order to enhance their independence and accelerate criminal prosecutions. Unfortunately, Russia has been slow to implement these changes and has been backsliding in other areas.

For example, government bureaucrats are often influenced by graft, and security agencies appear to participate in as many criminal activities as they prevent. Civil and political freedoms are insured more by financial contributions than the rule of law, and President Putin personally appoints most of Russia's political leadership. With the reemergence of corrupt and inefficient state agencies, the fragile independence of private enterprise is again being questioned by foreign investors.[26] Simply put, Russia is trying to find its niche in the world both economically (it is not yet a member of the WTO) and militarily (proposed expansion of NATO to former eastern satellites and U.S. missile plans). Russia is frustrated at having achieved neither, and is using oil diplomacy to leverage its position; creating instability in Europe and around the world. In due course, Russia will have to engage western economies, not rebuff them.[27]

Indonesian courts also are influenced by corruption, undercutting the rule of law. Decisions go to the highest bidder so that many government officials escape liability for misappropriating funds; bribing courts with the very funds they are accused of misappropriating.

Clearly the international economy cannot thrive when cronyism, fraud, and corruption substitute for sound economic practices. Bribery and corruption are disincentives to trade. Indeed, the great strength of established economies is market participants' ability to bring their complaints to impartial tribunals for objective resolution.

There will always be crime and criminals in the marketplace, from common street crime to intellectual property theft. The key is not to let it become so pervasive that crime seriously slows or cripples economic growth. The rule of law, an impartial judiciary, and a level of legal security are ultimately prerequisites to global trade.[28]

C. Equity and International Well Being

A third prerequisite to peace and security is a reasonably equitable distribution of resources. Often the maldistribution of resources between favored and disfavored groups reflects an illegitimate and/or corrupt government. These inequities can lead to disruptions that affect a nation's ability to engage in trade and attract investors.

For example, in 2003 Argentina defaulted on an extremely large loan, causing hyperinflation and unemployment rates exceeding twenty percent. One in two Argentineans lived in poverty. Militant groups of unemployed workers vented their frustration in violent protests. In France—an otherwise developed nation and global trader—economic stagnation increased joblessness, which disproportionately affected the poor and young foreigners, who rioted in Paris and elsewhere. Nations often suffer from their failure to address the needs of large subsets of the population (a particularly common problem in emerging economies). The resulting chaos can dampen trade and investment.[29]

When popular dissatisfaction with government reaches critical mass, the result is a breakdown of law and order further stunting economic growth and global trade. Perhaps one of the best examples of this is the Middle East, which has some of the highest rates of unemployment in the world. While the world-wide unemployment rate averages just over 6 percent, the Middle East's rate is twice that. Countries such as Saudi Arabia and Iran, with unemployment rates from 11 to 25 percent, rely on authoritarian regimes to maintain security. Lacking such control, Palestine is one of the world's most insecure economies, where unemployment exceeds 40 percent. Hence, it is not surprising that Palestine is one of the riskiest places for global investment, and the Palestinian economy is stagnant while political factions such as Fatah and Hamas battle for superiority.[30]

This insecurity radiates globally. Middle Easterners register their frustrations through regional and international terrorism; violent protests against perceived inequities attributed to western powers. To some extent, globalization's progress has been unhindered by these violent protests, even in the wake of September 11. But, prosperity is not the sole measure of security.

Just prior to World War I, the world was prosperous and interconnected. Yet that did not prevent growing divisions among European nations that eventually led to war. A retributive peace and economic depression led to more polarization, and ultimately World War II.

In order to prevent history from repeating itself, the beneficiaries of globalization must strive to resolve the disconnect between the rise of their economies and the inequalities experienced by persons residing in the Middle East and other developing counties around the world.[31]

South Africa faced its resource maldistribution problem by mandating land reform at the end of apartheid in 1994. During colonial times, the British reserved almost ninety percent of the land for themselves and other European colonists, while ethnic Africans were forcibly removed from their land by apartheid governments. After a decade of land reform, however, only three percent of the misappropriated land had been restored to ethnic Africans, precipitating a riot in May 2005. Indeed, record high rates of crime and violence have raised questions about the stability of Africa's most prosperous nation. Some persons have called for a wholesale expropriation of stolen land, similar to Zimbabwe. But that would be catastrophic for South Africa, since increased political and economic instability would further dampen trade and investment.[32]

Isolated dictatorships simply do not participate in or profit from global trade. Zimbabwe is a prime example. When President Mugabe became premier in 1980, it was "one of Sub-Saharan Africa's most diversified economies, founded on a highly efficient commercial farming sector with potential in manufacturing, mining and tourism." But, after nearly three decades of authoritarian rule, the farmers have been driven out, and no one will invest. "[T]wo-thirds of the population is close to starvation and living on less than a dollar a day," unemployment stands at eighty percent, and inflation exceeds 2,200 percent, the world's highest. Some three million of the country's 13 million population have fled the poverty and chaos, putting pressure on neighboring economies such as South Africa.[33]

Under these circumstances, one would think that neighboring states, the emerging African Union, or Zimbabwean natives themselves would intervene. But no one has.[34] Consequently, in Africa's poorest countries, resources are wasted and there is no economic growth. Their plight puts neighbors at risk as well.

Not all social unrest destabilizes an economy, of course. Spain endured nearly forty years of sporadic violence caused by Basque separatists. Yet its economy has experienced record growth. However, when a sufficiently large proportion of the population is disillusioned by its government's allocation of public resources, large scale instability can result. The authoritarian governments of China and other Asian nations are particularly concerned about this, since many Asians still live in extreme poverty. As a result of the communications revolution, the expectations of the chronically poor have risen, and governments have been forced to assuage them in order to maintain security. All members of society expect to profit to some degree from economic growth and global trade.[35]

The 21st Century is demonstrating how disproportionate resource allocation can slow the progress of globalization. As lower and middle class workers in developed nations lose jobs to workers in developing nations, they tend to elect politicians that pledge to increase trade barriers. China specializes in cheap labor, which has enticed various foreign companies to move some operations overseas. In 2005, the United States responded to this perceived threat by introducing 27 pieces of legislation to impose trade barriers on China. Anti-globalization initiatives are bound to be popular when average citizens feel that they don't benefit from liberalized trade.[36] But will retrenchment improve economic growth or blunt it?

Another example is found in the recent history of Latin American economies. In the mid to late nineties, much of Latin America pursued neo-liberal economic policies, privatizing many of the region's national industries. With some exceptions, foreign investment in technology and infrastructure helped those economies grow. Large, inefficient government bureaucracies gave way to private enterprises that streamlined business processes making many industries more productive. Some nations paid off large portions of their public debt, and new industries and markets quickly developed as Latin countries increased trade both locally and abroad.

However, large sectors of the population did not benefit proportionally from this prosperity. Less-well-to-do citizens in Latin American countries such as Venezuela, Bolivia, and Ecuador, became impatient with the slow pace of economic growth through market liberalization, and by occasional negative growth. Non-participating citizens expressed their frustrations through violence, and by supporting populist leaders who pledged social reform and economic redistribution. Recent elections have brought back neo-populists whose platforms recall the 1980s; an era of slow growth and economic nationalism. Their pledge to nationalize assets and restore socialism has increased insecurity in the region, threatening its future economic growth.[37]

In exchange for vast and often economically-unrealistic pledges, elected leaders such as Venezuela's Hugo Chavez, Bolivia's Evo Morales, Ecuador's Rafael Correa, and to a lesser extent Brazil's Lula da Silva, have sought to mend globalization's inequities by nationalizing private businesses and enacting a broad range of labor and social rights. The need for these is questionable when one considers that, in Brazil at least (Latin America's largest economy after Mexico), capital reforms had brought public debt and inflation under control, accelerated growth, and doubled exports. Whatever these leaders' motivation, the preemption of private property and undisciplined redistribution of wealth could create instability in Latin American countries that would overshadow any benefits.[38]

Fortunately, such backsliding has yet to gain serious traction in most Latin American nations. Emboldened by Chavez's anti-capitalist rhetoric, Ecuador threatened to default on foreign debt, notwithstanding its ability to pay. Repayment capital would supposedly be used to finance cash transfers to the poor instead. Rather than risking financial market backlash, however, President Correa chose to make Ecuador's scheduled loan payments on time.

There is evidence that some Latin leaders are only accommodating Chavez's extreme left-wing party line to get promised benefits, without any real intent to implement those policies. For example, Nicaragua's Daniel Ortega, once an advocate of communist reforms, who still supports Castro's Cuba, also favors strong relationships with the west and the Central America Free Trade Agreement. Latin populist leaders have learned or are learning that disassembling the progressive economic reforms of the nineties is likely to increase regional insecurity and slow economic growth in the long run. A stagnant economy and high inflation is the last thing they want. And too much nationalization is likely to result in the return of corruption and inefficiency.[39]

Even Venezuela's central bank has warned that Chavez's price controls and market regulation are harming the economy, giving rise to an extensive black market. Fortunately, his policies have not destabilized the entire region. Nations such as Uruguay and Chile provide a positive example by continuing to pursue progressive strategies while simultaneously addressing the inequalities that neo-liberalism has produced.[40] It also appears that South America's largest free-trade bloc—Mercosur—will reestablish itself (with Brazil in the lead) and eventually reengage the NAFTA partners (Canada, Mexico and the U.S.) in a trade relationship, and possibly a hemispheric trade pact.[41]

In order to prevent Latin America from backsliding into populism, global actors such as Europe, Asia, and the United States must continue to develop trade relations with the region and others like it around the world. Attention to proportionality in the distribution of resources will ensure that the benefits of international trade reach all corners of the developing world.

D. Global Security and the Global Economy

During much of the past century, developed nations were able to prosper without much concern for their developing neighbors. In today's increasingly interdependent world, however, insecurity in even isolated nations can have a global impact. Stabilizing factors such as legitimate governments, the rule of law, and reasonable attention to equality, discussed above, combine to promote growth in local, regional, and global markets. A nation's ability to participate in international markets is becoming more and more dependent on its ability to maintain security as a conduit to growth.[42] Conversely, economic isolation and inequality, regional instability, mass migration, and international terrorism all take a toll on global markets.

Preventing this often requires other nations to intercede to restore order and promote growth in the developing world. Each nation benefiting from global trade must ask: "am I my brother's keeper?" If a nation wants to participate in and benefit from global trade, the answer is increasingly "yes." Ignoring the challenges that developing economies face is costly to both exporter and importer. The United Nations was chartered to "save succeeding generations from the scourge of war." But if the disruption is less than warfare, what actions should countries take and when? Are those interventions likely to be beneficial? And how much money and effort, if any, should be invested in potentially "failed states" to reconstruct them and reduce the hardships they foster?[43]

First, nations can start with a policy of inclusion rather than exclusion. History has shown that the use of sanctions is largely ineffective. Countries such as Cuba, North Korea, Iraq, and Iran have been the subject of isolation strategies for years. But, instead of motivating locals to reject hostility toward the west, sanctions have provoked greater hostility. Indeed, North Korea has emerged as one of the world's newest nuclear threats despite a wide assortment of sanctions. Instead of dissuading North Korea's leadership from pursuing nuclear capability, sanctions chiefly hurt the nation's poor.

Iraq was the subject of heavy sanctions for years, yet Saddam Hussein continued to pursue hostile policies with a strong grip on power, while average Iraqis fell deeper into poverty. Ever since the end of the cold war, the United States has maintained sanctions against its neighbor Cuba, yet Castro's influence and control was threatened only by his failing health. Eventually, moderate Muslims will tire of the bloodshed and disruption, and peace will return to the Middle East. A move away from outdated policies of isolationism towards inclusion would improve the security of global markets, and benefit developing economies around the world.[44]

Second, secure nations can cooperate to assist regions into which conflict has spilled, threatening the stability and straining the economies of otherwise peaceful and stable nations. Regional security is critical to contain civil unrest where it breaks out. If uncontained and unaddressed, hostilities and/or refugees migrate to neighboring nations (many nearly as fragile), consuming public resources and slowing economic growth. Often this is viewed as a "regional problem." But frequently regional groups are too weak (the African Union) or too divided (the Middle East) to be effective. By the time the problem is addressed, the cost of containment is far higher and its impact on economic stability has increased. The Iraq war produced "the largest movement of civilians in the Middle East since the exodus of Palestinians after the creation of Israel." Two million Iraqis have fled the country and another 1.8 million are displaced within it. Without international intervention "a very limited number of countries [within the region are] paying a very heavy price." The same is true in Africa. Wouldn't the cost be lower and the social and economic disruption less if intervention and aid had been more timely?[45]

International organizations such as the North Atlantic Treaty Organization (NATO), the United Nations, and regional organizations such as the European Union and African Union, can play a role in promoting peace and security among their neighbors by injecting adequate security forces into areas of conflict. NATO's involvement in the Balkans proved a powerful example of international intervention that led to regional security. It slowed the stream of refugees, and contained the conflict, enabling the now-emerging economy to grow. Similar cooperation is needed in Darfur, where genocide has caused a mass migration that has depressed the entire Sub-Saharan region. With the deployment of around 100,000 U.N. peacekeepers to missions in the Congo, Liberia, and southern Sudan, the world is beginning to see the fruits of cooperative efforts by international organizations.[46] But intervention is not always timely or adequate.[47]

Increased political and economic coordination among nations and regional organizations should precede military intervention, of course. In most circumstances soft power is politically preferable and economically more efficient than military intervention. For example, in Kosovo millions of dollars were spent on costly weaponry to bomb infrastructure to rubble. Once peace was restored, millions more were spent to rebuild that very infrastructure. Although a military solution was needed to end Serbian ethnic cleansing, greater cooperation prior thereto may have prevented a tardy, costly, and deadly intervention.

A similar opportunity exists in Darfur. China could use more political and economic "soft power" to promote stability within the region, because it is Sudan's largest trade and investment partner. Although China's president has made behind-the-scenes efforts to persuade the Sudanese government to curtail genocide in Darfur and reconcile with rebel groups, it has many other options, such as applying economic pressure or using its influence in the UN Security Council to secure greater assistance for African Union forces. But China's efforts in Sudan may be disingenuous. For Chinese companies are deeply invested in arms sales and oil purchases there. So long as hostilities don't threaten Chinese interests, it practices a policy of "non-interference." China has also gotten permission to search for oil in a peaceful region of Somalia, with little concern for the chaos raging in Mogadishu.[48]

Neither was the European Union's soft power approach successful in getting Iran to abandon its nuclear ambitions. Nor have the quartet's soft power initiatives improved the Israeli-Palestinian standoff. However, soft power seems to be working fairly well in containing North Korea's nuclear program. But that is a multiparty effort, involving some of the world's strongest nations.[49]

Being less belligerent, polarizing, and costly, it is not surprising that soft power is preferred to "hard" (military) power. But one wonders whether soft power would work at all unless there was hard power in reserve.[50]

In the 20th Century, the United States emerged as the world's *de facto* policeman. It is a role the U.S. accepted; but a costly one, both economically and politically. In Afghanistan, the U.S. provided nearly one-half of the 35 thousand troops (from 37 countries) in the NATO-led security force. The U.S. defense budget is nearly as much as that of the rest of the world combined (although only about 4 percent of GDP). Much of the world is critical of U.S. military hegemony, and yet expects it to guard against potential threats from Russia, China and elsewhere. U.S. hard power allows its allies to withdraw their troops from hostilities (or not to send them at all) and to reduce military spending, diverting that money to domestic needs, or to disaster or overseas development aid, which is much better received in the developing world.[51]

It would be nice for all concerned if America could reduce its hard power role. But that is not possible unless soft power is more productive. Sooner or later, in one place or another, hard power may be needed to restore peace and allow economic growth.

America is beginning to realize that it is spread too thin, diplomatically and militarily. It needs to accept the limitations of unilateral, global diplomacy. Whereas the United States may be the world's dominant superpower, it is not the world's only superpower. Should the exercise of hard power prove necessary, the U.S. needs to align itself with other developed nations (including soft power advocates) to restore peace. It will not do for EU nations and leading Asian economies to cultivate emerging markets and dispense aid, while America alone keeps the peace.[52]

Hence, the third prerequisite to peace and security is to ensure that, should soft or hard power be needed, all developed nations that benefit participate. Recognition of this fact seems finally to be dawning.[53] With the increase in NATO and U.N. peacekeeping forces, discussed above, military cooperation is growing. However, there is much room for improvement. The United States still bears a majority of the costs of many U.N. peacekeeping missions. Its spending far exceeds that of any other country.

The United States should not be the world's sole policemen, or be criticized for warmongering when it merely responds to insecurity. Although there has been international cooperation in places like Afghanistan, many member nations place restrictions on their involvement. Intervention was clearly necessary in Kosovo and Afghanistan, and many believe greater intervention is needed in Darfur. However, regional and global stakeholders should share the responsibility. For example, African Union intervention is better suited to stabilizing Darfur, and is likely to be better tolerated than European or American forces. But it must be timely and effective.

Other major powers, such as China and the European Union, should contribute military resources as well, since they too benefit from peace and security. But many nations prefer soft power, and use that preference to avoid military involvement.[54]

Hostility and insecurity are not permanent conditions, although they may last for long periods. Eventually, people tire of the conflict and warring factions recognize the futility of their divisions and reconcile. Once peace and security return, economic growth is again possible.[55]

There is still much work to be done. Russia, and other concerned nations, must continue to pursue measures to limit the spread of nuclear capability.[56]

To some degree, crime is endemic to the global marketplace. Drugs, weapons, and other black market goods will never cease to circulate the globe. Dissidents and terrorists attack, often with no political agenda beyond destruction itself. Stopping their activities is virtually impossible. But containing them is. The harm created by widespread criminality needs to be held at levels low enough to allow global markets to prosper. Otherwise, the criminals will have won.[57]

The interdiction and punishment of criminal behavior is classically a state problem. And it will continue to be so. But, if crime knows no borders, neither should crime prevention. In a high-tech, globalized world, criminal activity that has regional or international impact must be addressed at that level. Terrorism is often funded internationally. So preemption may turn out to be a necessary option.

It is not easy to establish interstate cooperation in criminal matters. The burden falls disproportionately on established economies. They have the skills and resources, although the impact of criminal behavior often hurts marginal economies more. Nonetheless, trade depends upon the stability of one's trading partners as well as one's own. So, developed economies bear a disproportionate cost.[58]

Some developing economies, like Mexico, are taking steps to help themselves. But coalitions of nations are needed too; in order to control crime and corruption, and reduce the economic burden of containment. Fortunately, some networks are being developed under the aegis of the EU, NATO and UN.[59] Although it is politically difficult and economically costly for nations to address these issues, doing so will pay a dividend in the long run. Nations that wish to benefit from global trade must create and sustain an environment in which it can prosper.

Chapter XI

Globalization's Futures

A. Introduction

Has globalization a future, much less plural futures? While many people think (or hope) that it does not, I believe that it does. Of course, that future will be brighter and more secure if the globalization process benefits all—or at least most—participants, and reduces the gap between rich and poor nations. This process will require enforceable bilateral and multilateral agreements regarding the terms of globalization, and increase the role of international institutions; such as the World Trade Organization (WTO) and United Nations (UN).

The road toward an increasingly globalized world will not be smooth. Its impacts reverberate in economic, political, legal, and cultural spheres—to name just a few. And, as said previously, the process has both virtues and vices. Previous chapters have focused on some of the "problems" of globalization. This chapter demonstrates why, despite those problems, we should not give up on the process.

As globalization has accelerated over the past decade, some particularly strident books about its negative effects have been published.[1] One especially scathing and influential attack on globalization was Joseph Stiglitz's 2002 book, GLOBALIZATION AND ITS DISCONTENTS, for which he was praised as the "hero of the anti-globalization movement." In a later book, MAKING GLOBALIZATION WORK, however, Stiglitz sought "to show how globalization, properly managed ... can do a great deal to benefit both the developing and developed countries of the world."[2]

Nonetheless, globalization's opponents still attack the process; their most persistent claim being that the American economy and American workers will suffer in a globalized world. Remember forecasts of a "giant sucking sound"—representing the loss of jobs—if the United States entered NAFTA? Since NAFTA went into effect, American GDP has grown by $6 trillion, businesses have added 19.2 million private-sector jobs, and manufacturing production has increased by almost $500 billion.[3]

The truth is that globalization, and its concomitant international cooperation, has led to a reduction in poverty, stronger economies, more peaceful states, and a more secure world. Unfortunately, the process is poorly understood. And globalization's negative impacts (for example, job losses) are clear and immediate. Whereas its benefits (less-expensive goods, increased American exports, and foreign investment in the U.S.) are diffuse and longer term.

The public, politicians, and the media all play a role in spreading the anti-globalization myth. Bad news sells. So the media is quick to report the negative consequences of globalization.[4]

The positive results of globalization receive little attention. Rather than providing a balanced analysis, the media focus on the negative.[5] These alarmist reports fuel public angst, and that often leads to political action; generally protection.[6] But public and political responses often fly in the face of economic reality. Protection rarely works, and often backfires. It begets reciprocal protection, and is doomed to fail in the long term.[7]

While the politics of division is powerful, it is also hollow. The truth about globalization is that one nation rarely succeeds at the expense of another. More openness and inclusion tend to stimulate growth, and benefit most economies. Which product contributes more to the U.S. economy? A Ford assembled in Mexico with one-half of its content made in the U.S. or Canada, or a Toyota assembled in Indiana with 85 percent of its content from the U.S. or Canada?[8] The answer is, both, about equally.

Lester Thurow, writing in 1980, saw the American economy—and by extension the world economy—as something of a "zero-sum" game. The pie was just so large, and there was a loser for every winner.[9] The last two decades have shown that Thurow was incorrect. The world economy is not a zero-sum game. Indeed, since 1950, global trade has expanded by a factor of 25.

It is true that America has lost its hegemonic position, and is growing more slowly than many other economies; if for no other reason because its output is so huge. But the U.S. is still in a dominating position in the global sweepstakes.[10] How else would it be possible for the United States economy to be expanding at about three percent annually, while emerging economies like India, Brazil, South Korea, and China are growing at two or three times that rate?

The truth is the entire world economy is expanding, and more countries than ever are sharing in that growth. During the last half of the 20th Century, globalization has "led to the most rapid worldwide reduction in poverty and rise in living standards in the history of mankind."[11] In China alone market forces lifted 400 million people out of grinding poverty in just 25 years. Likewise, the prosperity achieved by Asia's "Little Tigers" (Hong Kong, Singapore, South Korea, and Taiwan) are the result of each country's robust participation in the international economy.[12]

Globalization has its problems, of course. The primary one is the inequitable distribution of its benefits. Remedying this situation is not a case of *nobelesse oblige*, but of enlightened self-interest. Without sustained growth, less-developed countries will not overcome poverty. And achieving that goal requires the assistance of developed countries and globalization. As developed countries grow richer, they have more assets to assist developing countries. With this aid (financial, technological, and otherwise), the latter can become market participants. When they do, they will purchase the goods and services of developed economies. Their benefactors' markets will expand.

Equitable distribution also needs to be addressed. Globalization can bring out the dark side of capitalism—an increasing gulf between the haves and the have-nots. European socialism is gradually being replaced with capitalism. European industries, such as Electricite de France, are being privatized in an attempt to increase productivity and profitability. However, efficiency should not overshadow the social inequality and environmental harm that may result.[13] That does not mean privatization should be abandoned. Rather, we need to build a relationship between government, businesses, and the populace that includes social safety nets such as education, job retraining, unemployment benefits, health care reform, and the environmental safeguards needed to buffer globalization's negative impacts. While unalloyed socialism is not an effective way to close the inequity gap, a capitalistic system that includes social safety nets could do so.[14]

Clearly, the process of globalization does not benefit all stakeholders all the time. But some modern changes are salutary. One is the growing influence of the private sector on international trade. Another is the increased inclusion of less-developed economies and non-governmental organizations (NGOs) in the process. This may—indeed, has—slowed the process somewhat. But a broader-based system benefits more people and is more immune to external shock. Global balance, sustainability, and a healthy competition are key.

Globalization is not an unalloyed success. But the sum of the evidence is that the world economy is steadily growing, and that more and more people are participating and benefiting from that growth.

B. Changes in the Global Economy

One of the most important changes in the global economy of late has been the rise of China, and by extension other Asian nations, including India. China is pushing America aside as the world's largest exporter, and already exports more to Europe than the U.S. does. Goldman Sacks expects China's GDP to exceed America's by 2027, and purchasing power parity to be achieved sooner. This has caused a great deal of consternation in America, which perceives its dominance as the world's leading economy to be slipping away.[15]

These estimates might be overblown, however. U.S. GDP in 2006 was $11.7 trillion (to China's $1.9 trillion) and per capita income was $39,430 (to China's $1,470). Furthermore the U.S. economy is hardly stagnant; although China's economy grows about three times as fast. Moreover, a recent reassessment of China's economy, based on better statistics, found it to be "smaller and poorer" than previously thought.[16]

The projections do not mean that the U.S. economy is in decline. Rather China and other emerging economies are catching up. While it is true that this reduces America's share of the global economy, that should be welcome. It is due in large part to the spread of democracy and capitalism, which the U.S. promotes. If our experiences in Iraq and Iran have eroded U.S. influence, they dramatically underscore the need for other market participants to promote the peace and security upon which market growth depends. The U.S. economy has grown at an average annual rate of 3.4 percent for the past 75 years and, although negative at the moment, may average 3 percent in the future. America remains preeminent among global traders despite the fact that its role has shrunk.[17]

Inevitably, the new world order will be greatly affected by the rise of China. It is already the world's third largest trading nation, and may eventually become the largest. It has overtaken the U.S. in trade with Japan, and has displaced the latter as the diplomatic and economic leader in Asia. China's bourses eclipse all others in Asia. And, since 2001, its trade balance has grown from $17 to $239 billion; a fourteen fold increase.[18] Because the Chinese market is so vibrant, it is able to bypass exchanges in Hong Kong, London, and New York, and raise investment capital through mainland IPOs (initial public offerings).[19] Chinese consumer spending has been growing at an average annual rate of 10 percent for the past decade. While this growth is not sustainable and needs to be slowed, China will remain an influential market player.[20]

China also is engaged in a number of "soft power" initiatives to increase its influence; not just in Asia (APEC, ASEAN, warmer relations with Japan), but also with potential competitors and/or enemies (India and Russia). Part of this charm offensive is aimed at expanding China's export markets beyond Asia, Europe and the U.S. But China also wants to insure steady energy supplies from Central Asia, the Mideast, and even Africa's Sudan to fuel its rapidly-expanding economy.[21]

Although Americans are concerned about China's rapid economic expansion, it can be a win-win situation for the United States. For example, American airline manufacturer, Boeing, was the recipient of a large airplane order from Chinese airline companies.[22] Microsoft and the International Finance Corp. are assisting China to expand its software industry. Chinese patent applications in the U.S. grew from 100 in 1994 to 1,655 in 2004.[23] Not only will the development of Chinese intellectual property grow the Chinese economy, it will also benefit United States IP designers and suppliers. And if China has its own IP to protect, it is more likely to respect the IP rights of others. As the Chinese economy continues to grow and mature it will require even more sophisticated goods and services. American firms like Boeing, Microsoft, and even General Motors, are unusually well-positioned to serve this rapidly-growing market, and help reduce a seriously-adverse U.S. trade balance.[24]

Although it may seem like more of a liability than advantage, China has now surpassed Japan as the world's largest holder of foreign reserves; about 70 percent of which are believed to be in U.S. dollars. Exactly what China does with those reserves is a matter for concern. But it doesn't make sense for China to damage America's economic stability, since it would be injuring its own investment. Likewise, the increased number of Chinese companies listed on the New York and London stock exchange exposes them to more oversight and transparency; an important *quid pro quo* for operating in foreign markets. Finally, an on-going China-US Strategic Economic Dialogue (SED) is producing more bilateral accommodation in a steadily-growing trade relationship.[25] China bears watching, but appears not to be the threat it once seemed.

China's rapid economic growth is just one-half of the story, however. The other one-half is less rosy. China's meteoric economic growth is bound to slow. One reason is that Chinese officials are trying to cool it down, lest it overheat. Even if their efforts aren't successful—and they haven't been to date—rapid growth contributes to inflation, which dampens consumption. Excess liquidity (export earnings; foreign investment) drives up asset prices which, uncontrolled, will lead to a major correction. China's export boom could also lead to market glut; driving prices down. And, in a robust economy, wage demands rise, taking a bite out profits. If none of these slow China's economic growth—and it is virtually certain some will—the mere fact that the economy ages and matures means that the numerator has trouble keeping up with the denominator. Steady, double-digit growth is impossible in the long term.[26]

But there are two other reasons why China's growth should ebb. One is its serious systemic problems. And the other is its increasing need to adhere to global trading standards.

With regard to China's problems, a veteran China-watcher observed—correctly I think—that "[marrying] a Communist party-state with the market is unsustainable." He calls it a "dysfunctional hybrid," the results of which "include rampant corruption, an absence of globally competitive ... companies, chronic waste of resources, rampant environmental degradation and souring inequality."[27] Air and water pollution are so serious in China that they are a grave threat to life. Some river water is so toxic it cannot even be used for irrigation. The government will need to spend billions to correct the problem, but billions would be needed anyway to address water and air-borne disease if unaddressed. And, since access to health care varies considerably based on wealth, it threatens social stability.[28]

Serious issues have also been raised about the safety of various Chinese products: pet food, drugs, and manufactures (lead paint in toys). This is bound to dampen demand in both the domestic and export markets. And require stricter (and more costly) regulations to rebuild confidence in Chinese brands.[29]

Moving up on the technological ladder also has exposed a shortage of skilled workers and produced concern about safe working conditions. Indeed, some people have questioned whether government-run, practically-oriented research and development will ever produce up-market innovations. Add all these problems to an overheated and under-regulated economy[30] and it is clear that eventually the Chinese will have to address matters that will improve fundamentals, but slow growth. Indeed, some corrections have already begun.

Beijing has launched an effort to improve energy efficiency and reduce pollution; balancing economic growth against its potentially crippling side effects. (Most of China's power plants rely on dirty coal that boosts greenhouse gas emissions). But, thus far the plan is behind its targets. Beijing has also invested heavily in improving food safety.[31]

Chinese companies also will have to adapt to international trade standards, and the government will have to prove that it is serious about enforcing those standards.[32] Being a member of the World Trade Organization, China is obliged to meet its commitments under the GATT treaty. Recent WTO complaints filed by the U.S. and others suggest that China's "honeymoon" is over.[33]

Notwithstanding its aversion to outside pressure (or perhaps because of it), China voluntarily took steps to liberalize its economy. Recently, ahead of schedule, a younger, more western-oriented cabinet was appointed, the tight trading band for its currency, the renminbi, was loosened, and the restrictions on individual Chinese investing abroad (as well as foreigners investing in China) were relaxed. The country is a global player, but still has many problems to surmount.[34] Anyone who dwells too much on China's rapid economic growth, without considering as well its manifold problems, is missing one-half of the story.

Whereas the growth of China's economic and political clout (in 2006 it was the world's sixth largest economy)[35] may be the greatest recent change in the global economy, it is certainly not the only one. China's Asian rivals, Japan and India, also have changed their positions. Indeed, India may ultimately prove to be a greater threat to America's economic hegemony than China. This is because the main engine of Indian economic growth is services (about 40 percent higher than the economy as a whole), and the U.S. is dominantly a service economy.

Even though India's infrastructure is sub par, its labor laws too restrictive, and its regulations burdensome, its fast-growing workforce has good English language and computer skills. These factors, combined with low wages, have allowed India to entice service industries to outsource jobs there. Despite its service sector growth, India will not be able to maximize economic growth until infrastructure is improved, and export-oriented manufacturing and agricultural production increase. Many of India's "best and brightest" work for multinationals both Indian and foreign, whereas domestic companies rank poorly in terms of operational efficiency. And there is a shortage of high-quality Indian employees.[36]

Moreover, there is reason to doubt India's ability to sustain growth—even at a pace lower than China's—without overheating. Share prices have risen four-fold in the past four years, and the current account deficit has widened, even while investment in education, health, and infrastructure has lagged. Although Indians are confident about their future, China seems to have the better game plan and attracts far more foreign companies and direct investment.[37]

Japan, once Asia's export leader and still the world's second-largest economy, has been in or near recession for over a decade. It has lost pride of place to China (with an economy one-half Japan's size), and been outflanked by other, more nimble, Asian traders like Hong Kong, South Korea, and Singapore. Indeed, the China-Hong Kong stock market has recently eclipsed Japan's in terms of market valuation.[38] Now, as Japan's manufacturing base shifts to lower-wage Asian countries, it must shore up its services sector. But will it? Indeed, can it?

Despite some painful restructuring, Japanese businesses are still interlocked in a "keiretsu" mode. Japan appears to welcome freer trade, but is ambivalent, even guarded, about its consequences.[39] Improving its relations with China and India may yet produce a formidable Eastern bloc, but their respective interests and Western relationships are not alike.[40]

Ten years after the Asian financial crisis, any number of East Asian nations have ramped up their economies. Many radically restructured their markets, and began to return to health after as little as one year. Pan-Asian consolidation is in vogue.[41]

Vietnam of all Asian countries has worked tirelessly over the past decade to gain membership in the WTO. It has improved its legal infrastructure and its banking system, and has made numerous economic reforms.[42] Recently, it reached its goal.

But all is not rosy in Asia. The necessary restructuring is far from complete. Rapid economic growth could lead again to a speculative bubble that bursts. Asian populations are aging, and in some countries, the workforce is shrinking and there is a shortage of talent. Whereas the rise of Asia is all the news, its cooling must be anticipated as well.[43]

The enlargement of the European Union and its improved economic health will also influence the world economy. As of January 1, 2009, twenty-seven countries were members of the EU. Despite its size and economic weight, however, the EU has only a moderate influence on global trade. Depending on how exchange rates are set, the EU accounts for one-fifth to one-third of the world economy, and its currency, the euro, is the second most heavily traded currency in the world. Four EU countries are members of the G8.

Despite its economic cohesion, the EU has been unable to speak with a collective voice on many issues. EU member countries must begin to think collectively, not nationally.[44] The impetus for this was the Lisbon initiative, which vainly called for the EU to become the world's premier technology economy by 2010. This almost certainly won't happen. But it has spurred the EU to increase its role in the global sweepstakes. As the American economy slowed, the European economy picked up some, although it is still sluggish. The euro is performing well against the U.S. dollar, the technology gap is shrinking, new members' economies are growing and, due to limited exposure, the European economy seems to be weathering the sub-prime market storm. Meanwhile the EU continues its outreach to other global traders—potentially undercutting U.S. influence.[45]

Considerable economic growth also typifies certain Latin America countries, with Brazil emerging as a new regional power.[46] Brazil is a founding and leading member of the so-called G20 group that is pressuring developed nations to open up their farm trade. Foreign direct investment in Brazil increased by eighty percent in 2004.[47] As its growth has moved inland, Brazil has recognized the need for a regional approach to economic planning; a trend that is likely to continue.[48] Despite their steady growth, however, Latin American countries—with the possible exception of Chile—have underinvested in the infrastructure needed to sustain growth. Without this infrastructure (roads, telecommunications, utilities, and water plants) Latin American economies will not continue to grow, or compete on the global stage.[49]

Of equal concern is the rise of populism in Venezuela (Hugo Chavez), Bolivia (Evo Morales) and Ecuador (Rafael Correa). Both Chavez and Morales have undertaken to nationalize their countries' oil and gas reserves; moves that will lose them favor with other Latin American countries and the United States. Moreover, Chavez has withdrawn Venezuela from the World Bank and IMF and sought to create an alternative South American lending bank. But his hubris may have run its course.[50]

Whereas anti-American populism may be popular with the lower classes, it undercuts the efforts of Latin American economies to become self sustaining economically, since they depend on America for both goods and markets (even Venezuela). Hence, embracing separatist strategies seems counter-productive. The very opposite may happen if South America's largest trading bloc, Mercosur, enlarges and cooperates on market fundamentals. That could lead to a bilateral deal with the EU, or the revival of negotiations for a free-trade area of the Americas (FTAA), which collapsed in 2003.

One thing is certain. The region is more insulated from external and internal shock than it was during the fiscal crises of 1998–99 and 2002. Indeed the stock markets of Mexico, Brazil and Chile all experienced double-digit growth by mid 2007 with a total inflow of $1.1billion—or five percent—into Latin American equity funds.

Rhetoric notwithstanding, many Latin American countries are experiencing steady economic growth, generally low inflation, financial stability and diminishing poverty. If this trend continues, they will become larger contributors to growth among emerging economies; and enjoy more clout as well.[51]

Of course, Mexico is a special case, not least because of the North American Free Trade Agreement. Under its new president, Calderon, it has begun to attract high-end investors (aerospace) and is restructuring its tax system so that infrastructure and social spending keep up with growth. Mexico is now the world's twelfth largest economy; just behind South Korea.[52]

Russia is a bit of a wild-card in the global sweepstakes. After a catastrophic experience with "instant capitalism," during which it defaulted on $40 billion in foreign debt, it has returned to something more like a state-managed economy. But the privatization of some of its most valuable assets and the economic and political chaos of the 1990s have cost Russia clout in both arenas. Russia has yet to be admitted to the World Trade Organization, although it has been included in the Group of Eight (G-8) leading economies (despite the fact that Russia's economy is sixty percent smaller than the next smallest G8 country, Canada). However, Russia's economy is growing fast thanks to oil revenue. It is also listed among of the BRIC emerging economies (Brazil, Russia, India and China), although it would be the poorest of that group as well.

Russia's exclusion from the WTO especially undercuts Russia's quest for global-power status.[53] Russian President Putin has called the collapse of the Soviet Union the "greatest geopolitical catastrophe" of the 20th Century. But, he feels hemmed in by the expansion of the EU and NATO to former Soviet satellites, criticism of Russia's human rights record, and the proposed European missile shield. Mr. Putin has responded by consolidating his hold on power, shaking down foreign investors in Russian oil and gas development, and aggressively and brutishly cutting off oil and gas supplies to break-away republics and some EU member states. These actions are testimony as much to Russia's weakness as its strength.[54]

Initially, EU leaders attempted to engage Russia in pacts regarding European "energy security," with Russia as a "strategic partner." (After all, the EU is Russia's largest market and Russia is the EU's third largest. And every seller needs a buyer.) But it appears that Russia is not inclined to be a reliable partner. And so the EU is cultivating other sources and promoting conservation.[55]

The Russians could use Western technology to limit waste and maximize oil and gas production. But their clumsy attempts to dominate the European energy market are likely to be rebuffed in the same way that Russia threatens others. The escalation of tensions does not bode well for Russia or the West.[56]

Conversely, Mr. Putin has brought stability and a degree of prosperity to the Russian economy. Forward planning has replaced crisis management. He has urged business leaders to modernize and diversity, and looked abroad for business partners and opportunities. Whether this or a more belligerent Russia is the real one, only time will tell.[57]

Even Africa—which I once called an economic basket case—is beginning to profit from globalization. It remains an economic laggard, and in some cases much worse, but the region as a whole has recorded 5 to 6 percent annual growth for the past several years and, with the establishment of the African Union (AU) in July 2002, fifty three African nations have pledged themselves to democratic principles, good governance, and the promotion of common African positions (evident in the Doha GATT negotiations). The first premise may be questioned, insofar as Somalia, Sudan, and Zimbabwe are all members. However, the new pact does give member nations the right to intervene in national conflicts which often spill across borders, and occurred (with UN backing) in Darfur. Whereas some AU countries have significantly improved their economies, with developed-country help and encouragement, other areas, like Darfur, are almost entirely dependent on foreign aid.[58]

This is not to depreciate the economic gains of certain African countries due to better governance, investment in education and infrastructure, and foreign capital. Many of them have mineral or oil resources, but need technical help to extract them. In Nigeria, for example, eight years of civilian rule has the economy growing at five percent annually. But Nigeria still depends on oil for 95 percent of its exports. What most African countries need is tariff-free access to developed country markets for their agricultural products—a sticking point in the Doha negotiations. With peace and security, dramatic improvements in health and productivity are possible; which attracts investment and eventually leads to self-sustainability. Africa has a way to go, but it may have turned a corner.[59]

The Middle East is also a mixed region economically. Some countries, for example Israel, Jordan, and Saudi Arabia, are reasonably well-run and prosperous. Others—such as Iraq and Afghanistan—are chaotic. Still others—Iran and Lebanon—are isolated, economically or militarily. This state of affairs is not healthy for the nations themselves or for progress in the region. Both hot war and cool relations are costly in terms of economic stability and growth. Speculation can also make developing economies appear more attractive than their fundamentals suggest, but punish them severely when sentiment turns.

In 2007, Turkey was on track to attract 25 times more foreign direct investment than it had six years earlier, but few Turks were engaged in the global market. Many Middle Eastern countries depend heavily on oil revenue, but have no contingency plans should oil prices drop or the oil run out.[60] Even devout Muslims and Islamic countries have entered the marketplace. But a lack of transparency and regulation makes their future risky as well. With the Middle East's need to diversity and other regions' need for energy, even reluctant Middle Eastern states are likely to be drawn more and more into the global trade and investment arena; at least once mutual suspicion is worn away and protectionist barriers reduced.[61]

Globalization also encourages cross-border mergers and acquisitions. In 2006, global M & A activity totaled $3.8 trillion, 38 percent higher than in 2005. These deals are increasingly being made from a company's capital reserves—yet another by-product of globalization. An Indian IT company, Wipro, acquired technology companies in Portugal, Finland, and California.[62] Swedish truck maker, Volvo, purchased the construction equipment division of Ingersoll-Rand.[63] Even China has allowed foreign enterprises to control some formerly state-run companies; while Chinese enterprises have sought to acquire American companies.[64]

The growth of multinational corporations has led to increased labor migration. As economies shift from agriculture to industry and then services, jobs and the people who fill them move more easily from one country to another. In some industries, it is not uncommon for workers to move to a new city, or a new country, every few years. Some workers describe themselves as "global citizens."[65]

While much of this migration is job related, conflict and poverty also contribute to migration, particularly in Africa. Approximately 23,000 doctors and nurses leave the continent every year. Diaspora networks allow emigrants to help those who have stayed, bolstering the economies of less-developed states.[66]

Given increased mobility, the growth of multinational corporations, and the rising demand for skilled labor, migration will not go away any time soon. Developing economies need to allocate resources intelligently, by investing in infrastructure, education, and social benefits. Improved infrastructure reduces the cost of transporting goods and services. Education prepares the workforce for changing technologies.[67] Finally, retraining helps workers to be more flexible and productive.

Not all countries have profited from globalization, however. The Doha Development Agenda (DDA) was meant to incorporate trade concessions that would spur economic growth in less-developed countries. After all, developed economies are better able to make trade concessions than their less developed neighbors. Unfortunately, the number of countries involved and the number of issues on the agenda caused the talks to become contentious and protracted. Developed and developing nations were so far apart that the talks were temporarily suspended in 2006. And a mini-ministerial failed in July 2008. No conclusion is likely until the United States and Europe alter their farm policies.[68] Until they do, existing subsidies, tariffs, and other trade barriers will slow the integration of developing countries into the global marketplace. The U.S. and EU need to use more carrots and fewer sticks, since their agricultural supports retard developing countries' escape from poverty.[69] If the Doha negotiations are successful, the elimination of tariffs and other protective measures could lift "at least 500 million people out of poverty within 14 years, and create long-term economic benefit [s for] ... developing countries."[70]

Conversely, developing countries are resistant to fully opening their markets to foreign non-agricultural goods.[71] So the stalemate continues. But what seems to be missed is that, by and large, developing economies gain from liberalizing their markets. And the very poor benefit as much as anyone from economic growth.[72] If the Doha talks fail, or even if their resolution is seriously delayed, both developed and less-developed countries will lose. But the latter will lose more; since they would reap greater gains from a new trade treaty.

If multilateral talks do fail, opportunities always exist for bilateral and regional agreements. These agreements are easier to negotiate, but they could be more damaging than helpful. Less-developed countries often lack negotiating skills and persistence and have less market leverage. Moreover, countries lose incentive to negotiate global agreements when bilateral deals are available.[73] Nevertheless, bilateral and regional agreements can lead to new multilateral agreements.

While prosperity has its benefits, increased consumption and the resulting depletion of natural resources are problematic. According to a UN report, industrialized countries will have to reduce their consumption ten-fold in order for adequate resources to be available for developing economies. That seems unlikely. On the other hand, sharing of resources through a global economic system, along with stabilization of population and reduction of consumption, will help avoid potential global environmental/humanitarian crises.[74] There is already competition for energy supplies. This could be very costly if it degenerated into competitive acquisition and exploitation, as it could increase maldistribution and waste. It would be far better if there was international collaboration on the development of alternative energy sources, husbanding those that currently exist, and addressing the pollution that energy consumption causes.[75] The recent spike in food prices illustrates the need for international cooperation.[76]

C. Increased Interconnection and Cooperation

Global problems invite global solutions. And so we have witnessed a large increase in international undertakings. Any number could be cited, for example: The United Nations (UN), the International Monetary Fund (IMF), World Bank, the North American Free Trade Association (NAFTA), the Group of Eight (G-8) industrialized nations, the European Union (EU), the Organization for Economic Cooperation and Development (OECD), and the Asian-Pacific Economic Cooperation (APEC) forum, to name just a few. But none of these are more important to global trade than the World Trade Organization (WTO).

As globalization has progressed, so has the impact of the WTO. From its original 33 members (then called the General Agreement on Tariffs and Trade, or GATT), the WTO has grown to 153, which account for over 96 percent of global trade.[77] WTO agreements set the stage for trade reform and growth, and are enforceable against signatory members.

WTO members are not the only drivers of globalization, however. The process has steadily become more inclusive. Business persons, consumers, and non-governmental organizations (NGOs)—all private sector stakeholders—have been invited to make their input as well. The two best-known business panels are the Trans-Atlantic Business Dialogue (TABD) and the APEC Business Advisory Council (ABAC). NGOs have gone from being opponents of globalization to participants that help shape its direction and impacts. While this broader base of participation may slow (indeed has slowed) the process somewhat, a more comprehensive system will be more widely supported. Broad participation also produces an important synergy. Collaborative efforts produce better results. Globalization's benefits and burdens can be distributed more equitably. Wide representation reduces the influence of any one nation — including the U.S. — on global growth. Moreover, downturns will be diluted by the breadth of the market.[78] The real story of globalization, however, is not greater cooperation among nations through international organizations in the public sphere, but the growing influence of businesses in the private sphere; below the public radar.

As the global economy has improved, the number of anti-dumping filings by the United States has declined. In 2001, 77 anti-dumping cases were initiated, compared to just 10 in 2005.[79] One reason for the decline is that U.S. manufacturers now recognize that less-expensive foreign goods will enter our market due to our own inefficiencies, not illegal dumping. U.S. manufacturers are challenged to abandon uncompetitive products or improve production. This does not mean that U.S. manufacturing is in a decline. On the contrary, manufacturing as a percent of GDP is holding steady, and American factories are still producing goods at a brisk pace, producing more than $1.5 trillion in goods in 2005 alone.[80]

While manufacturing has held steady, the United States is predominantly a service economy. In 2005, it provided approximately $190 billion of the world's $1,160 billion commercial services exports. And, unlike our negative balance of trade in goods, we have a positive balance in services.[81] We need to invest more in research and development and worker training in order to open new markets for American producers however.[82]

Globalization has also spurred cross-border investment. American manufacturers invested $39 billion in overseas plants in 2005.[83] Many people believe that this is a loss to the United States. Certainly U.S. assets are invested abroad, but they may be used to open new markets, increase efficiently, or produce a higher rate of return; all advantages to the U.S. economy. This is reminiscent of opponents of America's space program who seemed to think that NASA's rockets were loaded with U.S. assets and blasted into outer space. In fact, most space dollars stayed right here on earth in the pockets of workers and companies that supported the enterprise. They, in turn, paid taxes and produced technology that helped the U.S. economy grow.

People seem to forget that the United States is one of the largest beneficiaries of foreign direct investment (FDI). At the end of 2004, the United States had received some $1.53 trillion in FDI that builds businesses and creates jobs here in America.[84] From 2005 until April 2007, the U.S. invested $78 billion in foreign ventures, yet it received $100 billion in investment from abroad.[85]

Unfortunately, politicians pander to fears about foreign ownership of American assets. While security is important, the United States risks its economic well being if it discourages foreign investment. After all, U.S. corporations seek out foreign opportunities, so why shouldn't foreign businesses do the same? To protect one's market and indigenous industries from foreign acquisition is simply to send the business elsewhere.[86] Business consolidation, once chiefly limited to western economies, is accelerating and spreading to emerging economies as well. Cross-border merger and acquisition (M & A) activity shows little sign of abating, although it is slowed periodically by security concerns and economic downturns.[87]

Globalization leads to the convergence of national markets into a global market. Examples include NYSE's partnership with the Tokyo Exchange, and the NYSE's acquisition of Euronext NV. But a global financial market makes sense. There is probably no business sector in which consolidation and coordination is proceeding as quickly. This is due to its fungibility, and impact on all economies.[88] While these alliances are in their infancy, a permanently-open global exchange can become reality. If so, the United States will need to balance any regulatory concessions it makes against consumer protection.

The convergence of financial markets could also result in the creation of a third "world currency." At present, the U.S. dollar and the euro account for about 91 percent of the world's identified reserves, with the Japanese yen a very distant third. Given the rise of Asian economies, however, it is possible that the Chinese yuan—or more likely a basket of regional currencies based on the yuan and yen—will develop into an intra-regional currency. However, Asian countries are more diverse than the EU countries that created the euro, and presently trade less with one another. That does not mean a single Asian currency is impossible. The question is whether Asian countries are willing to cede some control over monetary policy in order to create a regional currency.[89]

Globalization is not just about the spread of capitalism or the growth of markets, however. It also increases the interdependence of nations. Advances in technology and communication fuel this process. And that suggests more uniform standards, a single regulator, and greater transparency. This seems to be particularly necessary in the turbulent field of financial services. In order for markets to be efficient they must be broadly-based and well-regulated. The global sweep of modern trade makes this difficult.[90]

Nonetheless, progress is being made in some areas. For example, financial accounting; which has now been reduced to two systems, one international and the other American. Another area needing harmonization is taxation. Diverse systems can create problems.[91] Whereas multilateral agreement on a common standard can make markets more efficient and competitive, unilateral behavior segments the market and raises trade tensions.[92] Collaboration is also the best way to interdict illegal behavior that increases the cost of international business.[93] Moreover, harmonization is a one-off event. Once a universal standard is adopted there is an end to most conflicts.

The United States cannot let globalization proceed unfettered, however. A laissez-faire attitude is risky. The best way to manage the long-term benefits (and short-term burdens) of globalization is through proactivity. In a globalized world, the social and economic problems of one country cannot be neatly contained. A collaborative approach generally produces the best results for all.

The comments above naturally raise concerns about the continued viability of the nation-state. It has not lost its importance, but its role is being reconfigured. Individual nations will continue to be the primary authority on domestic matters, but will have a shared voice in international decision-making. The latter is the most that participants can expect.

Globalization will probably erode cultural identify to some degree (the McDonald's effect). Language is one of the more obvious casualties. The world is harmonizing around English. But, foreign tongues are not dying out. Rather, the world is becoming more bilingual. While extreme cultural idiosyncrasies may be lost, treasured traditions and beliefs will be retained. The French will not cease being "French," nor Americans "American."

Today, no single nation-state has the power to dictate global policy; including the United States.[94] But some voice in decision-making is better than none. Additionally, problems such as aging, poverty, disease, environmental damage, and sustainability are now recognized as multinational issues. While certain countries may take the lead in addressing some of them, a collective effort is generally necessary to complete the task.

Participation results in some loss of autonomy. But nation-states are voluntarily bonding together in new configurations. They are disaggregating their national practices and reaggregating the best of them as international norms. The individual state remains important since it does not have to adopt those norms. But most elect to do so.

While the United States has balked at the EU's aircraft emissions standards, the EU's action could presage an international norm.[95] As world markets become more harmonized, international standards in areas such as climate change, banking, and competition will be developed. Presently, four so-called "Singapore issues" are waiting to be added to the Doha negotiating agenda: investment, competition policy, government procurement, and trade facilitation. Only the latter is presently being pursed. But international businesses support the Doha Round because it means more uniform standards and a wider market.[96] While those standards often reflect western practices, there is no reason that they must. Indeed, the negotiation process almost ensures that Western practices will be leavened. Rather than witnessing the end of the nation-state, we are simply witnessing its reconfiguration.[97]

Although globalization has had a powerful effect on the world, the issues that concern people most—education, social services, property ownership, inheritance, and welfare—continue to be locally (or nationally) regulated. While the spread of western business practices is criticized, its benefits are often overlooked. Without it the technology gap between developed and developing nations would continue to grow. American culture is often denounced, but our products are readily consumed.[98]

Of course, nation-states can choose not to participate in the globalization process. That decision is made at the local level. However, that choice could prove delimiting. In general, countries that embrace globalization profit the most. In the past twenty years, China's economic growth has lifted 400 million people (out of 1.3 billion) out of grinding poverty.[99] Thanks to its membership in the European Union, Ireland, which in 1990 had a per capita income 28 percent below Germany's, raised it to 26 percent above Germany's by 2004.[100]

If developing countries had the capital and know-how to develop their economies, they would not need assistance. But they do. So they rely on better-developed nations and, in the process, create opportunities for them to profit from foreign trade. Countries that are more prosperous have happier, more tolerant citizens who are willing to settle disputes peacefully and embrace democracy.[101] By helping developing countries, we help ourselves.

Well-managed, well-regulated Western businesses have something to contribute to the global marketplace. But foreign traders have something to contribute as well. The key is to identify and adopt measures that suit the greatest number and produce optimum growth with sustainability.

D. Leadership

With power comes responsibility. And so it falls to prosperous, post-industrial economies to make certain that all nations enjoy some benefit from globalization. And indeed wealthy countries have at times exhibited strong leadership; from U.S. Trade Representative Robert Zoellick's January 2004 letter that revived the Doha round of trade negotiations, to the EU's revision of its common agricultural to help developing economies participate in the global economy. But it is inappropriate for emerging economies such as China, Brazil, India, and Russia to insist upon the same trade concessions given least-developed nations. The former's insistence on preferential treatment stalls negotiations, further injuring the least-developed nations that already constitute a drag on global growth. All nations and international organizations must partner to reduce inequities and address a rising number of global concerns.

The United States should not always take the lead, either politically or militarily. It is appropriate for other developed countries to share the burden, especially since U.S. influence is declining. But they often do not. For example, America's NATO allies spend less than half as much of their GDP on defense as does America.[102]

America's style of leadership also needs to soften. The second Bush presidency began with a unilateralist agenda. While this may have been intended to inject reality into inert international negotiations, it upset friends and foes alike. Granted, no nation was meeting its Kyoto targets and the cold-war ABM treaty probably was anachronistic. However, the blunt rejection of these treaties was unnecessary. The key to America's global success has been consensus building, not imposition of its will.[103]

In the new global order, partnership is essential. The bipolar system died with the Cold War. Now, a brief unipolar system is morphing into a multipolar system. The United States remains a major force, but it needs allies to effectively address global issues.[104]

The United States' most likely partner is the European Union. Citizens of the EU favor globalization and believe it will benefit them and their families.[105] But they, as well as the U.S., have resisted deeper cuts in agricultural supports, while developing countries have resisted further opening their markets to manufactured goods. This impasse has virtually paralyzed the Doha trade negotiations. I believe it will be resolved in this or a future round, when the U.S. and EU accept that farm supports have little impact on their GDP and the G20 nations become more economically secure.[106] When the European Union and the United States cooperate, they generally enhance world trade.[107] But they do not always agree.[108] This allows other traders to increase their leverage by joining one or the other, forcing them apart. In general the EU is more protective of its market, and particularly shelters "national heroes" from foreign takeovers or even European consolidation.[109]

There is no such thing as a completely "free" market, of course. Even the freest in the world (probably the United States) is highly regulated. Just a few (of over one hundred) federal agencies, such as the FDA and SEC, have a profound effect on what goods and services can enter the U.S. market. Tariffs and non-tariff barriers, such as purity standards, are meant to protect against various threats. Some are perfectly legitimate. A nation does not want its food supply threatened by foreign pests or to have domestic industries compromised by subsidized foreign competitors. These are not the usual cases, however.

More often, local regulations simply perpetuate historical practices. For example, a beer purity law, Reinheitsgebot, has been in effect in Germany since 1516. In the U.S., a quota was imposed on Chinese socks, to protect the sock industry in Fort Payne, Alabama, because a local congressman agreed to vote for a Central American trade treaty only if the White House promised it would extend the quotas.[110] Whatever the political advantage, there is generally no economic benefit in market protection, and it invites retorsion.

I am not naïve enough to think that such practices can be prevented entirely. Local politicians are put under pressure to protect domestic businesses and jobs from foreign competition. This practice underpinned the hugely successful Japanese economy of the 1980s. By minimizing foreign competition and subsidizing exports, Japanese producers were able to build up a huge foreign trade surplus. But, following the Uruguay Round of GATT negotiations, Japan was forced to open its market, and it was uncompetitive. Because Japan failed to make periodic, short-term corrections, its market suffered a huge correction in 1993. Japan has been near or in recession ever since.[111]

Market regulations enacted merely to inhibit globalization are unwise. They may have some short-term benefits (if used to protect an inefficient industry while it restructures), but they are generally ill-conceived in the long run. They limit consumer choice, and sooner or later consumer preference seems to win out. Additionally, these measures distort competition. They can result in overpriced and low quality goods. Hence, protection is an inefficient use of both monetary and human capital.

The United States cannot afford to seal off its economy. Americans consume millions of dollars of foreign goods every day and export millions in U.S. goods and services to foreign consumers.[112] As nations erect walls around their economies to hold back the rising tide of globalization, they marginalize themselves. In the end, they will be the losers.

"True leadership" means telling constitutes the bad news as well as the good. World trade and its effects on the U.S. economy are more complex than politicians and the popular media admit. No one benefits by pretending it is otherwise. Both must stop pandering to the populist view that globalization is a curse, and address its complexities.

For example, Americans object to the outsourcing of jobs overseas. But most of the industries and jobs that are lost are reaching obsolescence anyway and will eventually be phased out. Moreover, outsourcing is nothing new, and affects but a small percentage of American jobs. Finally, globalization has the ability to create more and better jobs. Now is the time for America to retool and adjust to the changing world economy. We cannot be content with the status quo.[113]

Politicians' pledge to "fight for American jobs" is disingenuous. It inflates expectations and fosters an "us vs. them" mentality. No country is entitled to any
particular jobs. Some would disappear with or without globalization. Globalization just forces the issue. It forces the United States to develop competitive
sectors and to eliminate inefficient ones.

Lack of leadership is not limited to the United States, of course. Many European citizens also decry globalization. And European leaders fail to explain
that open markets underpin Europe's prosperity and the social models it favors.[114]

Another difference between the U.S. and EU is the latter's heavy reliance on
"soft power." It is certainly to be preferred to "hard" power, *if* it works. But, if
it means indecision and reluctance to get involved as conditions worsen, then
it is hardly the leadership expected of an economic superpower. The EU was
unable to handle ethic cleansing in Europe, and lately has been inert in dealing with Zimbabwe's pariah-president Mugabe. Part of the reason is that the
EU doesn't have a functional foreign policy, but shares power with its constituent states. They often don't agree on the way forward. On the other hand,
America's "war on terror" has undermined its legitimacy and exhausted its resources. It has offended friend and foe alike.[115]

The EU exerts its soft power chiefly through the process of enlargement; draw-
ing more and more European states into an "area of freedom, security and justice"
(Article Z, EU treaty). The EU also has reached out to other neighbors and less-
developed African, Caribbean, and Pacific (ACP) nations; most of them former
colonies. But these preferential agreements terminated in 2008, when a temporary dispensation from WTO rules ended. However, they could be replaced by bilateral trade agreements.[116] But, so long as the EU remains fragmented, both with
respect to foreign policy and the single market, it will "punch below its weight."

That said, Europe has led dramatically on some issues; such as foreign aid
and climate change. And it has joined the U.S. in threatening China with tariffs to compensate for its export subsidation. Moreover, the European economy
has begun to pick up after many year's of trailing America's. But Europe's pre-
occupation remains its economic health and status in the world.[117]

These manifold differences may foretell a schism in western leadership—a
decoupling—rather than increased global influence for the transatlantic alliance. If the two collaborate they can probably drive the global agenda. But
their separate interests and approaches makes that unlikely at present. And,
the EU's new "reform" (Lisbon) treaty (October, 2007), if adopted, will give the
Community a leaner management structure and more competencies.[118] So it
could act as a "federal" counterweight to the U.S.

Japan, the world's second largest national economy, also has given support
to the U.S., both militarily (the Gulf) and politically (North Korea). However,

it is struggling to recover from fifteen years of low or negative growth. Japan inclines to cooperate with that U.S. (patent registration; piracy; and competition law), but it wants to protect certain sensitive economic sectors, such as agriculture, and must get along with its neighbors—especially China. All this definitely limits Japan's international clout.[119]

Two other nations that are generally supportive of the U.S. and western economic policy are Canada and Mexico; in large part because of their close ties with the U.S. economy. But they too lack significant international clout.

So the most important new influence on global leadership is China; or more generally the so-called BRICs; Brazil, Russia, India and China. But, China is the main story. It contributed to global stability through the North Korea nuclear negotiations. But, by and large, China seems focused on managing the exponential growth of its increasingly capitalistic economy; with little concern for collateral impacts.

It wants to maintain stable relations with the U.S. enough to agree to a military hotline, and allow American businesses to participate in Chinese markets. For, being export-oriented, China needs foreign consumers.[120] And, as an emerging economy, China is also looking for export and investment opportunities elsewhere in the world. Chinese companies are expanding globally, particularly searching for resources that China needs to grow its economy. They have focused on African and South-East Asian targets, but may eventually turn to western targets. At present, however, Chinese investors seem largely unconcerned about environmental, governance, and human rights issues.[121] Indeed, it seems the Chinese would rather do nothing than alienate a trader with whom they might do business.[122]

Such behavior is untenable in the longer term. China is a member of the WTO, and sooner or later will be forced to meet its obligations thereunder. China's tightly regulated currency, the renminbi, distorts international trade. One day it will need to float as other currencies do.[123] Moreover, China has serious systemic problems, including pollution, over-population, inflation, agrarian collapse, corruption, and unemployment as state-owned enterprises are closed.[124] At present much of its energy is focused on these problems. So China contributes very little to international leadership.[125]

Russia is no better. After a period of what can only be described as "failed capitalism," Russia reverted to a more-autocratic state under President Putin. Although Russia also helped negotiate the North Korean nuclear agreement (in its national interest), and recently agreed with the U.S. about the safe disposal of its weapons-grade nuclear material and to continue missile talks, Russia's foreign policy has been decidedly anti-American and anti-European; as if being anti-west improved Russia's status in the rest of the world.[126]

In his effort to restore Russia's former status, Mr. Putin has used the country's oil and gas supplies as political leverage; pleasing neither producers (worried about security of demand) and consumers—particularly those in Europe (anxious about security of supply). Indeed, Russia has used the threat of legal action (for environmental pollution) and expropriation to force foreign co-venturers to reduce their stake in petroleum enterprises.[127] This "pipeline diplomacy" strains Russian relations with energy-consuming countries that one expects it would want to cultivate rather than rebuff by building vast state monoliths and cultivating relations with Iran and Venezuela. The prospect of genuine energy independence may by illusory, but Russia's strategic policy is brutish and its economic policy chaotic.[128]

The remaining two BRIC nations, India and Brazil, are more democratic, have economies of roughly Russia's size, and are less strident. India in particular is very entrepreneurial, has a growing middle class, and global companies that are keen to expand. But this exacerbates its skills shortage. Rapid growth also threatens inflation, which could be explosive in a country with so many poor. Nevertheless, a growing microfinance market in India (with an estimated 36 million borrowers in 2007) suggests that class disparity is finally being addressed. American angst about competition from China and India seems misplaced. In the near term at least, they are assemblers and servers, not innovators. Moreover, they will increasingly be consumers.[129]

Brazil is also a strong voice in the emerging-economy sector. But, due to its many small political parties, shifting coalitions, and a tradition of patronage and corruption, its voice is somewhat muted. Nonetheless, it has sued the U.S. in the WTO and won (agricultural subsidies). And it is a leader within the so-call Group of 20 emerging economies that is holding the Doha GATT negotiations to ransom until those economies get agricultural concessions in return for market access.[130]

However, the rapid growth of the BRIC economies has produced greater world economic balance, and that may presage more stability and productivity. Although India and Brazil's foreign policy is less strident than China or Russia's, it is just as self-interested and has helped the Group of 20 emerging economies join the global mainstream.

As for other nations, they have less impact on international relations, but are sensitive to shifts in power and influence. Asia's influence is increasing. Latin America's is also. Even Africa is in play.[131] But handicapping every nation's contribution to global leadership would require a book in itself. Suffice it that many nations make some contribution. But, among smaller states, the influence of oil-rich Middle-Eastern states such as Saudi Arabia, Qatar, and Dubai may be among the most important. They too are caught in a trading world that is governed as much by political concerns as it is by economic ones.[132]

Of course, nations are not the only leaders in the globalization process. A number of international organizations—many of them created after World War II—were expressly designed to address global issues. Most of them now confront issues they were not created to tackle, however. Their composition is also suspect. In the words of one critic, they are "to varying degrees, fragmented, unrepresentative and ineffective;" their legitimacy is in decline.[133] It will take very strong leadership to change that.

Take the United Nations (UN) for example. It is difficult to say that any global issue is beyond its responsibilities, because its membership is so large and its remit so vast. And yet its very size and diversity makes consensus difficult to achieve; and it has no real adjudicative or enforcement powers.

The UN's most ambitious recent undertaking is the Millennium Development Goals (to reduce extreme poverty and hunger by one-half and halt the spread of HIV/AIDS and malaria by 2015, among others; nine goals in all). But many goals will not be met because developed nations have not kept their promise to contribute .7 percent of their GDP to overseas development (Johannesburg World Summit on Sustainable Development). If the first goal is reached at all, it will be thanks to the booming economies of India and China. Africa has no chance whatever of meeting it.[134]

A second large—and critical—UN initiative is to cut carbon emissions and global warming; particularly because it threatens many developing countries (beneficiaries of the Millennium Goals) that are not serious polluters themselves. A general acceptance of the problem presaged the UN launch of a climate "summit" in Bali in December, 2007. But a successful outcome is far from certain. Major polluters such as China and India do not feel that they should bear any sizable portion of the reduction because they are developing nations. Developed nations respond that India and China are very inefficient energy users, and huge polluters. They should not be exempt from any reduction plan. Meanwhile, the present (Kyoto) agreement is due to lapse in 2012, and a climate change "crisis" could arrive as early as 2015. Achieving an effective treaty in time will be a real test of the UN system.[135]

A third important UN mission is peacekeeping. The UN relies entirely on volunteered national troops, many from developing countries; troops that are poorly trained and equipped, and sometimes accused of misbehavior. Since 1998 there has been a six-fold increase in the number of UN peacekeepers, serving on 18 separate missions; aided by a similar number of NATO and African Union troops. But the blue-helmeted UN troops generally are more successful (they generally have the easier tasks) and enjoy greater international legitimacy.[136]

The UN cannot begin to address all the problems it has accepted—or had thrust upon it—given its meager (and uncertain) budget.[137] Nevertheless, the

UN has done a credible job. But institutional reform is a must. However, the five nations that hold permanent seats on the Security Council with veto power (the US, Britain, China, Russia and France), have very different perspectives, and are almost certain to block any reforms that threaten their status or interests. In all, the UN still may be best *political* overseer of globalization, but its lack of adjudicative and enforcement capability weakens it.[138]

Another World War II initiative is the General Agreement on Tariffs and Trade (GATT), which morphed into the WTO in 1993.[139] Its remit is narrower than the UN's, but by no means small. More important, the 1993 overhaul modernized its institutions and gave them adjudicative and enforcement powers. That alone has made the WTO effective in carrying out its mandate.[140]

But not all WTO members (Cape Verde became the 153rd member in 2007) meet its high standards. Hence, there is "special and differential" treatment for emerging economies and some flexibility for countries with "implementation issues" (inability to implement all their obligations). The Doha Development round of GATT negotiations, launched in late 2001, was meant to reconcile the differences between developed and developing nations. But both groups have proved somewhat intransigent, so the future of these talks is uncertain. This is sad because the one thing that all parties seem to agree upon is the importance of trade facilitation.[141] Even if these talks fail, however, others are bound to be initiated. Global trade is that strong an inducement. And the WTO, with its narrow but critical function, may be the most modern and effective international institution.[142]

The World Bank and International Monetary Fund (IMF) are two additional post-World War II institutions, both based in Washington, D.C. In times past, both performed their functions tolerably well, if for no other reason than that their clients were desperate for financial help. But, as those countries' economies improved, they became less willing to submit to formulistic Washington-imposed reforms; the so-called "Washington Consensus."

In the case of the IMF, demand for its help is greater when countries are in fiscal crisis. During prosperous recent times, there has been less demand for its support, and hence its earnings shrank. Now many potential borrowers can fund themselves from their foreign-exchange reserves or by borrowing from other sources with fewer conditions than the IMF imposes. The sub-prime loan crisis may reduce liquidity, but its impact seems greater in profligate Western countries than elsewhere. Even if emerging economies do need to borrow from the IMF, they want a greater say about its lending policies.[143]

The World Bank is in a slightly different situation. There remain many poor countries world wide that need a hand up. Under its new president, Robert Zoellick, the institution has committed to spur growth by ending conflict, building infrastructure, developing financial markets, encouraging good governance, ending corruption (a systemic problem in weak economies), and stimulating export trade; particularly agricultural products. But this will require several institutional changes. First, the Bank must allow borrowers to participate more fully in their own development through "differentiated business model[s]." Second, it must reduce the influence of lender nations by courting the private sector. And finally, it must funnel more money into the agricultural sector, where extreme poverty is the worst. (The proportion of aid that went to agriculture fell to a low of 3.4 percent in 2004).[144]

Will these overhauls save the IMF and World Bank? No one knows for certain. But the need to shore up marginal economies will not go away. And the global marketplace will not be secure until that happens.

The group of seven industrialized states (G7; Britain, Canada, France, Germany, Italy, Japan, and the U.S.) is another international body. It is not broadly representative, even when it includes Russia (G8). But the G7 nations represent well over one-half of global GDP. And, when you add three nations — deserving but not presently included (China, the sixth largest economy in the world; Spain 8th; and India 10th) — they equal about three-quarters of global GDP. (Canada is 9th and Russia 15th).

The G7 used to be able to form a consensus around chiefly economic issues, and then take some concerted action. Today the issues are more complex, consensus is harder to reach, and the impact of their action more muted. But, under the right conditions, concerted action by the G7 can still have influence. Even if the G7/8 is nothing more than a "talking shop," their meetings are useful and they have the potential to lead on a variety of matters.[145]

The Organization for Economic Co-operation and Development (OECD) is a 30-nation Paris think tank devoted to research and promotion of best practices in economic governance. However, its success has been modest. Although its work thoroughly documents the advantages of good practices, its own research reveals that structural reforms were most likely to be adopted by countries in crisis. That is, reform is impolitic unless there is a crisis. Once the crisis is past, it is common to return to the status quo. That does not bode well, for these crises are increasingly global. And some require a global response. But political inertia is hard to overcome.[146]

The last international grouping I will discuss is the North Atlantic Treaty Organization (NATO). It was formed after World War II principally to protect democracy in Europe from the spread of Russian socialism. With the collapse of the Soviet Union, however, and aside from Mr. Putin's belligerence, that objective has ceased to be significant. Still, trouble spots in the world require a police presence, and preferably one of international composition. With Europeans reluctant to put their forces at risk and inclined to negotiation,

NATO's future is fragile, if still necessary at this juncture. Europe's reluctance to police even its own theater leaves NATO alive but largely inert.[147]

Even within Europe, NATO members cannot agree about how fast or how far to extend its membership, particularly when confronted with Russian objections to admitting former satellites. There is also contention about America's proposed missile defense shield in Eastern Europe. So, even European defense leadership seems somewhat rudderless.[148]

Numerous other international groupings could be named: for example, APEC, ASEAN, ACP, Mercosur (the Southern Market), The Andean group, the African Union, and so forth. But none have the impact of those discussed above.

Part of the reason for the failure of international leadership may be that the participants are too numerous and the agenda too diverse. To fill the gap many nations have resorted to negotiations among small groups of homogenous nations. Others have resorted to bilateral free-trade agreements (FTAs).[149] These may be stepping stones to broader agreements. But they could also conflict with or delay them.

So exactly what is happening to the world economy? Quite simply, it is re-balancing. For many years, the U.S. and western European nations drove the global trade agenda. Now the west has lost its hegemonic position, and won't recover it.[150] That is not so bad; for there is no balance in a unipolar world.

Today emerging Asian economies account for more global GDP growth than America. And China and India's consumer spending is growing faster too. Moreover, East Asia's growth is less likely to be effected by the current economic slow-down than Europe or America. Of course, China can't continue to grow at its present pace, but other Asian economies could pick up the slack. And, as economies mature, trade imbalances leaven. This assumes that continued growth in emerging economies will be fueled by domestic (as well as export) demand. And that is a big if.[151]

For the time being, America will remain a primary force in the world economy. But a broader balance in economic and political affairs should be welcome. If the U.S. dollar is losing favor with global investors (and it is), it only means that there is a greater need for global fiscal coordination. Sadly, residual nationalism can thwart both regional and international leadership.[152]

Of course, global leadership can come from the private sector too. Witness the work of the Gates Foundation; and the growing notion that prosperous multinational corporations have social responsibilities.[153]

At present the forces that favor globalization and those that oppose it are about equally balanced. There are variations, of course, depending upon the stakeholder, region, or issue involved. But often there is national retrenchment even while the globalization process pushes slowly ahead.[154] This condition can't prevail.

America will stand on the sidelines at its peril. To do so means that it will not influence the agenda, although it will be affected by it.[155] But the U.S. will not be a credible negotiator until Congress restores trade promotion authority (TPA) to the executive.

Exactly which actors, groups, or organizations take the initiative, and in what areas, remains to be seen. It may be the WTO, which will undoubtedly expand its membership (including Russia) and its remit. Or it may be bilateral or regional free trade agreements (FTAs) that add more and more sectors to trade pacts and help harmonize markets.[156] Although improbable, it is even possible that the Doha negotiations may be completed soon.

It is certain that every stakeholder—rich and poor alike—will seek some advantage. And the process will not be sound unless there is broad support. But achieving this is difficult politically. So, in the end, the drivers of globalization may be private individuals, non-governmental organizations (NGOs), and multinational businesses, which have a large stake in its success, but no political constituency to appease. All of them fly below the political radar.[157]

It's a false yardstick to measure America's well-being by another country's. Excepting the extremes, there will always be countries better off or less well off. Moreover, one-half of any numerical listing has to be "below average," which can't always be so terrible. And yet Americans grow anxious at the suggestion that we are number two—or worse.[158] First the good news. The U.S. is the world's largest trading nation; measured by both imports and exports of goods and services. (Although Germany is the largest goods exporter, having surpassed the U.S. in 2003). The U.S. is also the world's leading manufacturer (based on market value); which most people would tend to doubt, considering the steady loss of manufacturing jobs. But efficiency is the key.[159] The U.S. leads in many other categories as well, such as gross domestic product (GDP); innovation; and Nobel laureates. But it is ninth in GDP per-capita; tenth in quality of life, and forty-first in life expectancy.[160]

What if the yardstick was not wealth, but comfort across a range of important criterion such as health, happiness, security, and freedom? Globalization presents the opportunity for participating countries to achieve a level of comfort never before experienced.

E. Conclusion

Change is inevitable; we all know that. And yet "globalization" is often portrayed as a problem, rather than an opportunity.[161] The failure to anticipate and adjust to change can be worse than the change itself. The real issue is how to manage it. Properly managed, globalization can improve the standard of living for many, if not all, participants. It is, after all, a process and not a destination. So it will proceed only as far and fast as the majority of participants, and circumstances, will allow. There are virtues and vices to every step. The question is the degree to which one outweighs the other.

Unfortunately, Americans often view globalization as a threat. Its losses are evident and immediate. Its benefits are longer-term and diffuse. Hence the often-exaggerated losses to the American economy due to globalization produce anxiety and pushback. For example, one study suggests that we will lose our position as the world's top manufacturer by 2020. (Don't most American's believe that we have already done so?) It may, or may not, happen. But globalization's impact on our economy is a lot more complex.[162]

The greatest challenge for the U.S. is to adjust to an increasingly globalized world. The world is not flat, and it never will be.[163] But it is flattening. The U.S. has lost its economic hegemony. But whether this means a huge loss of economic influence is far less clear. After all, in the 1980s and early '90s Japan was expected to become the world's economic superpower, and that never came to pass. Yes, the U.S. percentage of world GDP is shrinking. That is to be expected as more and more nations enter in the global marketplace. But America remains foremost among those competitors. And participation in that market actually helps U.S. firms to excel. Just recently, General Motors seized back from Toyota kudos as the world's largest automaker. And Caterpillar saw its exports rise 44 percent from 2004 to 2006.[164]

The shift away from being a comprehensive, self-sufficient economy involves some risks. Chief among these is dependence on other economies to supply certain consumption needs. But there is no large economy in the world that is truly self-sufficient. Being dependent is a vulnerability shared by all. And there is a greater risk of friction if economies are independent rather than interdependent.

What is happening is a necessary, and salutary, rebalancing of the world economy. This is good for America and the rest of the world. America remains an efficient producer, and at the top in global competitiveness. But other nations are inevitably catching up. The global economy is not static. The U.S. should not always be its principal engine. It will be as hard for the rest of the world to "decouple" from the U.S. economy as it would be for the U.S. to separate from the rest of the world. But, it will take time for political and social changes to catch up with globalization's economic thrust.[165]

We are witnessing the slow death of nation states as independent operators, and the emergence of a broader-based global economy that defuses risk, but also control. It is the triumph of economics over politics. This assumes however that all participants play by the same rules, equitably and fairly.[166]

It matters not where the process begins. Open markets are synergistic. Witness the enormous strides countries like Taiwan, South Korea, and China made once they embraced global trade. On the other hand, developing economies are, by definition, "works in progress." They are fragile, poised between growth and collapse. Although the latter is felt most acutely by emerging economies, it is shared by all globalists. Any nation that fails to grow economically constitutes a drag on the system.[167]

It is inevitable that developing economies will increase their market share. So, strong leadership is required to remain competitive. Cutting farm supports, reforming health care and public education, increasing investment in research and development, and remaining flexible in a changing world will help America keep its edge.[168]

Economic dislocations are nothing new of course, and globalization will not prevent them altogether. But today economic shocks reverberate around the globe. The U.S. has been aided by foreign investors' thirst for the dollar. But the dollar's share of foreign reserves is shrinking. We cannot count on foreign funds to favor the U.S. forever.[169]

There is another problem. Rapidly developing economies like China and India, have substantial problems of their own. One is the increasing gap between rich and poor; contributing to political instability. Another is a shortage of skilled labor, and rising wages and inflation. Rapid economic growth creates competition for resources and taxes infrastructure. Eleven percent growth year-on-year isn't sustainable. Hence, their torrid growth must slow.[170]

And that is where "globalization" plays its primary role. All commerce is regulated to some extent. Much of this regulation is national in scope; intentionally or unintentionally biased in favor of local products and practices. This segments the market. Of course, some regulation is needed in a competitive market. But where national regulations are inconsistent, and retard international trade, then global systems are needed. Trade in the 21st Century is more dynamic than ever before; more participants and more sectors are in play. Yet regulatory systems are scarcely adequate to the 1990s.

Take the capital crisis of 2007-2008 as an example. The failure may have been due to U.S. bankers and regulators, but the impact was global. Simply put, regulation has not kept up with the pace of business. Fortunately, international cooperation insured a degree of liquidity once lending tightened. In due course better national and international regulation is likely to result.[171] But something similar happened in South East Asia in the late 1990s. You would think that international bankers would have learned something by now; particularly since the risks are generic, and the volume of global trade is absolutely staggering.[172]

Other potential financial threats are posed by sovereign wealth funds and initial public offerings (IPOs). The former are huge amounts of reserve cash (chiefly in U.S. dollars) built up by export-oriented economies (China, Saudi Arabia) and now being invested in financial markets to maximize returns. But these investors are not private individuals like venture capitalists or hedge fund operators. Rather, they are public entities (the wealth-holding sovereign). This gives sovereign nations the potential to manipulate the markets of other nations, although they foreswear this intention. The potential is there, and there is no international regulation to prevent it.[173] Perhaps that is unnecessary, since to destabilize another nation's economy in which you are invested puts your own investment at risk. But the shift from private to public foreign investment is alarming, and certain to spur protection; including the outright refusal to sell "sensitive" assets to foreigners. But this restraint cuts both ways.[174]

IPOs are the means used by private companies to raise capital by offering shares to the public. This practice is well regulated in the U.S. and Europe, but far less so in emerging economies. Yet the growth opportunities in emerging markets are such that IPOs there are more and more common; with the risk absorbed by in the global market.[175]

The flattening that is now so evident in global trade suggests that participants begin playing by similar rules. While allowances might be made for countries unable to do so, those exceptions should be limited and temporary. Otherwise there is no incentive for developing countries to reform their economies. Long-term market protection benefits no one. Indeed, it retards trade and investment. Improved market conditions in less-developed countries will help them grow.[176]

Generally speaking, broader markets are more stable. And, whereas the harmonization of standards and systems is a burden for those who must adjust, it is a one-off event. This presumes, I think, that developing economies will be given a larger role in international decision-making; which until recently has been driven by developed economies and their organizations.[177]

A successful conclusion to the Doha round of trade negotiations (or some successor thereto) also is needed to establish a balance between developed and developing nations; calibrated to satisfy both groups. The current stalemate is political more than economic. And increasing developing-country consumption is important for developed-county export trade; just as inexpensive developing-country products keep prices in check in developed countries. But finding common ground has not been easy. Each side wants more than the other is willing to give; despite the fact that there seems to be a clear consensus in favor of facilitating international trade.[178]

Despite increased cooperation, trade disputes will continue. But they are becoming less common (of 369 disputes filed with the WTO from its inception to December 2007, only 89 were filed since 2002). Moreover, many disputes are resolved before the dispute settlement process is completed. Nonetheless, resolution would be expedited by reforming the WTO's Dispute Settlement Understanding (DSU) system. Currently, trade disputes fester far too long. (The so-called "banana dispute" between the U.S. and EU, begun in 1993, still wasn't concluded in 2008). Although the process is long and secretive, it does bind WTO members to their trade agreements, and provides restitution if they fail to meet them. But delays in compliance weaken the system; one of the few international agreements that has an enforcement mechanism.[179] DSU decisions also fill gaps purposely left vague by negotiators in GATT treaties, enlarging trade consensus free of political influence. In doing so, trade rules are harmonized and the playing field flattened.

Ongoing discussions among trading nations need to continue; indeed, accelerate. These meetings correct misunderstandings and assuage antipathy that can persist in isolation. Face-to-face meetings help participants to better understand one another's concerns; find common ground; and move forward together.

It took the terrible events of 9/11 to shock nations into the realization that there were many serious problems confronting them and that a coordinated response was better than individual ones. Among those problems are: climate change, poverty, disease, energy supply, environmental degradation, population growth and aging, and migration.[180] The scale and scope of the list suggests that none of these problems is likely to be effectively addressed by nations acting alone. Only a prioritized and collective response is likely to produce positive results.[181] At a UN-sponsored framework convention on climate change in Bali in December 2007, the U.S. finally agreed to "go forward and join [a growing international] consensus." Will the appropriate steps be taken in time? Only time will tell. But reducing chlorofluorocarbon release, and thereby arresting the growth of the Arctic ozone hole, shows what concerted action can accomplish.[182] That is what makes it so galling when individual nations respond to inflation and potential food shortages by enacting embargos on domestic products, rather than pursuing an international solution.[183]

Immigration has long been a social and economic "safety valve" that, in the long term, benefited both immigrant and host country. America is, after all, a nation of immigrants. Regulating immigration is one thing. But stopping it altogether seems both costly and improbable.[184]

The worst possible reaction to globalization and the problems it creates is to try to wall it out. If the U.S. erects walls, it will be the loser in a flattened world. Exclusion begets exclusion; whereas cooperation benefits all. A competitive, open market makes efficient use of resources. And sustainability is the ultimate key to continuing life on earth.

"Globalization" is still in its infancy, so ambivalence toward it is under-standable. But hostility toward it is not.[185]

On balance, globalization has been kind to America. We have profited from expanded markets abroad; inexpensive imports; and massive foreign invest-ment in the U.S., financing our national debt and creating good jobs. If other nations are profiting as well from a more-inclusive trading environment, we should be pleased, not anxious.[186]

America's preeminence as a global power is founded largely on its re-sourcefulness, efficiency, and competitiveness. Why should those characteris-tics fail us now? And, if they do, can we blame others?[187]

Globalization is the challenge du jour. It is likewise an opportunity. The human race has evolved tremendously in a very short period of time. Much of that growth is due to multilateral cooperation. Globalization has the poten-tial to grow diverse economies in an equitable manner; to produce enough to meet the needs of the entire world.[188] What is lacking are vision, political will, and leadership.

Notes

Preface

1. Thomas C. Fischer, The Europeanization of America: What Americans Need to Know About the European Union (Carolina Academic Press, 1995).

2. Thomas C. Fischer, The United States, The European Union, and the 'Globalization' of World Trade: Allies or Adversaries? (Quorum, 2000).

3. For example, Thomas L. Friedman, The World is Flat: A Brief History of the Twenty First Century (Farrar, Straus and Giroux, 2005).

4. For example, Amy Chau, World on Fire (Doubleday, 2003); George Soros, The Crisis of Global Capitalism (Public Affairs, 1998); Joseph Stiglitz, Globalization and its Discontents (W.W. Norton, 2002).

Chapter I

1. "Big shots," Newsweek, December 22, 2003, p. E6.

2. Diana Farrell, "U.S. offshoring: Small steps to make it win-win," Economist's Voice, March 2004, available at: www.bepress.com/ev, last visited April 9, 2004.

3. See Lester C. Thurow, The Zero-Sum Society (Basic Books, 1980). Cf. Dan Hamilton and Joe Quinlan, "Outsourcing is out, insourcing is in," Transatlantic, July/August 2004, p. 14.

4. Between 1990 and 2004 (the last available figures) the gross national income (GNI) of China grew from $368 billion to $1.94 trillion; South Korea's from $246 billion to $673 billion; India's from $331 billion to $673 billion; Mexico's from $236 billion to $705 billion; and Brazil's from $415 billion to $552 billion. Whereas U.S. GNI grew from $5.8 trillion to $12.2 trillion. Table 1324,

STATISTICAL ABSTRACT OF THE UNITED STATES: 2007 (126th edition, U.S. GPO, 2006), p. 845.

5. See Edward Gresser & Sarah West, "Race to the Top II," available at: www.ppionline.org, citing Historical Almanac of Statistical Abstracts, last visited October 2001.

6. Progressive Policy Institute, "World exports reached $12.5 trillion in 2005," available at: admin@newsmail.dlc.org, last visited November 21, 2006.

7. DANIEL S. HAMILTON & JOSEPH P. QUINLAN, PARTNERS IN PROSPERITY: THE CHANGING GEOGRAPHY OF THE TRANSATLANTIC ECONOMY (Johns Hopkins University/SAIS, 2004) p. xii. "Corporate America pumped $87 billion in [FDI] into Europe in 2003 [alone].... a jump of 30.5% from 2002." Meanwhile Europeans accounted for 65% FDI into America [in 2003]." "A creaking partnership," THE ECONOMIST, June 5, 2004, citing PARTNERS IN PROSPERITY (supra).

8. See "Race to the Top II," op. cit.

9. Progressive Policy Institute, "One-ninth of all U.S. production is for export," available at: ppi_admin.main.dlc@ppionline.org, last visited March 21, 2008; Geoffrey Colvin, "Saving America's socks—but killing free trade," FORTUNE, August 22, 2005, p. 38.

10. The 1957 list is available at: http://money.cnn.com/magazines/fortune/fortune500archive/full/1957; and the 2007 list is available at: http://money.cnn.com/magazines/fortune/fortune500/2007/fulllist/index.html, both visited August 24, 2008.

11. "Trade experts agree on need to make better case for globalization," 15 ITR 1008, June 10, 1998, p. 1.

Chapter II

1. DANIEL S. HAMILTON & JOSEPH P. QUINLAN, PARTNERS IN PROSPERITY (Johns Hopkins, 2004), p. 24. Indeed, European affiliates account for one million more American jobs than U.S. affiliates created in Europe. Id., p. 30

2. Id., pp. 26–27.

3. However, the U.S exports substantially more to the world ($731 billion) than either Japan ($384 billion) or China ($313 billion). John D. Sparks, "The power game," NEWSWEEK, December 22, 2003, p. E16.

4. PARTNERS IN PROSPERITY, op. cit., pp. 5, 13 & 15; Stephen Fidler, "FDI inflow 'is good for growth'," FINANCIAL TIMES, April 11, 2001, p. 15. Financial flows to 31 developing countries rose 37 percent in 2000.

5. The world's richest 20 percent receive about 83 percent of world income, and consume a comparable share of its resources. While the world's

poorest 20 percent survive on 1.4 percent of total income. The gap between the top and bottom 20 percent has doubled since 1950. Taken from a speech by David Korten, "Sustainability and the Global Economy: Beyond Bretton Woods," October 1994, quoting a UN Human Development Report, 1992.

6. Lionel Barber, "The case for globalization," EUROPE, December/January 2000–2001, p. 15; MARTIN WOLF, WHY GLOBALIZATION WORKS (Yale, 2004) pp. 33–35.

7. "Reaping the European Union harvest," The Economist, January 8, 2005, p. 44.

8. "A question of justice?" THE ECONOMIST, March 13, 2004, p. 13.

9. "Measure first, then cut," THE ECONOMIST, September 11, 2004, p. 71.

10. Jagdish Bhagwati, "Cheap liberal talk," FINANCIAL TIMES, August 17, 1999, p. 10.

11. "We are the champions" in "Behind the mask: A survey of business in China," THE ECONOMIST, March 24, 2004, pp. 13–15; David S. Broder, "Schizophrenic China: Roaring cities, reeling villages," SEATTLE POST INTELLIGENCER, June 27, 2004, p. D2.

12. GLOBAL ECONOMIC PROSPECTS: REALIZING THE DEVELOPMENT PROMISE OF THE DOHA AGENDA, 2004 (The World Bank, 2003) pp. xiv–xvi.

13. Marc Gunther, "Cops of the Global Village," FORTUNE, June 27, 2005, p. 158; Progressive Policy Institute, "Haiti's HOPE Act is one year old," available at: ppi_admin.main.dlc@ppionline.org, last visited March 27, 2008.

14. "Cops of the global village," op. cit., pp. 164–166.

15. PARTNERS IN PROSPERITY, op. cit., p. xi. Of the nearly 9.8 million workers employed by US foreign affiliates in 2001, roughly 43 percent worked in Europe.

16. Janet Guyon, "The American way," FORTUNE, November 26, 2001, p. 114.

17. AMY CHUA, WORLD ON FIRE: HOW EXPORTING FREE MARKET DEMOCRACY BREEDS ETHNIC HATRED AND GLOBAL INSTABILITY (Doubleday, 2003), p. 6.

18. David Kirkpatrick, "China won't protect IP until it gets its own IT," FORTUNE, June 27, 2005, p. 50.

19. Stephen Fidler, "Developing countries: FDI inflow 'is good for growth'," FINANCIAL TIMES, April 11, 2001, p. 15.

20. "A survey of the world economy," THE ECONOMIST, September 28, 2002, p. 25.

21. Dan Hamilton & Joe Quinlan, "Outsourcing is out, Insourcing is in," TRANSATLANTIC, July/August 2004, p. 14.

22. Edward Gresser, "Chinese Challenge" (BLUEPRINT MAGAZINE) available at: http://www.ppionline, last visited August 29, 2005; Stephanie Mehta,

"India on the march," FORTUNE, July 25, 2005, p. 191; "Globalization with a third-world face," THE ECONOMIST, April 9, 2005, p. 66.

23. Progressive Policy Institute, "Currency trading totals $3 trillion a day," available at: ppi_admin@dlcppi.org, last visited March 26, 2007.

24. "Bad loans made good," THE ECONOMIST, October 1, 2005, p. 70.

25. George Soros, "The crisis of global capitalism," NEWSWEEK, December 7, 1998, p. 78; "Turning global finance," THE ECONOMIST, April 10, 1999, p. 8.

26. Samuel Brittan, "Who's afraid of globalization?" FINANCIAL TIMES, January 8, 1998, p. 21.

27. George Soros, op. cit., Daniel Pruzin, "Africa fails to attract foreign investment despite improved economic performance," 16 ITR 1230 July 21, 1999.

28. "A survey of the world economy," THE ECONOMIST, September 28, 2002, p. 25.

29. "Shell games," THE ECONOMIST, October 26, 2002, p. 69.

30. "A Survey of Outsourcing: A world of opportunity, why the protectionists are wrong," THE ECONOMIST, November 13, 2004, p. 20; "Factory workers in China still toil for Nike," SEATTLE TIMES, July 3, 2005, p. E1.

31. "A Survey of Outsourcing: Sink or Schwinn," THE ECONOMIST, November 13, 2004, p. 18 (citing in part McKinsey Global Institute). Even a critic of U.S. trade policy like Paul Krugman allows "[T]he U.S. economy would be poorer and less productive if we turned our back on world markets." But, "free trade is *politically* viable only if it's backed by effective job-creation measures...." "Global trade fears can't be ignored," SEATTLE POST-INTELLIGENCER, February 29, 2004, p. F2 (emphasis added).

32. "Economic focus: trade disputes," THE ECONOMIST, September 18, 2004, p. 80 (citing Forrester Research).

33. Jeffery Garten, "America's fast-track trade needs a domestic safety net," FINANCIAL TIMES, May 8, 2007, p. 9.

34. Robert J. Samuelson, "Real issues, not rhetoric," NEWSWEEK, September 20, 2004, p. 42.

35. George F. Will, "The perils of protectionism," NEWSWEEK, March 29, 2004, p. 84.

36. "Bird flu spurs fear of human pandemic," SEATTLE POST-INTELLIGENCER, June 29, 2004, p. A2.

37. INVESTING IN DEVELOPMENT: A practical plan to achieve the Millennium Development Goals, Jeffrey D. Sachs, Director, (c) 2005 by the United Nations Development Programme, pp xviii–xxii. See also, JEFFERY D. SACHS, THE END OF POVERTY; ECONOMIC POSSIBILITIES FOR OUR TIMES (Penguin, 2005).

38. "Economic focus: Ends without means," THE ECONOMIST, September 11, 2004, p. 72.

39. "[I]n China, the scale of environmental problems is mind-boggling. [It] is home to five of the world's ten most polluted cities in terms of air quality ... water is in short supply and deserts are expanding rapidly....," "Cops of the global village," op. cit.; Denis Hayes, "Making China green," SEATTLE POST-INTELLIGENCER, August 21, 2005, p. D1.

40. John Lloyd, "Cultivating the world," FINANCIAL TIMES, September 20, 2000, p. 12.

41. Richard Steiner, "The real clear and present danger," SEATTLE POST-INTELLIGENCER, May 30, 2004, p. F1.

42. See generally, THOMAS L. FRIEDMAN, THE WORLD IS FLAT (Farrar Strauss and Giroux, 2005)

43. "Emerging economies: coming into flower," THE ECONOMIST, October 16, 2004, pg 67.

44. "Democracy in Asia: That other miracle," THE ECONOMIST, April 24, 2004, p. 10.

45. Daniel Pruzin, "Developing countries set out common position for Doha," 18 ITR 1683 (October 25, 2001).

46. Michael Schrage, "Nationality matters more than ever," FORTUNE, November. 13, 2000, p. 462.

47. Richard Pells, "The local and global loyalties of Europeans and Americans," THE CHRONICLE OF HIGHER EDUCATION, May 2, 1997, p. B4.

48. Martin Wolf, "Comment and Analysis," FINANCIAL TIMES, September 5, 2001, p. 17.

49. JOSEPH E. STIGLITZ, GLOBALIZATION AND ITS DISCONTENTS (W.W. Norton, 2003), p. 133.

50. Id.

51. WHY GLOBALIZATION WORKS, op. cit., pp. 34–35 and 38–39.

52. "Democracy in Asia: That other miracle," op. cit.

53. Anne-Marie Slaughter, "The Real New World Order," 76 FOREIGN AFFAIRS No. 5, September/October 1997, p. 184.

54. WORLD ON FIRE, op. cit., p. 6.

55. Jerry Useem, "There's something happening here," FORTUNE, May 15, 2000, p. 244.

56. Clive Crook, "Unfounded new fears on free trade," FINANCIAL TIMES, May 10, 2007, p. 11.

Chapter III

1. According to the Progressive Policy Institute, a Washington, D.C. think tank, the U.S. imported $1.8 trillion in goods and services in 2004, while exporting some $1.2 trillion. Taken together, exports and imports amount to almost 25 percent of America's estimated $12 trillion GDP. Export/import trade almost trebled between 1960 (9.2%) and 2000 (25.6%) as a percentage of U.S. GDP. Available at: ppi_admin@dlcppi.org, last visited October 12 and 18, 2005.

2. Paul Krugman, "Global trade fears can't be ignored," SEATTLE POST-INTELLIGENCER, February 29, 2004, p. F2.

3. Fareed Zakaria, "What the world is hearing," NEWSWEEK, March 10, 2008, p. 45.

4. "U.S., EU sign veterinary MRA covering more than $3 billion in trade," 16 ITR No. 29 July 21, 1999; "U.S., EU sign mutual recognition agreement on product standards for marine equipment," 21 ITR No. 10 (March 4, 2004), no pages on line. A mutual-recognition agreement (MRA) is one in which each trader agrees to recognize the suitability of a product of the other trader, if it has satisfied that trader's technical standards, and vice versa.

5. See, for example, "Technical discussions dominate US-Thai FTA round," 9 BRIDGES WEEKLY TRADE NEWS DIGEST (hereinafter BRIDGES) No. 33, October 15, 2005, p. 9.

6. "US-SACU [Southern African Customs Union] talks underway again," 9 BRIDGES No. 33, October 15, 2005, p. 10.

7. Among these, one might list the information technology agreement (ITA), concluded in late 1996, chiefly between the U.S. and EU. It eventually embraced about twenty traders, and covered 90 percent of the market. "New nations join U.S.-EU info tech pact," 12 ITR 1941 (December 18, 1996).

8. For example, the U.S. free trade agreements with Oman, 9 BRIDGES No. 33, October 5, 2005, p. 11.

9. To get some sense of the integration and prospects of the European Union, see: THOMAS C. FISCHER, THE EUROPEANIZATION OF AMERICA, (Carolina Academic Press, 1995), Chapters 5–7; THOMAS C. FISCHER, THE UNITED STATES, THE EUROPEAN UNION AND THE "GLOBALIZATION" OF WORLD TRADE, (Greenwood Press, 2000), Chapter 9; and Thomas C. Fischer, "An American Looks at the European Union," 19 EMORY INTERNATIONAL LAW REVIEW 1489 (Fall, 2005).

10. "The importance of being good neighbors." THE ECONOMIST, August 27, 2005, p. 130.

11. "Summit of the Americas fails to resurrect FTAA," 9 BRIDGES No. 38, November 9, 2005, p. 6.

12. "CAFTA-DR narrowly wins House vote," 9 BRIDGES No. 28, August 3, 2005, p. 3; "ASEAN summit draws attention to slow pace of regional trade liberalization," 9 BRIDGES No. 34, October 25, 2005, p. 9

13. See Thomas C. Fischer, "A Commentary on Regional Institutions in the Pacific Rim: Do APEC and ASEAN Still Matter?" 13 DUKE JOURNAL OF COMPARATIVE & INTERNATIONAL LAW 337 (2003); APEC ministers call for progress in Doha Round negotiations," 9 BRIDGES No. 39, November 16, 2005, p. 12; "Uncle Sam visits his restive neighbors," THE ECONOMIST, November 5, 2005, p. 41.

14. "US Doha offer welcomed by EU Trade Commissioner," NEWS @ EU No. 84, October 13, 2005, p. 3; "EU links progress on ag[riculture] to deep NAMA [non-agricultural market access] tariff cuts," 9 BRIDGES No. 34, October 12, 2005, p. 13.

15. "ASEAN summit draws attention to slow pace of regional trade liberalization," *op. cit.*; "EU-Mercosur trade talks hit stalemate," 8 BRIDGES No. 8, September 1, 2004, p. 5.

16. "The farmer's friend," THE ECONOMIST, November 5, 2005, p. 77.

17. C. Fred Bergsten, "Globalizing Free Trade," FOREIGN AFFAIRS, May/June 1996, p. 105.

18. Since a GATT negotiating round is viewed as a "single undertaking ... nothing is agreed until everything is agreed," "Quote: Mariann Fischer Boel," NEWS @ EU No. 85, October 21, 2005, p. 1; "Brazil and India to G-7: Will cut NAMA tariffs if EU, U.S. cut ag[ricultural] tariffs," 9 BRIDGES No. 42, December 7, 2005, p. 11.

19. For example, "Brazil requests USD 3 billion retaliation against US in cotton disputes," 9 BRIDGES WEEKLY No. 26, July 20, 2005, p. 60.

20. "Rich countries seeking 'round for free', say nine developing countries," 9 BRIDGES No. 41, November 30, 2005 p. 4; "In the rough," THE ECONOMIST, November 5, 2005, p. 77; "Cape Verde," BRIDGES DAILY UPDATE [to Doha miniministerial], No. 4, July 24, 2008, p. 4.

21. A brief history is given in THOMAS C. FISCHER's THE UNITED STATES, THE EUROPEAN UNION, AND THE "GLOBALIZATION" OF WORLD TRADE, (Greenwood Press, 2000), pp. 201–202.

22. There are four "Singapore issues: trade facilitation (now included in the Doha negotiations); competition; investment; and public procurement. See "The WTO under fire," THE ECONOMIST, September 20, 2003, p. 26.

23. "What is Doha all about?" EUROPA NEWSLETTER No. 65, September 22, 2005, p. 4. Originally the group involved 21 developing countries. A list is given in the article referenced above, along with an account of their uncompromising negotiating stance and "miscalculation" at Cancun. See also, "Cancun's charming outcome," THE ECONOMIST, September 20, 2003, p. 11.

24. The Doha Ministerial Declaration (14 November 2001) is found at: WTIMIN (01)/Dec/1 (20 November 2001)

25. "The WTO under fire," *op. cit.*; "Agriculture negotiations: Paris meet yields no concrete results," 9 BRIDGES No. 32, September 28, 2005, p. 1.

26. "Lamy outlines Doha Round roadways for Hong Kong and beyond," 9 BRIDGES No. 35, October 19, 2005, p. 3.

27. "US Doha offer welcomed by EU Trade Commissioner," NEWS @ EU No. 84, October 12, 2005, p. 3; "Ag subsidies on negotiating table; haggling underway," 9 BRIDGES No. 34, October 12, 2005, p. 1; "EU tables bold and realistic agriculture market access offer," NEWS @ EU No. 86, November 2, 2005, p. 3; "G-20 calls on rich countries to respond constrictively to ag proposals," 9 BRIDGES WEEKLY No. 30, September 14, 2005, p. 6.

28. Progressive Policy Institute, "WTO members account for 96 percent of trade," available at: ppi_admin@dlcppi.org, last visited November 2, 2005.

29. "SPC Committee [of WTO] looks at ways forward on S&D," 9 BRIDGES No. 36, October 26, 2005, p. 12. Civil society groups believe that LDCs will continue to be marginalized in global trade unless "rich countries ... provide special and differential treatment to developing countries." "Civil Society groups adopt 'Doha Declaration on LDC interest in Doha," 9 BRIDGES No. 35, October 19, 2005, p. 11; "LDCs granted limited extension for implementing TRIPS commitments," 9 BRIDGES No. 41, November 30, 2005, p. 6.

30. "The farmer's friend" and "The harnessing of nature's bounty," both in THE ECONOMIST, November 5, 2005, pp. 58 and 73, respectively.

31. "Cambodia ratifies WTO membership," 8 BRIDGES No. 28, September 1, 2004, p. 9; "Saudi Arabia set to join WTO [in December, 2005]," 9 BRIDGES No. 38, November 9, 2005, p. 8; "Vietnam accession [to WTO] by Hong Kong [ministerial] looking unlikely," 9 BRIDGES No. 31, September 21, 2005. There were 153 WTO members in July, 2008; up from 78 that signed the WTO treaty on April 15, 1994 in Marrakech, Morocco.

32. According to the Progressive Policy Institute, a Washington D.C. think tank, WTO members include 23 of the worlds 25 largest economies; and 38 of the 40 largest exporters; The addition of Saudi Arabia in December, 2005 will raise each of these numbers by one and cover 97 percent of world trade. "WTO members account for 96 percent of trade," available at: ppi_admin@dlc.ppi.org, last visited November 2, 2005.

33. All goals are set forth in the preamble to the Uruguay Round (WTO) treaty, 33 I.L.M. 13 at 15.

34. "Fearful fortress France," THE ECONOMIST, October 29, 2005, p. 49.

35. A brief exploration of this concept can be found at: THE UNITED STATES, THE EUROPEAN UNION, AND THE "GLOBALIZATION" OF WORLD TRADE, *op. cit.*, pp. 35–39.

36. "Africa suffers from textile quota phase-out, says ILO'" 9 BRIDGES No. 34, October 26, 2005, p. 10.

37. DANIEL S. HAMILTON & JOSEPH P. QUINLAN, PARTNERS IN PROSPERITY (Johns Hopkins University, 2004), p. 3.

38. "EU offer of deeper farm tariff cuts fails to restart [Doha] talks," "EU's price for NAMA market access too steep, say developing countries," both in 9 BRIDGES No. 37, November 2, 2005, pp. 1 and 4, respectively; "[Americas] trade summit ends without agreement," THE SEATTLE TIMES, November 6, 2005, p. A14.

39. "Tired of globalization," THE ECONOMIST, November 5, 2005, p. 11.

40. "Lamy outlines Doha Round roadmaps for Hong Kong and beyond," 9 BRIDGES No. 35, October 19, 2005, p. 3.

41. "LDCs, Africans ask for more time to revise S&D proposals" 9 BRIDGES No. 34, October 12, 2005, p. 12; "Civil society groups adopt, 'Dhaka Declaration', on LDC interests in Doha [negotiations]," 9 BRIDGES No. 35, October 19, 2005, p. 3.

42. "Lamy meets with Asian civil society organizations in Hong Kong," 9 BRIDGES No. 35, October 19, 2005, p. 3.

Chapter IV

1. "The paradox of plenty," THE ECONOMIST, December 24, 2005, p. 46.

2. "The brain-drain cycle," THE ECONOMIST, December 10, 2005, p. 57.

3. Hugh Williamson, "Germany looks east as skills shortage bites," FINANCIAL TIMES, July 26, 2007, p. 3.

4. The greatest threat to economic growth comes from those who feel they have no stake in it. Jerry Useem, "Is it a small world after all?" FORTUNE, October 15, 2001, p. 38.

5. Allen Beattie, "Reduce inequality, says World Bank," FINANCIAL TIMES, September 13, 2000, p. 8; "The paradox of plenty," *op. cit.*

6. See Public Law 106-200, 106th Congress (May 18, 2000); 114 STAT 251, entitled the "Trade and Development Act of 2000," the largest portion of which (sects 101–131) addresses sub-Saharan Africa, with other sections dealing with Caribbean Basin countries (sects 201S-213), Albania (301) and Kyrgystan (302). Among the many things the Act envisions are the creation of loosely defined public and private fora to "foster close(r) economic ties between the United

States and sub-Saharan Africa" (105), and such specific goals as "comprehensive debt relief for the world's poorest countries" (121) and "[encouragement for U.S. businesses] to provide assistance to sub-Saharan countries to prevent and reduce incidences of HIV/AIDS [in these countries] (128).

7. "Oxfarm calls for global trade reforms to help developing nations fight poverty," 19 ITR 730 April 15, 2002; "Reduce inequality, says World Bank," *op.cit.*

8. "Global trade: weighed in the balance," THE ECONOMIST, December 10, 2005, p. 81.

9. "More or less equal?" THE ECONOMIST, March 13, 2004, p. 69; "East, West and the gap between," THE ECONOMIST, November 26, 2005, p. 63. Concerning the rapid growth of East European economies.

10. Progressive Policy Institute, "The United States collects more tariff money from Cambodia than from Britain," available at: ppi_admin.main.dlc@ ppionline.org, last visited February 21, 2008.

11. Edward Gresser, "Toughest on the poor: America's flawed tariff system," FOREIGN AFFAIRS, November/December 2002, p. 9; "A question of justice?" THE ECONOMIST, March 13, 2004, p. 13.

12. One authoritative source concludes that "sub-Saharan Africa plainly suffers not from globalization, but from a lack of it." "More or less equal?" *op.cit.*, p. 71; "U.S. downturn poses 'considerable risk' to developing countries, UN agency warns," 18 ITR 741 (May 10, 2001).

13. Overall, the gap between developed and developing economies seems to be decreasing, not increasing. "More or less equal?" *op. cit.*; "A question of justice?" *op.cit;* "East, West and the gap between," *op.cit.*

14. "The next green revolution," THE ECONOMIST, February 23, 2008, p. 81.

15. "U.N. agency warns that e-commerce could widen countries' development gap," 18 ITR 1900 (November 29, 2001); David Kirkpatrick, "Tech into plowshares," FORTUNE, October 15, 2001, p. 211; "The world promises to narrow the digital divide," EUROPA NEWSLETTER No. 70, December 1, 2005, p. 7; commenting on the World Summit on the Information Society (Tunis, November 16–18) under the auspices of the U.N., agreeing to create an international Internet Governance Forum (IGF), referred to as the Tunis Commitment.

16. "East, West and the gap between," *op. cit.*; "Weighed in the balance," *op. cit.*

17. "EU aims to help developing countries harvest 'green gold'," EURECOM, September 2002, p. 4; "The paradox of plenty," *op.cit.*, also called the "curse of oil"; failing to develop government institutions or alternate resources because of a plentitude of one valuable resource.

18. Peter Goodman, "Factory labor runs short in China: Workers finding better options/manufacturing wages to rise," THE SEATTLE TIMES, September 26, 2004, p. A13; "Is it a small world after all?" *op.cit.* at p. 40.

19. Anne-Marie Slaughter, "The real new world order," 76 FOREIGN AFFAIRS No. 5 (September, 1997) p. 183.

Chapter V

1. Thomas C. Fischer, "An American Looks at the European Union," 12 European Law Journal No. 2 March 2006, pp. 269–270; "Citing data, biotech panel delays report again," 9 BRIDGES No. 28 August 3, 2005, p. 14.

2. THOMAS C. FISCHER, THE UNITED STATES, THE EUROPEAN UNION, AND THE "GLOBALIZATION" OF WORLD TRADE; ALLIES OR ADVERSARIES? (Greenwood Press, 2000) pp. 187–198; "Emerging economies: Coming of age," THE ECONOMIST, January 21, 2006, p. 10.

3. Robert J. Samuelson, "God is in the details," NEWSWEEK, April 20, 1998, p. 47.

4. "Spring Council: more jobs and increased energy security," No. 77 EUROPA NEWSLETTER, March 27, 2006, p. 1; "Not yet free to serve," THE ECONOMIST, February 18, 2006, p. 52.

5. THOMAS C. FISCHER, *supra* note 2," Chapter 4: Four Economic 'Models'," pp. 30–31.

6. Briefly stated, capitalism expects the government to protect the citizen/consumer from business. Macro-socialism, expects government and business to work together to improve the lot of the citizen. In micro-socialistic societies, there is not much difference between government and business, and citizens expect to benefit. With communism (not by design, but in practice) autocrats run government and business, but benefits for the citizen/consumer can be strangulated by a lack of opportunity and incentive.

7. Daniel Gross, "The U.S. economy faces the guillotine," NEWSWEEK, February 4, 2008, p. 39.

8. "Economic and financial indicators," THE ECONOMIST, January 28, 2006, p. 100

9. Alan Sloan, "Trial by fire: The real Enron lesson," NEWSWEEK, February 6, 2006, p. 14; "Enron: The drama goes to trial," THE ECONOMIST, January 28, 2006, p. 61.

10. "Greatest danger, or greatest hope," THE ECONOMIST, November 18, 2003, p. 11

11. "Economic and financial indicators," *op.cit.* In 2005, The Eurozone (EU member states adopting the Euro currency) grew only 1.6 percent relative to the U.S. growth of 3.6 per cent. See also "An American Looks at the European Union," *op.cit.*, pp. 234–260.

12. Id., p. 235; "Head in the clouds," THE ECONOMIST, September 10, 2005, p. 9; "Europe must reform to keep its social model: Ecofin," NEWS @ EU No. 66, May 20, 2005, p. 4; "Reform or die" THE ECONOMIST, January 28, 2006, p. 52.

13. "Set Airbus free to soar," THE ECONOMIST, November 11, 2006, p. 16.

14. "An American Looks at the European Union," *op.cit.*, p. 252.

15. Id., p. 233; Jeffrey Gedmin, "Europe's unilateralist leaders" FINANCIAL TIMES, August 22, 2001, p. 130. Europeans profess to "favor" globalization, although there is little evidence that they do. EUROPA NEWSLETTER No. 23, November 26, 2003, p. 1.

16. See e.g., LESTER THUROW, HEAD TO HEAD: THE COMING ECONOMIC BATTLE AMONG JAPAN, EUROPE AND AMERICA (William Morrow, 1992), "Chapter 4, Japan: The Challenge of Producer Economics," pp. 113–151.

17. THOMAS C. FISCHER, *supra* note 2, "Chapter 11, Japan: Asia's Disintegrating Colossus," and "Chapter 13, Asia's Emerging Economies: 'Miracle, Myth or Neither?'" pp. 145–159 and pp. 178–198, respectively; Paul Abrahams & Michiyo Nakamoto, "Japan 'in recession' as GDP contracts 1.4 %, FINANCIAL TIMES, December 4, 1997, p. 12; Paul Abrahams & Beth Hutton, "Japan jobless rate hits 4.1 % amid fears of deflation," FINANCIAL TIMES, May 30–31, 1998, p. 1.

18. "The sun also rises," THE ECONOMIST, October 8, 2005 (A survey of Japan) pp. 3–18; "Locking in the legacy," THE ECONOMIST, January 28, 2006, p. 41.

19. "Asian capitalism: The end of tycoons," THE ECONOMIST, April 29, 2000 p. 67

20. Bill Powell & Yevgenia Albats, "The end of the miracle," NEWSWEEK, January 25, 1999, p. 37; "Putting up with Putin," THE ECONOMIST, May 22, 2004, p. 11. See generally, "A survey of Russia," THE ECONOMIST, May 22, 2004, p. 3 et seq.

21. "Jiang's restructuring plan wins praise," [ASIAN] WALL STREET JOURNAL, September 15, 1997, p. 1. (For the full text of this part of Jiang Zemin's Report to the 15th Party Congress, see: http://www.geocities.com/wallstreet/8038/jiang5.html#part 5.) See also, Richard Tomlinson, "A Chinese giant forges a capitalist soul," FORTUNE, September 29, 1997, p. 184; James Kynge, "Beijing tears up proletarian roots," FINANCIAL TIMES, November 16/17, 2002, p. 3.

22. For example, Guy de Jonquières, "China may lead world output by 2020," FINANCIAL TIMES, May 27, 1997, p. 9. For a more sober view, see: "Inside the New China," FORTUNE (Special Issue), October 4, 2004; Peter Marsh,

"US to lose role as world's top manufacturer ... [but not before] 2020," FINANCIAL TIMES, May 24, 2007, p. 8.

23. "China: A demo turns bloody," THE ECONOMIST, December 17, 2005, p. 40; "How the other 800m live," THE ECONOMIST, March 11, 2006. See generally, Thomas C. FISCHER, *supra* note 2, "Chapter 12: China; The Middle Kingdom in the Middle," pp. 160–177.

24. David Broder, "Schizophrenic China: Roaring cities, reeling villages," SEATTLE POST INTELLIGENCER, June 27, 2004, p. D2; Minxin Pei, "The Chinese split personality," NEWSWEEK, October 28, 2002, p. 44D.

25. "How the other 800m live," *op.cit.*

26. THOMAS C. FISCHER, *supra* note 2, p. 168; "Parts that the bulldozers have not yet reached," THE ECONOMIST January 10, 2004, p. 59; "We are the champions," THE ECONOMIST (A survey of business in China), March 20, 2004, p. 13.

27. "Don't bank on a bail-out," THE ECONOMIST, December 6, 2003, p. 66; "Beyond bail-out," THE ECONOMIST, January 10, 2004, p. 13.

28. Michael Sheridan, "Chinese army wins trade war," THE LONDON TIMES, March 9, 1997, p. 3.6; "Chinese army-owned firm hopes to rank in Fortune 500 by next decade," 14 ITR 1817 (October 22, 1997).

29. "Shooting the messenger," THE ECONOMIST, September 4, 2004, p. 43; Julie Chao, "Progress comes with moral decay in China," SEATTLE POST INTELLIGENCER, April 18, 2005, p. A4.

30. James Kynge, "Beijing pledges support for private investment" FINANCIAL TIMES, January 5, 2000, p. 18; "Chinese entrepreneurs: On their way back," THE ECONOMIST, November 8, 2003, p. 59; "On the capitalist road," THE ECONOMIST, March 20, 2004 (A survey of business in China), p. 15.

31. "China, a difficult place for foreign firms to invest," SEATTLE POST INTELLIGENCER, August 8, 2004, p. F3; "Behind the mask" and "Bulls in a China shop" both in THE ECONOMIST, March 20, 2004 (A survey of business in China), pp. 3 and 9, respectively.

32. Progressive Policy Institute, "Trade Fact of the Week: Three-Quarters of Foreign Direct Investment in China is Asian," available at: ppi_admin@d/cppi.org, last visited on October 26, 2005.

33. Brad Wong, "Great wall breached," SEATTLE POST INTELLIGENCER, September 21, 2005, p. C1; "Over the Great Wall," THE ECONOMIST, November 5, 2005, p. 71.

34. Peter Montagnon & James Kynge, "China probe signals corruption purge," FINANCIAL TIMES, January 24, 2000, p. 14; "Uncooking the books," THE ECONOMIST, July 9, 2005, p. 34.

35. "Gate-crashing the party," THE ECONOMIST, November 15, 2003, p. 39; "Communist Party calls for better government," SEATTLE POST INTELLIGENCER,

September 27, 2004, p. A4; "Hu Wen, How?" THE ECONOMIST (The World in 2006), circa December 1, 2005 (no publication date), p. 44; "The emperor is not always obeyed," THE ECONOMIST, November 13, 2004, p. 46.

36. Alex Taylor, "A tale of two factories," FORTUNE, September 18, 2006, p. 118.

37. Edward Luce, "India stirs," FINANCIAL TIMES, August 29, 2002, p. 10; "Can India work?" THE ECONOMIST, June 12, 2004, p. 67; Clay Chandler, "India's bumpy ride," FORTUNE, October 31, 2005, p. 134; "The tiger in front," THE ECONOMIST, March 5, 2005, p. 10; "The next wave," THE ECONOMIST, December 17, 2005, p. 57.

38. "Wall-Mart still waits," THE ECONOMIST, July 16, 2005, p. 39; "India's economy: Fast track," THE ECONOMIST, March 4, 2006, p. 38; "'Cybercoolies' resist efforts to unionize," SEATTLE POST INTELLIGENCER, September 20, 2005, p. C1.

39. Progressive Policy Institute, "Trade Fact of the week: South Korea-North Korea Trade Topped $1 billion last year," available at: ppi_admin@d/cppi.org, last visited on February 1, 2006.

40. "Glittering economic prizes," THE ECONOMIST, April 10, 1999, p. 19.

41. DEMOCRACY IN AMERICA, p. 311 (Gryphon edition, 1988).

42. "Set Airbus free to soar," THE ECONOMIST, November 11, 2006, p. 16; "Japan: Locking in a legacy," THE ECONOMIST, January 28, 2006, p. 41.

43. "Emerging economies: Coming of age," *op.cit.*

44. "A backlash against the free market, THE ECONOMIST, August 17, 2002, p. 12; "Enter the man in the stripey jumper," THE ECONOMIST, January 21, 2006, p. 38.

45. *Id.*; "Uruguay's bold new oil policy," THE ECONOMIST, December 13, 2003, p. 34; "Evo ready or not," THE ECONOMIST, January 8, 2006, p. 37.

46. "Bolivia takes on the superpower," THE ECONOMIST, January 21, 2006, p. 10; "Democracy clings on in the cold [Latin American] climate," THE ECONOMIST, August 17, 2002, p. 29; "The magic of Lula," THE ECONOMIST, March 4, 2006, p. 11.

47. Robert Samuelson, "The European predicament," Newsweek, February 9, 2004, p. 51.

48. Jody Miller & Matt Miller, "Get a life," FORTUNE, November 28, 2005, p. 109.

49. "Unfinished battle," THE ECONOMIST, April 10, 1999, p. 77.

50. "Emerging economies: Climbing back," THE ECONOMIST, January 21, 2006, p. 69.

51. Klaus Schwab, "Capitalism must develop more of a conscience," NEWSWEEK, February 24, 2003, p.E10.

52. David Kirkpatrick, "I'd like to teach the world to type," FORTUNE, November 28, 2005, p. 63.

Chapter VI

1. The Progressive Policy Institute, a think-tank in Washington, D.C., reports that export/import trade (goods and services) reached about 25 percent of U.S. gross domestic product (GDP) in 2000–2004 whereas goods trade (alone) represented just 6.7 percent of U.S. GDP in 1950. (Of course, the value of U.S. GDP grew tremendously over this period as well.) "The United States is the world's biggest exporter, but also the 5th-smallest," available at: http://www.ppionline.org, last visited October 12, 2005.

2. Martin Wolf, "Bush's free trade responsibility," FINANCIAL TIMES, April 25, 2001, p. 23; "Trade winds," THE ECONOMIST, November 8, 1997, p. 85; Progressive Policy Institute, "World exports reached $12.5 trillion in 2005," available at: admin@newsmail.dlc.org, last visited November 21, 2006.

3. According to the POCKET WORLD IN FIGURES, THE ECONOMIST, 2006 Edition (circa December 15, 2005), services account for 80.8 percent of U.S. GDP; industry for 18.2 percent; and agriculture 1 percent (p. 234). U.S. imports ($1.26 trillion) exceeded exports ($725 billion), but were measured entirely in terms of goods (p. 23).

4. In 1996, the WTO estimated that trade in services was worth about one-quarter the value of goods, "Trade winds," *op. cit.*; Richard Milne & John Reed, "Ghosn sees sales shift to emerging markets," FINANCIAL TIMES, March 5, 2008, p. 21; "U.S. families reaping up to $2,040 in benefits due to trade pacts, USTR says," 18 ITR 1525 (September 27, 2001).

5. Robert Samuelson, "Will America pass the baton," NEWSWEEK, March 6, 2006, p. 47; "Euro-area economy on track," 76 NEWS @ EU, April 7, 2006, p. 3; "The sun also rises," THE ECONOMIST, October 8, 2005 p. 11; "Testing all engines," THE ECONOMIST, February 4, 2006, p. 65.

6. Sameena Ahmad, "The end of the affair," in THE WORLD IN 2006, THE ECONOMIST, circa December 15, 2005, p. 46; Progressive Policy Institute, "U.S. exports to India have doubled since 2003," available at: http://www.ppionline.org, last visited September 21, 2005.

7. Fareed Zakaria, "India rising," NEWSWEEK, March 6, 2006, p. 32; "Coming out," "Keep growing" and "No time like the present," in "Balancing act: A survey of China," THE ECONOMIST, March 25, 2006, pp. 3, 12, and 19, respectively; Joe McDonald, "China turns gaze to its rural poor," SEATTLE POST INTELLIGENCER, March 2, 2006, p. A7.

8. Peter Goodman, "Factory labor runs short in China," THE SEATTLE TIMES, September 26, 2004, p. A13; Progressive Policy Institute, "Residents of China filed 1,655 patent applications in the United States in 2004," available at: admin@newsmail.dlc.org, last visited November 22, 2005; Todd Bishop, "Real windows in China PCs," and Martin Crutsinger, "U.S. trade deficit with China drops," both in SEATTLE POST INTELLIGENCER, April 12, 2006, p. E1.

9. POCKET WORLD IN FIGURES, *supra*, at p. 235; STATISTICAL ABSTRACT OF THE UNITED STATES: 2004–2005 (U.S. Census Bureau), Chart No. 1279, "U.S. Balances on International Transactions by Area and Selected Country: 2002 and 2003; No. 1278, "U.S. International Transactions by Type of Transaction: 1990 to 2003 (using 2003); and No. 1280, "Private International Service Transactions by Selected Type of Service and Country: 2000 to 2003, pp. 801 and 799.

10. "Services cluster under way, plurilateral requests in works," 10 BRIDGES No. 5, February 15, 2006, p. 9.

11. Geoffrey Colvin, "Saving America's sox—but killing free trade," FORTUNE, August 22, 2005, p. 38.

12. "World Trade Report downplays off-shoring impact," 9 BRIDGES No. 24, July 6, 2005, p. 10; "Not yet free to serve," THE ECONOMIST, February 18, 2006, p. 52; Geoffrey Colvin, "Our leading export? Nonsense about China," FORTUNE, May 16, 2005, p. 58.

13. "Where next?" THE ECONOMIST (A survey of World Trade), October 3, 1998, p. 6; "Growing pains," THE ECONOMIST (A survey of Agriculture and Technology) March 25, 2000; Edward Gresser, "America's hidden tax on the poor," Progressive Policy Institute, March 2002; Progressive Policy Institute, "The United States collects more tariffs on Cambodian goods than French goods," available at: http://www.ppionline.org, last visited March 22, 2006; "Textile exporters express 'grave concern' with protectionist policies in rich countries," 5/28/2002 (BNA) BTD d 9.

14. Progressive Policy Institute, "Two-thirds of American farmers receive no subsidies," and Ron Kind, "America's farm policies and their effects on international trade," both available at: www.ppionline.org/ppi, last visited on July 25, 2007.

15. "Growing pains," *op. cit.* p. 9; "EU face[s] calls for farm reform at WTO," THE KITSAP DAILY, July 21, 2008, p. 8.

16. Susanna Hecht & Charles Mann, "How Brazil out farmed the American farmer," FORTUNE, January 21, 2008, p. 93.

17. "Agriculture lags in world trade reform," 15 ITR 2025 (December 2, 1998); "WTO Chief Moore urges abolition of agriculture subsidies," 19 ITR 180 (January 31, 2002); Robert Samuelson, "A sad primer in hypocrisy," NEWSWEEK, February 11, 2002.

18. Michael Smith & Others, "Anything but agriculture," FINANCIAL TIMES, November 19, 1999, p. 16.

19. "WTO Ministerial agrees on setting course for final stage of talks; some disappointed," 22 ITR No. 50 (December 22, 2005), p. 2046; Tobias Buck & Others, "Fischler's surprise for Europe's farmers," FINANCIAL TIMES, June 27, 2003, p. 17; "Joint effort for Doha success: EU ag commissioner in Oz," NEWS @ EU No. 79, August 29, 2005, p. 3; "Farm monopolists: Jurassic twilight," THE ECONOMIST, July 30, 2005, p. 59.

20. "Floundering in a tariff-free landscape," THE ECONOMIST, November 30, 2002, p. 31.

21. "EU-U.S. head for possible collision on exports of genetically-modified maize," 13 ITR 1424 (September 11, 1996), p. 87; "Precautionary tales," in "Growing pains," *op. cit.,* p. 10; "WTO panel rules against EU import ban in beef hormone case," 12 BRIDGES, No. 11, April 2, 2008, p. 1.

22. "Japanese farm trade proposal at WTO echoes EU call to protect multifunctionality," 18 ITR 104, (January 18, 2001), p. 47; "EU farmers will not be sacrificed: Fischer Boel," NEWS @ EU No. 75, August 1, 2005, p. 3.

23. "NAMA negotiations remain deadlocked," 10 BRIDGES No. 11, March 29, 2006, p. 7; "Slow progress on industrial goods talks in final push to ministerial," 12 BRIDGES No. 25, July 9, 2008, p. 3.

24. In a famous EU case, Rewe-Zentral AG v. Bundesmonopolverbaltung fur Brantwein [1979] ECR 649, Germany attempted to exclude a French wine (Cassis de Dijion) because it wasn't alcoholic enough!; "Greenspan says slowdown in growth could give in to protectionist pressures [in the U.S.], 17 ITR 1773 (November 23, 2000), p. 28.

25. "U.S., EU to sign new MRAs this month facilitating trans-Atlantic trade," 15 ITR 809 (May 13, 1998), p. 12; "Japan, European Union agree to launch mutual recognition accord on standards," 18 ITR 2034 (December 20, 2001), p. 60.

26. "Bethlehem files for bankruptcy, blaming imports and sagging economy," 18 ITR 1640 (October 18, 2001), p. 33; "U.S. attacked for protectionism during OECD ministerial meeting," 19 ITR 909 (May 23, 2002), p. 27; Andrew Jack, "Brussels warms to rescue for French bank," FINANCIAL TIMES, March 15, 1995, p. 3.

27. "U.S. steel industry seeks relief from surge of imports resulting from Asian crisis," 15 ITR 1529 (September 16, 1998), p. 8; "E.U. to slap anti-dumping duties on Chinese and Vietnamese shoes," 10 BRIDGES No. 6, February 27, 2006, p. 11; "U.S. makes concession in WTO agenda talks on clarifying [GATT] dumping, subsidies agreements," 18 ITR 1819 (November 15, 2001), p. 19; Progressive Policy Institute, "The United States has initiated only 10 anti-dumping cases this year," available at: http://www.ppionline.org, last visited on December 2, 2005.

28. "China to keep telecom market closed to foreign operators," 14 ITR 1460 (September 3, 1997), p. 23; Guy de Jonquieres, "China to impose regulation on insurers in competition with state-owned company," 14 ITR 1464 (September 3, 1997), p. 38; "Unlocking business," THE ECONOMIST, September 17, 2005, p. 77.

29. "Telecom groups call for greater regulatory independence in China, and Japan," 19 ITR 273 (February 14, 2002), p. 48.

30. See generally, THOMAS. C. FISCHER, THE EUROPEANIZATION OF AMERICA, "Chapter 12: Competing Completion Laws and Policy" (Carolina Academic Press, 1995), p. 177 *et seq.*; "Giving the invisible hand a helping hand," THE ECONOMIST, November 9, 2002, p. 14; "More news," EUROPA NEWSLETTER No. 77, March 27, 2006, p. 8.

31. "WTO cites need for competition rules for business practices that restrict trade," 12/19/97 BNA-BTD d7 (December 19, 1997) p. 1; "Monti: Two tracks toward a global competition policy," EUROCOM, September 2002, p. 1.

32. "Finance ministers OK VAT imposition on digital goods sold via internet in EU," 19 ITR 839 (May 9, 2002), p. 1.

33. Tony Walker, "U.S. and China avert trade war over copyright piracy," FINANCIAL TIMES, February 27, 1995, p. 1; "China claims new piracy crackdown," 13 ITR 24 d15 (June 12, 1996), p. 30.

34. "Transshipment charges levied against China," 18 ITR 2039 (December 20, 2001), p. 76.

35. "Growing consensus on internet management," EUROCOM, September 1998, p. 2.

36. "OECD cautions on trade imbalances; works against protectionist measures," 16 ITR 1047 (June 23, 1999), p. 1; Robert Samuelson, "Competition's quiet victory," NEWSWEEK, February 7, 2005, p. 43; "Free trade on trial," THE ECONOMIST, January 3, 2004, p. 13; "WTO Ministerial agrees in setting course for final stage of talks"; some disappointed," 22 ITR No. 50 (December 22, 2005) p. 2046.

37. Willard Berry, "Why sanctions don't work," FINANCIAL TIMES, December 1, 1997, p. 14; "Unilateral sanctions are not effective, private sector witnesses tell senate panel," 15 ITR 387 (March 4, 1998), p. 97; "Trade facilitation talks resume with flurry of new proposals," 10 BRIDGES No. 6, February 22, 2006, p. 6; "Altogether now…," THE ECONOMIST, November 22, 2003, p. 69.

38. POCKET WORLD IN FIGURES, *op. cit.*, p. 235.

39. Renee Sauers & Kelly Pierce, "U.S. international transactions: First quarter of 2005," SURVEY OF CURRENT BUSINESS, July 2005, p. 72, Table A; Progressive Policy Institute, "The U.S. 'commercial services' trade surplus reached $100 billion last year," available at: http://www.ppionline.org, last vis-

ited March 1, 2007; Progressive Policy Institute, "U.S. exports to India have doubled since 2003," available at: http://www.ppionline.org, last visited September 27, 2005.

40. James Hardin, "More winners emerge in [China's] three Gorges scramble," FINANCIAL TIMES, August 20, 1997, p. 4; "Exports and the [U.S.] economy: A few good machines," THE ECONOMIST, March 15, 2008, p. 25.

41. "Why trade is good for you," in "A Survey of World Trade', THE ECONOMIST, October 3, 1998, p. 4.

42. David Dollar & Aart Kraay, "Growth is Good for the Poor," The World Bank (Development Research Group), March 2001, available at: www.worldbank.org/research/growth, last visited October 21, 2003.

43. "WTO member states agree to launch development round at rough talks in Doha," 18 ITR 1814 (November 15, 2001), p. 8; "Trade officials assess winners, losers in aftermath of Doha ministerial meeting," 18 ITR 1856 (November 22, 2001), p. 7.

44. "U.S. surprise initiative to restart trade talks," 8 BRIDGES No. 1, January 14, 2004, p. 1; "World trade talks: A step forward," THE ECONOMIST, August 7, 2004, p. 11.

45. "Ag Chair to draft 'reference papers' on issues where convergence apparent'; "Trade facilitations talks resume with flurry of new proposals," both in 10 BRIDGES No. 6, February 22, 2006, pp. 1 and 6, respectively; "Plans set for S & D talks," 10 BRIDGES No. 7, March 2, 2006, p. 10; "WTO members reach 'moment of truth' on sensitive farm products," 12 BRIDGES No. 12, April 11, 2008, p. 1; "Services talks pick up momentum," 11 BRIDGES No. 44, December 19, 2007, p. 10; "WTO mini-ministerial ends in collapse," BRIDGES DAILY UP-DATE, Issue 10, July 30, 2008, available at: bridges_weekly@ictsd.ch, last visited July 31, 2008.

46. "The tiger in front" and "Rivals and partners" in "A survey of India and China," both in THE ECONOMIST, March 5, 2005, pp. 10 and 14, respectively; "Trade talks all about give and take," NEWS @ EU No. 26, June 21, 2004, p. 3; "AMTAC says China gets free ride," in "WTO ministerial agrees on setting course for final stage of talks," op. cit.

47. "Developing nations want to drop issues from trade talks," "Mexico vows to fight agricultural subsidies," "China to resist calls for further concessions in Cancun WTO talks," all in WTO-Watch, available at: WTO-watch@iatp.org, last visited September 4, 2003.

48. "Cancun trade talks collapse over rich-poor rift," in Cancun Update, available at: cancunupdate@iatp.org, last visited on October 8, 2003.

49. Brian Knowlton, "Failed Cancun talks give impetus to bilateral deals," THE INTERNATIONAL HERALD TRIBUNE, September 23, 2003, available at:

http://www.tradeobservatory.org/news/index.cfm?=4827, last visited October 9, 2003; "World trade talks: A step forward," *op.cit.*; "WTO ministerial agrees on setting course for final stages of [GATT] talks," 22 ITR 2046 (December 22, 2005).

50. Progressive Policy Institute, "Turkey and the European Union have opened membership talks," October 5, 2005, available at: ppi_admin@dlcppi.org, last visited April 17, 2006.

51. Thomas C. Fischer, "A Commentary on Regional Institutions in the Pacific Rim: Do APEC and ASEAN Still Matter?" 13 Duke Journal of Comparative & International Law 337 (2003).

52. Christopher Lockwood, "The club that excludes America," in "The World in 2006," THE ECONOMIST, circa December 15, 2005, p. 48; "Dead on arrival," THE ECONOMIST, December 17, 2005, p. 40; "The enigma of SAARC: Summit or trough?" THE ECONOMIST, November 19, 2005, p. 44; Anita Snow, "Nations sign alternative to U.S.-led trade pacts," THE SEATTLE TIMES, April, 30, 2006, p. A 12; "Nine African nations agree to create free-trade area, move toward greater union," 17 ITR 1722 (November 9, 2000), p. 75

53. "What GATT did," in "Where next?" (A survey of World Trade), THE ECONOMIST, October 3, 1998, p. 9; Progressive Policy Institute, "Last Multilateral Trade Agreement: 1998," April 12, 2006, available at ppi_admin@dlcppi.org, last visited on April 13, 2006.

54. For example, Public Law 107-210 (HR 3009), the Andean Trade Preference Act, August 6, 2002; and "U.S. says 58 African, Caribbean nations will receive new trade benefits under law," 17 ITR 1508 (October 5, 2000),p. 10, commenting on the Trade and Development Act of 2000.

55. Claire Gooding, "Standardize and deliver," FINANCIAL TIMES (Survey: International standards), October 13, 1995, p. 1; World Trade Organization, Agreement on the Implementation of the Ministerial Declaration on Trade in Information Technology Products, 36 I.L.M 375 (1997); "U.S., EU to hold talks aimed at salvaging pact on trade in pharmaceutical products," 19 ITR 993 (June 6, 2002), p. 31.

56. "The tiger in front," *op. cit.*

57. George Russell, "The Power of Globalization," 16 NBR [National Bureau of Asian Research] No. 2, November 2005, p. 9. "Even with the weak economic policies of [2000–2005] and the spectacular emergence of China and India as industrial challengers, America's economy is larger ... and more Americans are on the job. Since NAFTA went into effect in 1994, American gross domestic product has grown by $6 trillion, businesses have added 19.2 million private-sector jobs, manufacturing production has risen by almost $500 billion, and average unemployment rates have dropped by one [percentage] point."

Edward Gresser, "Trading in Myth," February 9, 2006, available at: http://www.ppi online.org, last visited February 16, 2006. Michael Smith, "Trade reform promises $400 billion bonus for world," FINANCIAL TIMES, May 26, 1999, p. 8; Robert Samuelson, "Competition's quiet victory," NEWSWEEK, February 7, 2005, p. 43.

58. "Weighing up the WTO," THE ECONOMIST, November 23, 2002, p. 72; Fareed Zakaria, "Conservative contradictions," NEWSWEEK, April 25, 2005, p. 33; "The key to trade and aid," THE ECONOMIST, June 4, 2005, p. 15.

59. "GAO says small, medium-sized firms exporting U.S. goods doubled in five years," 17 ITR 701 (May 4, 2000), p. 36; "Buying the future" in "A survey of consumer power," THE ECONOMIST, April 2, 2005, p. 15.

60. Fareed Zakaria, "Conservative Contradictions," *op. cit.*; Paul Krugman, "Is Capitalism Too Productive?" FOREIGN AFFAIRS, September/October 1997, p. 79.

61. Robert Samuelson, "The buyer of last resort," NEWSWEEK, August 24, 1998, p. 42; Zanny Minton Beddoes, "Tipping-point: America's economy is set to slow," in "The World in 2006," *op.cit.*, p. 31; Nancy Dunne, "U.S. slips behind in key emerging markets," FINANCIAL TIMES, October 29, 1997, p. 8.

62. "Europe's new protection is in," THE ECONOMIST, July 2, 2005, p. 49; Daniel Yergin, "Over a barrel," FORTUNE, May 16, 2005, p. 114; Vivienne Walt, "China's African Safari," FORTUNE, February 20, 2006, p. 41; Jia Lynn Yang, "Shanghaied in Florida," FORTUNE, March 6, 2006, p. 45.

63. "Altogether now...," THE ECONOMIST, November 22, 2003, p. 69; "Testing all engines," THE ECONOMIST, February 4, 2006, p. 65.

64. "U.S., EU business leaders call for 'ambitious' new round of WTO trade talks," 18 ITR 1733 (November 1, 2001), p. 37.

Chapter VII

1. See generally, LESTER THUROW, THE FUTURE OF CAPITALISM (William Morrow, 1996) pp. 273–274.

2. ALVIN TOFFLER, POWER SHIFT (Bantam, 1990), p. 58, emphasis added; Progressive Policy Institute, "Currency trading totals $3 trillion a day," available at: http://www.ppionline.org, last visited March 14, 2007.

3. FREDERIC MISKIN, THE NEXT GREAT GLOBALIZATION (Princeton, 2006); "The domino effect," THE ECONOMIST, July 5, 2008, p. 86.

4. In the United States, public consumption (at all levels) represents only 18.6 percent of GDP. POCKET WORLD IN FIGURES, THE ECONOMIST (2007 ed.), p. 234. Of that, large percentages go to defense, health (including Medicare), social security, and debt service. Very little of the federal budget goes toward

infrastructure building. U.S. Census Bureau, STATISTICAL ABSTRACT OF THE UNITED STATES: 2006 (GDP, 2005), table 463, p. 319.

5. William Dawkins, "Japan unveils record $ 137 billion recovery plan," FINANCIAL TIMES, September 21, 1995, p. 1; Paul Abrahams & Gillian Tett, "Japan slips into recession as economy shrinks 5.3%," FINANCIAL TIMES, June 13–14, 1998, p. 1.

6. POCKET WORLD IN FIGURES, op. cit., p. 218.

7. Progressive Policy Institute, "The Japan postal service is the world's largest bank" (at $1.7 trillion), available at http://www.ppionline.org, last visited February 22, 2006; "Non-performing," THE ECONOMIST, (A survey of business in China), March 20, 2004, p. 18.

8. Saikat Chatterjee, "Indian banks prepare bevy of bond offerings," THE WALL STREET JOURNAL (London), May 30, 2006, p. 21; "Out in Africa," THE ECONOMIST, June 10, 2006, p. 72.

9. Progressive Policy Institute, "Foreign governments and banks hold $2.1 trillion of [U.S.] Treasury securities," available at http://www.ppionline.org, last visited January 17, 2006; "Current account deficits: Still waiting for the big one," THE ECONOMIST, April 8, 2006, p. 19; Peter Garnham, "Chinese cash turns in new directions," FINANCIAL TIMES, November 30, 2007, p. 24; Song Jung-a & Others, "South Korea pension fund shuns low-yield US securities," FINANCIAL TIMES, March 27, 2008, p. 15.

10. "In 2005 foreigners adventured a net of $61.4 billion in emerging market equities ... and a further $237.5 billion in direct investments. At the end of the year, the shares in all exchanges in emerging economies were worth $4.4 trillion, up from $1.7 trillion three years before." "A nasty spillage," THE ECONOMIST, June 19, 2006, p. 71.

11. "Latin American bonds: Kicking the habit," THE ECONOMIST, March 4, 2006, p. 69.

12. STATISTICAL ABSTRACT OF THE UNITED STATES, op. cit., tables 1285 and 1286, pp. 830 and 831, respectively; Robert Chote, "Aid to poor nations falls to 18-year low," FINANCIAL TIMES, April 8, 1999, p. 5; James Wolfenson, "Ending the unilateral approach to aid," FINANCIAL TIMES, September 26, 2002, p. 13; Homi Kharas & Abdul Malik, "Short term fixes for development assistance," available at: www.brookings.edu/opinions/2008, last visited April 21, 2008.

13. "Which is the victim?" THE ECONOMIST, March 6, 2004, p. 63; "The new man at the Fund," THE ECONOMIST, June 5, 2004, p. 69; "Nestor unbound," THE ECONOMIST, December 24, 2005, p. 14; "Not even a cat to rescue," THE ECONOMIST, April 22, 2006, p. 69.

14. Stephen Fidler, "The danger of a safety net," FINANCIAL TIMES, June 4, 1998, p. 13; "Bad loans made good," THE ECONOMIST, October 1, 2005, p. 70.

15. "A regime changes," THE ECONOMIST, June 4, 2005, p. 65; "Just saying no," THE ECONOMIST, March 4, 2006, p. 69; "The World Bank: That empty nest feeling," THE ECONOMIST, September 8, 2007, p. 61.

16. "Not even a cat to rescue," *op. cit.*

17. Richard McGregor, "State funds join China's hunt for foreign deals," FINANCIAL TIMES, October 31, 2007, p. 2; "China's sovereign wealth fund to follow strictly 'politics-free' goals," FINANCIAL TIMES, October 17, 2007, p. 1.

18. See generally, GEORGE SOROS, OPEN SOCIETY: REFORMING GLOBAL CAPITALISM (Public Affairs, 2000) pp. 177–178, 183–185, and 215–217.

19. "Third thoughts on foreign capital," THE ECONOMIST, November 18, 2006, p. 82.

20. STATISTICAL ABSTRACT OF THE UNITED STATES: 2006, tables 1278 and 1283, pp. 824 and 827, respectively; Scheherazade Daneshkhu, "FDIs near $1,500 bn [annual] world record," FINANCIAL TIMES, October 17, 2007, p. 7.

21. GEORGE SOROS, OPEN SOCIETY, *op. cit.*, pp. 168–169 and 177–178.

22. In 2000, the so-called "triad" (the EU, U.S. and Japan) accounted for 82% of FDI outflows and 71% of FDI inflows. EURECOM, October, 2001.

23. STATISTICAL ABSTRACT, *op.cit*, note 20; Progressive Policy Institute, "Three-quarters of foreign direct investment in China is Asian," available at: http://www.ppionline.org, last visited October 26, 2005.

24. Frances Williams, "Global foreign investment flows 'set to fall by 40%'," FINANCIAL TIMES, September 19, 2001, p. 9; "Borders of finance: FDI inflows," THE ECONOMIST, January 17, 2004, p. 7.

25. "Globalization with a third-world face," THE ECONOMIST, April 9, 2005, p. 66.

26. "China seeks more private investment in state-owed firms," 14 ITR 1543 (September 17, 1997); "Thailand to enforce intellectual property law, move to attract more FDI," 18 ITR 1988 (December 13, 2001); Stephen Fidler, "FDI inflow is good for growth," FINANCIAL TIMES, April 11, 2001, p. 15.

27. "Cooling down," THE ECONOMIST, January 28, 2006, p. 73; "The last, best game," THE ECONOMIST, October 22, 2005, p. 78; "A nasty spillage," *op. cit.*; Martin Wolf, "Dangers of poor institutions, skills and moral hazard," FINANCIAL TIMES, October 6, 1998, p. 13.

28. "Can India fly?" THE ECONOMIST, June 3, 2006, p, 13; "The tiger in front (A survey of India and China), THE ECONOMIST, March 5, 2005, p. 3; "Africa fails to attract foreign investment despite improved economic performance," 16 ITR 1230 (July 21, 1999); "Emerging markets: The global gusher," THE ECONOMIST, January 6, 2007, p. 59.

29. "Exporting success," THE ECONOMIST, February 4, 2006, p. 69; "A first gentle shake," THE ECONOMIST, April 29, 2006, p. 75; James Kynge, "China plans bold move to give entrepreneurs power," FINANCIAL TIMES, August 28, 2002, p. 1; "Creeping towards the marketplace," THE ECONOMIST, February 4, 2006, p. 38; "Non-performing," THE ECONOMIST, March 20, 2004; p. 18; Alan Beattie, "Investors see corruption as a barrier," FINANCIAL TIMES, October 17, 2000, p. 8.

30. Frances Williams & Guy de Jonquireres, "WTO pact to open up global financial markets [during the Asian meltdown]," FINANCIAL TIMES, December 15, 1997, p. 1; "Liberalism lives [in Latin America]," THE ECONOMIST, January 2, 1999, p. 59; "The battle for Latin Americas soul," THE ECONOMIST, May 20, 2006, p. 11.

31. "Middle-age spread," THE ECONOMIST, December 17, 2005, p. 76.

32. Robert J. Samuelson, "The mysterious merger frenzy," NEWSWEEK, October 16, 2000, p. 55.

33. "Global foreign investment flows set to fall by 40%," op.cit.; "Love is in the air," THE ECONOMIST, February 5, 2005, p. 9; "Once more onto the breach, dear clients, once more," THE ECONOMIST, April 8, 2006, p. 71.

34. David Henry & Others, "Have dealmakers wised up?" BUSINESS WEEK, February 21, 2005, p. 36; "Riding the wave," THE ECONOMIST, April 8, 2006, p. 18.

35. "The global merger boom: The beat goes on," THE ECONOMIST, May 12 2007, p. 77; "Bank consolidation: Under the hammer," THE ECONOMIST, July 12, 2008, p. 81; "European banking consolidation: Braveheart," THE ECONOMIST, April 28, 2007, p. 13; "Globalization's offspring," The ECONOMIST, April 7, 2007, p. 11; Peter Larsen, "Activity soars beyond western horizons," FINANCIAL TIMES (Special Report on Corporate Finance), February 28, 2007, p. 2; "Cross-border mergers: Heavy mittal," THE ECONOMIST, February 4, 2006, p. 11.

36. "Breaking down the walls," FOCUS EUROPE, Summer 2006, p. 7; "Arcelor wobbles," THE ECONOMIST, June 17, 2006, p. 70; "Big deals," FOCUS EUROPE, op. cit., pp. 14–15.

37. Greg Hitt, "Europe and China watch U.S. investment debate," THE WALL STREET JOURNAL (Europe) May 30, 2006, p. 1.

38. "Private equity: Size matters," THE ECONOMIST, January 29, 2005, p. 72; "Capitalism's new kings," THE ECONOMIST, November 27, 2004, p. 9. See also, "A survey of private equity," Id.

39. Paul Abrahams, "Venture capital investment plummets," FINANCIAL TIMES, August 14, 2001, p. 1; "After the drought," THE ECONOMIST, April 3, 2004, p. 71; "The great tech buy-out boom," THE ECONOMIST, February 25, 2006, p. 65; "Anglo-Saxon attitudes," THE ECONOMIST, December 17, 2005, p. 69.

40. Clay Chandler, "Rolling the dice on China's banks," FORTUNE, December 25, 2006, p. 181; Joe Leahy, "China and India to head steep rise in Asian IPOs," FINANCIAL TIMES, July 10, 2007, p. 25; Robin Kwong & others, "China on course to lead world IPO league," July 5, 2007, p. 1.

41. "On top of the world," THE ECONOMIST, April 29, 2006, p. 11; "Bigger footprints," THE ECONOMIST (Survey of international banking), THE ECONOMIST, April 17, 2004, p. 12; Lionel Barber, "How to harmonize financial services?" (in the EU), EUROPE, September 2000, p. 5. See generally, "Final Report of the Committee of wise men on the Regulation of European Securities Markets" (Brussels, February 15, 2001).

42. Jenny Anderson & Heather Timmons, "NYSE group reaches deal to acquire Euronext," NEW YORK TIMES, June 2, 2006, p. 3; Edward Luce & Vincent Boland, "NASDAQ goes global," FINANCIAL TIMES, November 7, 1999, p. 6; "European exchanges: Crowding the dance floor," THE ECONOMIST, May 20, 2006, p. 77; European insurance: Thirst for growth," THE ECONOMIST, June 17, 2006, p. 79; "Exchanges: A look into the future," THE ECONOMIST, March 24, 2007, p. 85; "Nasdaq OMX trading system 'will slash fees'," FINANCIAL TIMES, March 20, 2008, p. 17; Tony Tassell, "European bourses eclipse US markets by value," FINANCIAL TIMES, April 3, 2007, p. 1; Gerrit Wiesmann & Jeremy Grant, "SGL to seek delisting from New York," FINANCIAL TIMES, March 27, 2007, p. 15; James Mackintosh, "Emerging market funds prefer London," FINANCIAL TIMES, February 12, 2008, p. 21.

43. Scheherazade Daneshkhu, "Global balance but domestic finances on edge," FINANCIAL TIMES, May 25, 2007, p. 2.

44. "Thinking big" (A survey of international banking), THE ECONOMIST, May 20, 2006, p. 3; "A blurred Euro-vision" (A survey of international banking), THE ECONOMIST, May 21, 2005, p. 10; "Still getting to know you," THE ECONOMIST, May 1, 2004, p. 75; "What single market?" (A survey of international banking/2006) op. cit., p. 12.

45. "Technology and exchanges: Moving markets" THE ECONOMIST, February 4, 2006, p. 68; "Open wider," A survey of international banking/2005) op. cit., p. 3; "China under fire at WTO over banking, insurance, express delivery commitments," 19 ITR 1048 (June 13, 2002); Henry Kaufman, "A lack of leadership," FINANCIAL TIMES, October 7, 1998, p. 11; "One Basel leads to another" (A survey of international banking/2006), op. cit., p. 10; Geoffrey Colvin, "Keep America's edge," FORTUNE December 25, 3006, p. 99.

46. Progressive Policy Institute, "The U.S. trade deficit is falling," available at: http://www.ppionline.org, last visited November 20, 2007; "Falling dollar may benefit some American companies," THE KITSAP DAILY, November 28, 2006, p. 5.

47. "The passing of the buck?" (Special report: The future of the dollar), THE ECONOMIST, December 2, 2004, p. 71; Robin Bew, "The currency crisis of 2006," in THE WORLD IN 2006 (THE ECONOMIST, *circa* December 15, 2005), p. 15; "Capital goes global," THE ECONOMIST, October 25, 1997, p. 87; "Monetary policy: Imperfect foresight," THE ECONOMIST, May 13, 2006, p. 13. See also, Paul Krugman, "The Return of Depression Economics," FOREIGN AFFAIRS, January/February 1999, pp. 73–74.

48. "Monetary policy: Imperfect foresight;" *op.cit.*; Peter Norman & Richard Waters, "G-7 resolves to put brakes on strong dollar," FINANCIAL TIMES, February 10, 1997, p. 1; Gerard Baker, "Dollar could be buoyed in spite of G-7," FINANCIAL TIMES, February 11, 1997, p. 7.

49. James Kynge, "China to add the euro to its foreign currency reserves," FINANCIAL TIMES, October 31/November 1, 1998, p. 3; Progressive Policy Institute, "World euro reserves: $1.7 trillion" (26 percent), available at: ppi_admin.main. dlc@ppionline.org, last visited June 16, 2008.

50. Slovakia joined the euro area in January 2009. "EU welcomes Slovakia to the euro area," NEWS @ EU, July 9, 2008, p. 4; "When countries don't count," THE ECONOMIST, November 11, 2000, p. 92.

51. See generally, "The Single Market on Steroids: Economic and Monetary Union" in THOMAS C. FISCHER, THE UNITED STATES, THE EUROPEAN UNION, AND THE "GLOBALIZATION" OF WORLD TRADE, *op. cit.*, pp. 116–125; and "European Monetary Union and the Euro" in Thomas C. Fischer, "An American Looks at the European Union," 12 EUROPEAN LAW JOURNAL 226, at 239–243.

52. "Euro blues," THE ECONOMIST, April 29, 2006, p. 58; "The Euro and trade," THE ECONOMIST, June 24, 2006, p. 75; Wolfgang Munchau, "Early steps towards an assertive eurozone," FINANCIAL TIMES, November 19, 2007, p. 13.

53. Actually, the British pound sterling edged out the Japanese yen by a small margin in 2007, but the yen may strengthen again. At any rate, the pound is subservient to the Euro, moves with it, and may eventually be replaced by it. Phillip Wooldridge, "The changing composition of official reserves," BIS QUARTERLY REVIEW (2006), pp. 33–37; "[D]ollars comprise most of Asia's total [monetary] reserves of more than $2 trillion." "A need for flexibility," THE ECONOMIST, November 27, 2004, p. 75.

54. "Japan's monetary policy: Situation cloudy," THE ECONOMIST, June 10, 2006, p. 75; "A need for flexibility," *op. cit.*; "Please release me…," THE ECONOMIST, November 6, 2004, p. 12; "How far will it go?" THE ECONOMIST, July 23, 2005, p. 67; "The Chinese yuan: Revaluation by stealth," THE ECONOMIST, January 12, 2008, p. 69.

55. James Harding & Tony Walker, "Beijing backs regional currency fund," FINANCIAL TIMES, November 18, 1997, p. 8. See generally, Zanny Beddoes,

"From EMU to AMU? The case for Regional Currencies," FOREIGN AFFAIRS, July/August 1999, p. 8; Wolfgang Munchau, "Asian monetary integration poses many problems," FINANCIAL TIMES, May 7, 2007, p. 9.

56. "The invasion of the sovereign wealth funds," THE ECONOMIST, January 19, 2008, p. 11; Progressive Policy Institute, "Chinese direct investment abroad has grown twenty-five fold since 2000," available at: http://www.ppi-online.org, last visited October 29, 2007; John Burton, "Wealth funds exploit credit squeeze," FINANCIAL TIMES, March 24, 2008, p. 14; Lawrence Summers, "Sovereign funds shake the logic of capitalism," FINANCIAL TIMES, July 30, 2007, p. 9.

57. "China's sovereign wealth fun to follow strictly 'politics-free' goals," *op. cit.*; Daniel Dombey & Simeon Kerr, "Wealth funds strike deal with Washington," FINANCIAL TIMES, March 22–23 2008, p. 4.

58. Shawn Tully, "What's wrong with Wall Street," FORTUNE, April 14, 2008, p. 70; "What went wrong," and "Wall Street's crisis," both in THE ECONOMIST, March 22, 2008, pp. 77 and 11, respectively.

59. "Financial engine failure," THE ECONOMIST, February 9, 2008, p. 79; Progressive Policy Institute, "World stock market losses this week: $3 billion," available at: ppi_admin.main.dlc@ppionline.org, last visited January 28, 2008.

60. "Waiting for Armageddon," THE ECONOMIST, March 29, 2008, p. 81; Robert Samuelson, "A darker future for us," NEWSWEEK, November 10, 2008, p. 26; Scott Nelson, "The real Great Depression," THE CHRONICLE OF HIGHER EDUCATION, October 17, 2008, p. 98; Daniel Gross, "How a lack of faith pounded the markets," NEWSWEEK, March 31, 2008, p. 48; "G 20 meeting [15 November 2008, Washington, D.C.]," NEWS @ EU, November 19, 2008, p. 2; Joseph Coleman, "APEC [leaders] confident on economy," SEATTLE POST-INTELLIGENCER, November 24, 2008, p. A4; "Mission creep at the Fed," THE ECONOMIST, August 9, 2008, p. 67.

61. "Latin America economies: A coming test to virtue," THE ECONOMIST, April 12, 2008, p. 41.

62. Progressive Policy Institute, "Foreign government and banks hold $2.1 trillion worth of treasury securities," available at: ppi-admin@dlcppi.org, last visited January 11, 2006; "Asian squirrels," THE ECONOMIST, September 17, 2005, p. 80; "Current-account deficits: Still waiting for the big one," THE ECONOMIST, April 8, 2006, p. 19; "Wide gap, wide yawn," THE ECONOMIST, March 19, 2005, p. 78; "What is it on?" THE ECONOMIST, December 10, 2005, p. 37; "Mr. Hu finally goes to Washington," THE ECONOMIST, April 15, 2006, p. 43.

63. Doug Cameron, "Accountancy standards review mooted," FINANCIAL TIMES, February 14, 2001, p. 8; "China to join in international accounting rules," 14 ITR 1024 (June 11, 1997); Jim Kelly, "US rejects plan for world ac-

counting body," FINANCIAL TIMES, April 15, 1999, p. 1; "Accounting standards: Common ground," THE ECONOMIST, December 20, 2003, p. 105; "International accounting: Fair's fair," THE ECONOMIST, March 6, 2004, p. 65.

64. "Financial reporting: AIG's accounting lesson," THE ECONOMIST, March 6, 2004, p. 64; "China falsifies economic statistics, financial reports, Xinhua discloses," 13 ITR 12 d 26 (March 20, 1996).

65. Tangled taxes need simplification," FINANCIAL TIMES, July 30, 2007, p. 8; "Overhauling the old jalopy," THE ECONOMIST, August 4, 2007, p. 16.

66. "World's tax system 'at risk' because of WTO ruling, U.S. warns," 18 ITR 1890 (November 29, 2001); "A taxing battle," THE ECONOMIST, January 31, 2004, p. 71; "Corporate tax: Time to hiss," THE ECONOMIST, January 31, 2004, p. 14; "Corporate tax signs of relief," THE ECONOMIST, December 17, 2005, p. 62; "Flat is beautiful," THE ECONOMIST, March 5, 2005, p. 54. See generally, Stephen Utz, "Tax harmonization and coordination in Europe and America," 9 CONNECTICUT JOURNAL OF INTERNATIONAL LAW 767 (Summer, 1994); Reuveu Aui-Yonah, "Globalization and Tax Competition," Law Quadrangle Notes (University of Michigan Law School), Summer 2001, p. 60.

67. "The world economy: Rebalancing act," THE ECONOMIST, December 2, 2006, p. 75.

68. THOMAS C. FISCHER, THE UNITED STATES, THE EUROPEAN UNION AND THE "GLOBALIZATION" OF WORLD TRADE, op. cit., "Chapter 13: Asia's Emerging Economies: 'Miracle,' Myth or neither?" pp. 178–198; "Cool nerves at the central banks [in wake of 9/11]," FINANCIAL TIMES, October 1, 2001, p. 2; "History finance," THE ECONOMIST, April 5, 2008, p. 13.

69. Robert Samuelson, "Global boom and bust?" NEWSWEEK, November 10, 1997, p. 35; "Finance: Trick or treat?" THE ECONOMIST, October 23, 1999, p. 91; John Plender, "Revisiting of a deadly disease," FINANCIAL TIMES, September 21, 1998, p. 17; "U.N. agency cites sharp drop in global foreign investment for 2001," 18 ITR 1512 (September 27, 2001); "Bear Stearns fall-out," op.cit.

70. Allen van Duyn, "Bond insurance crisis talks," FINANCIAL TIMES, February 16–17, 2008, p. 1; Chris Giles & David Pilling, "Rich nations unmoved by urgent need for action," FINANCIAL TIMES, January 6, 2008, p. 2.

71. Id.; "Central banks: A dangerous divergence," THE ECONOMIST, March 22, 2008, p. 83; David Pilling & Others, "G7 finance chiefs wary of overreaction," FINANCIAL TIMES, February 9–10 2008, p. 2.

72. Jennifer Hughes, "Emerging markets hit at 'key' moment," FINANCIAL TIMES, May 20, 2006, p. 1; Kimberly Blauton, "Perils of a fast buck," BOSTON GLOBE, September 2, 1998, p. E1; Robert Chote, "Investors retreat from emerging markets," FINANCIAL TIMES, September 30, 1998, p. 6. Cf, "Going with the flow," THE ECONOMIST, August 21, 1999, p. 68.

73. Stephen Fidler, "Market turmoil 'threatens open economies'," FINANCIAL TIMES, September 15, 1998, p. 12. See generally, George Soros, "The Crisis of Global Capitalism," NEWSWEEK, December 7, 1998, p. 78, although Mr. Soros' views were revised and toned down in a new edition of his book, entitled OPEN SOCIETY: REFORMING GLOBAL CAPITALISM (Public Affairs, 2000).

74. "No pain, no gain," THE ECONOMIST, December 13, 2003, p. 77; "Market turmoil 'threatens open economies'," *op. cit.*; "Emerging markets hit at 'key' moment," *op. cit.*

75. Stephen Fidler & Robert Chote, "Rubin spells out U.S. ideas for global financial reforms," FINANCIAL TIMES, October 2, 1998, p. 6; Stephen Fidler, "Capital curbs seen in more favourable light [by IMF]," FINANCIAL TIMES, September 15, 1998, p. 12; Alan Beattie, "Call for big changes to global financial system," FINANCIAL TIMES, November 5, 2001, p. 8.

76. John Plender, "Taming wild money," FINANCIAL TIMES, October 20, 1998, p. 17; "Still gushing forth," THE ECONOMIST, February 5, 2005, p. 67; Louise Lucas & Peter Montagnon, "Temptations of controlling capital," FINANCIAL TIMES, September 2, 1998, p. 3; Stephen Cecchetti, "Halfway to vanquishing volatility," FINANCIAL TIMES, August 22, 2001, p. 13.

77. Robert Chote, "Report says IMF needs to improve global surveillance," FINANCIAL TIMES, August 2, 1999, p. 12; "IMF to seek to redress global economic imbalance," 10 BRIDGES No. 14, April 27, 2006, p. 16.

78. "A host of problems," THE ECONOMIST, April 29, 2006, p. 82; "G-force," THE ECONOMIST, October 9, 2004, p. 72; "G-7 and the currencies," FINANCIAL TIMES, April 27, 1995, p. 13.

79. "Bothersome Basel [2]," THE ECONOMIST (A survey of international banking), April 17, 2004, p. 5; Harold Benick & George Kaufman, "Turmoil reveals the inadequacy of Basel II," FINANCIAL TIMES, February 28, 2008, p. 11.

80. James Tobin, "A Proposal for International Monetary Reform, 4 E. ECON. J. 153 (1978); International Chambers of Commerce, "The 'Tobin tax'—A business viewpoint," December 14, 2001, available at: http://www.globalpolicy.org/socecn/gtotax/currtax/2001/ICCTobin0114.htm, last visited May 30, 2006; "Revisiting a deadly disease," *op. cit.*

81. "Significant issues remain in stalled MAI talks," 15 ITR 774 (May 6, 1999), p. 23; Global Policy Forum, "Multinational agreement on Investment and Related Initiatives," available at: http://www.globalpolicy.org/socecon/bwi-wto/indexmai.htm, last visited May 30, 2006; "Trade by any other name: Does the WTO need special rules for foreign direct investment?" THE ECONOMIST, October 3, 1998 (World Trade Organization: A Survey of World Trade), p. 10.

82. Bethany McLean, "Where were the cops?" FORTUNE, September 3, 2007, p. 53; "When to bail out," THE ECONOMIST, October 6, 2007, p. 90; "Fixing fi-

nance," April 5, 2008, p. 13; John Kay, "Why more regulation will not save us from the next crisis," FINANCIAL TIMES, March 26, 2008, p. 15; "Caveat counterparty," THE ECONOMIST, March 22, 2008, p. 86.

83. "Will it fly?" THE ECONOMIST, April 5, 2008, p. 77; Jeremy Grant, "US market regulator revises its foreign policy," FINANCIAL TIMES, March 8, 2007, p. 6; "Central banks: A dangerous divergence," *op.cit.*

84. "A dirty job, but someone has to do it," THE ECONOMIST, December 15, 2007, p. 81; Chris Giles & Krishna Guha, "UK central bank to join battle on liquidity," FINANCIAL TIMES, March 27, 2008, p. 1; Gillian Tett, "Banking code to top agenda at Rio talks," FINANCIAL TIMES, March 5, 2008, p. 2; John Grieve Smith, "Wanted: a guardian of the world's financial system," FINANCIAL TIMES, April 13, 2007, p. 13.

85. Stephen Fidler, "IMF admits drawbacks to free flow of capital," FINANCIAL TIMES, September 22, 1998, p. 9; Ted Bardacke, "Asian crisis victims win greater voice," FINANCIAL TIMES, May 17, 1999, p. 3; "Senate ratifies bilateral treaties on investment with 10 countries," 17 ITR 1631 (October 26, 2000), p. 21.

86. "Emerging markets: Spot the difference," THE ECONOMIST, July 8, 2006, p. 68; "The insidious charms of foreign investment," THE ECONOMIST, March 5, 2006 (A Survey of India and China), p. 7; "Economic zones in India: Playing catch-up," THE ECONOMIST, June 24, 2006, p. 48; "Rivals and partners," (A survey of India and China), *op. cit.*, p. 14; "China's trade policy review highlights economic dynamism, points to challenges," 10 BRIDGES No. 14, April 27, 2006, p. 14.

87. "China: Engulfed by pyramids," THE ECONOMIST, July 17, 2004, p. 46; "Money laundering: Shell games," THE ECONOMIST, October 26, 2002, p. 69; Progressive Policy Institute, "The U.S. 'C-note' is the favorite target of counterfeiters worldwide," available at ppi-admin@dlcppi.org, last visited January 26, 2006.

88. Robert Samuelson, "Global capitalism, R.I.P.?" NEWSWEEK, September 14, 1998, p. 41; Judy Dempsey, "Liberalization key to growth, says IMF," FINANCIAL TIMES, November 17, 1997, p. 5; "Service cluster underway, plurilateral requests in the works," 10 BRIDGES No. 5, February 15, 2006, p. 9; "How China runs the world," THE ECONOMIST, July 30, 2005, p. 11; E.S. Browning, "Will stocks' rising tide ebb? Global markets rose in step….," WALL STREET JOURNAL (International), May 30, 2006, p. 17.

Chapter VIII

1. See generally, LESTER THUROW, THE FUTURE OF CAPITALISM (William Morrow, 1996), pp. 273–274; "Vietnam: Changing gear," THE ECONOMIST,

November 26, 2005, p. 49; "Ladders out of poverty" (A survey of South Africa), THE ECONOMIST, April 8, 2006, p. 9.

2. David Lynch, "Some would like to build a wall around U.S. economy," USA TODAY, March 15, 2006, p. B1; Progressive Policy Institute, "The number of 'globalized' workers has quadrupled since 1980," available at: ppi_admin@dlcppi.org, last visited September 7, 2007.

3. "A world of work" (A survey of outsourcing), THE ECONOMIST, November 13, 2004, p. 3. According to McKinsey Associates, 87 percent of foreign direct investment (FDI) is made to develop local markets. *Id.*, p. 4.

4. Although America imports much more from China than it exports to China (witness our trade imbalance), China is a huge consumer of foreign products. Its imports grew by 40 percent in 2003. Indeed, "China spends virtually all its export revenue on imports." "The dragon and the eagle," THE ECONOMIST (A survey of the world economy), October 2, 2004, pp. 4, 11–12.

5. Robert Litan, "Services Offshoring: How Much, How Fast?" The Brookings Institution, Policy Brief #132, April 2004.

6. Marc Gunther, "Cops of the global village," FORTUNE, June 27, 2005, p. 158; "The great hollowing-out myth," THE ECONOMIST, February 21, 2004, p. 27.

7. Alwyn Scott, "Bridging two worlds: a new life for Susie Cheng," SEATTLE TIMES, July 9, 2006, p. A1; "Minimum monthly wages are raised in Shanghai, Beijing," SEATTLE POST-INTELLIGENCER, July 5, 2005, p. E 2; Progressive Policy Institute, "Koreans work the longest hours [30 percent more than Americans]," available at: ppi_admin@dlcppi.org, last visited December 7, 2005.

8. "Services offshoring: How much, how fast?" *op. cit.*

9. Almost 81% of American jobs are in the service sector, 18.2% are industrial (with manufacturing making up the bulk at 12.1%), and agriculture accounts for a paltry 1.2% of American employment. POCKET WORLD IN FIGURES, THE ECONOMIST, 2007 ed. (Profile Books Ltd., 2006), p. 234.

10. "The great job switch," THE ECONOMIST, October 1, 2005, p. 13; Brad Stone, "Should I stay or should I go?" NEWSWEEK, April 19, 2004, p. 52; "Indian call centers: Busy signals," THE ECONOMIST, September 10, 2005, p. 60; "Outsourcing: Time to bring it back home?" THE ECONOMIST, March 5, 2005, p. 63.

11. Dan Hamilton & Joe Quinlan, "Outsourcing is out, insourcing is in," TRANSATLANTIC July/August 2004, p. 4; "Relocating the back office," THE ECONOMIST, December 13, 2003 (Special report: Offshoring), p. 67; "Smile, these are good times. Truly.," THE ECONOMIST, March 14, 2004, p. 29; Robert J. Samuelson, "Keeping U.S. jobs at home," NEWSWEEK, May 3, 2004, p. 41.

12. "WTO, ILO release joint study of trade and employment," 11 BRIDGES No. 6, February 21, 2007, p. 7.

13. Robert Taylor, "Unions aim for global labour pacts," FINANCIAL TIMES, January 29, 1997, p. 4; Jagdish Blagwati, "Break the link between trade and labour," FINANCIAL TIMES, August 29, 2001, p. 13.

14. PAUL KRUGMAN, POP INTERNATIONALISM (MIT Press, 1996), p. 157.

15. "The new jobs migration," THE ECONOMIST, February 21, 2004, p. 11; Robert J. Samuelson "Keeping U.S. jobs at home," NEWSWEEK, May 3, 2004, p. 41; "The great hollowing-out myth," *op. cit.*

16. "The wages of fear: Are poor countries pinching the rich ones' jobs?" THE ECONOMIST, October 3, 1998, p. 3; "The allure of low technology," THE ECONOMIST, December 20, 2003, p. 99; "The dragon and the eagle," *op. cit.*, p. 10; "Busy signals', *op. cit.*; "A world of opportunity" in "A world of work," *op. cit.*, p. 20; "Relocating the back office," *op. cit.*; "Should I go or should I stay?" *op. cit.*

17. "Relocating the back office," *op. cit.*; "The jobless boom," THE ECONOMIST, January 14, 2006, p. 46.

18. "The allure of low technology," THE ECONOMIST, December 20, 2003, p. 99; Progressive Policy Institute, "China is the world's top IT exporter, in a way," available at: ppi_admin@dlcppi.org, last visited July 20, 2006.

19. By one estimate, 6.4 million U.S. jobs (5 percent) were attributable to FDI in 2001, two-thirds of it from Europe. And of course these workers, as consumers, support additional workers. Moreover, the former are mostly high-end jobs. "A creaking partnership," *op. cit.*

20. "Busy signals," *op.cit.*; Peter Goodman, "Factory labor runs short in China," SEATTLE TIMES, September 26, 2004, p. A13; "Minimum monthly wages are raised in Shanghai, Beijing," SEATTLE POST-INTELLIGENCER, July 5, 2005, p. E2; "Relocating the back office," *op. cit.*

21. "Changing gear," *op. cit.*; "Bridging two worlds: a new life for Susie Cheng," SEATTLE TIMES, *op.cit.*; "The dragon and the eagle," *op. cit.*, pp. 9–11.

22. "The halo effect," in "The dragon and the eagle," *op. cit.*, pp. 10–11.

23. George Will, "The perils of protectionism," NEWSWEEK, March 29, 2004, p. 84; Paul Krugman, "Global trade fears can't be ignored," SEATTLE POST-INTELLIGENCER, February 29, 2004, p. F2.

24. Paul Krugman, "Toyota, moving northward," NEW YORK TIMES, July 25, 2005, p. A19.

25. Robert J. Samuelson, "Competition's quiet victory," NEWSWEEK, February 7, 2005, p. 43; "Higher wages or more job security?" THE ECONOMIST, September 18, 2004.

26. Diana Farrell, "U.S. offshoring: Small steps to make it win-win," ECONOMISTS' VOICE, available at: www.bepress.com/ev (March 2006); "The wages of fear," *op. cit.*; "DOL proposes new program to help workers who lose their jobs

to trade," 19 ITR 97 (January 17, 2002), p. 1; "In praise of Finland," THE ECON-OMIST, July 8, 2006, p. 48.

27. Peter Goodman, "Factory labor runs short in China," SEATTLE TIMES, September 26, 2004, p. A 13; "Break the link between trade and labour," *op. cit.*

28. "Foreign, redirected investment," THE ECONOMIST, May 29, 2004, p. 58; "Footloose firms," THE ECONOMIST, March 27, 2004, p. 77; "Cops of the global village," *op. cit.*

29. "A dubious deal," THE ECONOMIST, May 19, 2007, p. 30; Geoff Dyer, "China's labor debate spurs war of words for US interests," FINANCIAL TIMES, May 3, 2007, p. 7; Richard McGregor & Geoff Dyer, "Big US unions court Chinese counterparts," FINANCIAL TIMES, May 23, 2007, p. 2.

30. *Id.*; Progressive Policy Institute, "Child labor rates are falling [by 33 percent in hazardous work since 2000]," available at: ppi-admin@dlcppi.org, last visited June 5, 2006.

31. "Manufacturing employment: Industrial metamorphosis," THE ECON-OMIST, October 1, 2005, p. 69.

32. "Be my guest," THE ECONOMIST, October 8, 2005, p. 86; Todd Bishop, "Microsoft chairman makes pitch for foreign workers," SEATTLE POST — IN-TELLIGENCER, August 18, 2005, p. E1; "A turning tide?" THE ECONOMIST, June 28, 2008, p. 30.

33. "Cops of the global village," *op. cit.*; "China: How the other 800m live," THE ECONOMIST, March 11, 2006, p. 12.

34. Brookings Institution, Policy Brief No. 132, *op. cit.*; Ben Edwards, "Learning to love outsourcing," in "The World in 2005," THE ECONOMIST, January, 2005, p. 16.

35. "Vietnam: Changing gear," THE ECONOMIST, November 26, 2005, p. 49; "Ladders out of poverty," THE ECONOMIST (A survey of South Africa), p. 9; James Kynge, "5 m Chinese state workers to lose jobs," FINANCIAL TIMES, March 8, 2000, p. 6.

36. Progressive Policy Institute, "The world has become more peaceful," available at: admin@newsmail.dlc.org, last visited December 27, 2005; "Cops of the global village," *op. cit.*; "U.S. signs free-trade pact with Jordan that in-cludes labor, environmental rules," 17 ITR 42 (October 26, 2000), p. 1653.

37. "EU's Lamy opposes addressing social issues such as workers' rights in trade agreements," 18 ITR 536 (April 5, 2001), p. 33.

38. Julie Chao, "Progress comes with moral decay in China," SEATTLE POST-INTELLIGENCER, April 18, 2005, p. 18.

39. Richard Read, "Factory workers in China still toil for Nike," SEATTLE TIMES, July3, 2005, p. E1.

40. Stephen Fidler, "FDI inflow is good for growth," FINANCIAL TIMES, April 11, 2001, p. 15.

41. "From hand to mouth," THE ECONOMIST, October 8, 2005, p. 55; "Tuberculosis killed 1.7 million globally in 2006, WHO says," THE KITSAP DAILY, March 18, 2008, p. 6; "Dengue fever: A deadly scourge," THE ECONOMIST, April 21, 2007, p. 42; Andrew Jack, "WHO forecasts deaths to double," FINANCIAL TIMES, April 25, 2007, p. 22.

42. Clive Cookson, "WHO warns of jump in infectious diseases," FINANCIAL TIMES, May 20, 1996, p. 5; Tom Paulson, "Gates keys project on global health," SEATTLE POST-INTELLIGENCER, October 31, 2005, p. A7; "EU gives [euro] 58 m to fight AIDs, malaria and tuberculosis," NEWS @ EU No. 76, August 5, 2005, p. 6.

43. Tom Paulson, "Gates gives millions for malaria vaccine," SEATTLE POST INTELLIGENCER, October 31, 2005, p. A1; "Gates give PATH $75 million," SEATTLE POST-INTELLIGENCER, April 3, 2006, p. A1; Nicholas Timmins, "World trade liberalization 'damaging to child health'" FINANCIAL TIMES, November 5, 2001, p. 8; "WHO warns of jump in infectious diseases," op. cit.

44. Richard Steiner, "The real clear and present danger," SEATTLE POST-INTELLIGENCER, May 30, 2004, p. F1.

45. "From hand to mouth," op.cit.

46. Paul Drain, "Africa's devastating challenge: HIV/AIDs and extreme poverty," SEATTLE POST-INTELLIGENCER, August 6, 2006, p. D1; "Gates gives millions for malaria vaccine," op. cit.

47. "The real and present danger," op. cit.

48. John Zubrzycki, "Fertility clinics in demand as India's population soars," THE AUSTRALIAN, November 25, 1996, p. 15.

49. James Lamont, "Aids pandemic stunts Southern Africa growth," FINANCIAL TIMES, August 20, 2002, p. 3.

50. "World trade liberalization 'damaging to child health'," op. cit.; "Health crisis plagues rural areas of China," op. cit.; John Saul, "Pillaging Africa: a surreal case study," SEATTLE TIMES, August 6, 2006, p. J10.

51. "Health crisis plagues rural areas of China," op. cit.

52. "WTO members agree on draft text on consistency in food safety measures," 17 ITR 484 (March 23, 2000), p. 1; "Franken food approved," THE ECONOMIST, March 13, 2004, p. 57; "The bubble-and-squeak [Johannesburg] summit," THE ECONOMIST, September 7, 2002, p. 79; Alan Beattie, "Food safety clash gives taste of battles ahead," FINANCIAL TIMES, August 1, 2007, p. 2; Geoff Dyer, "Chinese regulator warns that food safety could threaten social stability," FINANCIAL TIMES, August 10, 2007, p. 1.

53. "Health care: America's headache," THE ECONOMIST, January 28, 2006, p. 12.

54. "U.S. loses ground in latest draft of reform proposal on TRIPs/medicines," 10 ITR 2162 (December 19, 2002); "WTO TRIPs chair restarts talks on breaking TRIPs/medicines deadlock," 20 ITR 162 (January 23, 2003); "Developing countries prepared to use new WTO accord to import cheap medicines," (BNA) WTO REPORTER, September 3, 2003; "WTO members, industry welcome deal incorporating TRIPs/medicine agreement," (BNA) WTO REPORTER, December 7, 2005.

55. *Id.*; "Brazil set to grant compulsory license for AIDs drug," 9 BRIDGES No. 24 (July 6, 2005), p. 7; "Compromise averts compulsory AIDs drug license in Brazil," BRIDGES ICTSD No. 6-7 (June/July 2005) available at: www.ictsd.org, last visited July 20, 2005; "Thailand authorizes generic production of two more patented drugs," 11 BRIDGES No. 3, January 31, 2007, p. 3.

56. Tom Paulson, "Gateses give PATH $75 million," *op.cit.*; "Push and pull," THE ECONOMIST, March 25, 2006, p. 82; "WTO members adopt resolution on pharmaceutical innovation," 11 BRIDGES No. 18, May 23, 2007, p. 3; "Tackling the research gap on neglected diseases," BRIDGES ICTSD No. 7 (November–December, 2007), p. 25.

57. Jeffery Sachs, "Doing the sums on Africa," THE ECONOMIST, May 22, 2004, p. 19; "A glimmer of light at last?" THE ECONOMIST, June 24, 2006, p. 51; "The UN's Millennium Goals: Aspirations and obligations," THE ECONOMIST, September 10, 2005, p. 67; (The original document is "5512/ UN Millennium Declaration," doc. A/RES/55/22, September 18, 2000); Jeffery Sacks, "Weapons of mass salvation," THE ECONOMIST, October 26, 2002, p. 71; "Doubling EU development aid," EUROPA NEWSLETTER (Development Special), August 11, 2005, p. 4; "The bubble-and-squeak summit," *op.cit.* (The "Key Outcomes," are available at: UN, Johannesburg Summit 2002, UN/DESA, September 2002); James Lamont & John Mason, "A long way to go for a little success," FINANCIAL TIMES, September 2, 2002, p. 11.

58. "Doubling EU development aid," *op. cit.*; "EU gives [euro] 58 million to fight AIDs, malaria, and tuberculosis," NEWS @ EU No. 76, August 5, 2005, p. 6; "Eradicating hunger: Europe pledges [euro] 197 m in 2006," NEWS @ EU, June 27, 2006, p. 2; "Text of U.S.-EU Declaration on HIV/AIDs, Malaria, and Tuberculosis" (Dromoland Castle, Shannon, Ireland), White House, Office of the Press Secretary, June 26, 2004; "Global fund to fight AIDs, Tuberculosis and Malaria," EUROPA NEWSLETTER, (Development Special) *op. cit.*, p. 8.

59. "The business of giving" (A survey of wealth and philanthropy), THE ECONOMIST, February 25, 2006; Tom Paulson, "Gates keys projects on global health," *op.cit.*; Carol J. Loomis, "Warren Buffett gives it away," FORTUNE, June

10, 2006, p. 57; "The new powers in giving," THE ECONOMIST, July 1, 2006, p. 63; "Give and make," THE ECONOMIST, June 24, 2006, p. 12.

60. "The side-effects of doing good," THE ECONOMIST, February 23, 2008, p. 77.

61. David Stipp, "The coming war against bird flu," FORTUNE, March 7, 2005, p. 115.

62. "How Dr. Chan intends to defend the planet from pandemics," THE ECONOMIST, June 16, 2007, p. 67; Andrew Jack & Amy Kazmin "WHO seeks 'solidarity stock pile' of flu vaccine," FINANCIAL TIMES, March 23, 2007, p. 4.

63. "A mixed prognosis," THE ECONOMIST, November 29, 2003, p. 77.

64. "Help at last," THE ECONOMIST, November 29, 2003, p. 11; "A saving embrace," THE ECONOMIST, November 22, 2003, p. 40; "Anatomy of an epidemic," THE ECONOMIST, July 30, 2005, p. 36; "Too much morality, too little sense," THE ECONOMIST, July 30, 2005, p. 13.

65. "Compromise averts compulsory AIDS drug license in Brazil," BRIDGES ICTSD No. 6-7, June/July 2005.

66. "Anatomy of an epidemic," THE ECONOMIST, July 30, 2005, p. 36.

67. Found at http://www.globalissues.org/Geopolitics/Africa/AIDS.asp: last visited, April 5, 2005.

68. "Aids: Getting the message," THE ECONOMIST, June 7, 2008, p. 91; "Help at last," op. cit.; "Moving targets," THE ECONOMIST, July 2, 2005, p. 70.

69. "Not half as bad," THE ECONOMIST, July 21, 2007, p. 42; "Who's counting," THE ECONOMIST, November 24, 2007, p. 65.

70. "A mixed prognosis," op. cit.; "Help at last," op. cit.; "AIDs pandemic stunts southern Africa growth," FINANCIAL TIMES, August 20, 2002, p. 3.

71. David Brown, "AIDs conferees broaden strategies to reduce its toll," SEATTLE TIMES, August 20, 2006, p. A12; "Look to the future," THE ECONOMIST, August 19, 2006, p. 11.

72. "On a wing and a scare," THE ECONOMIST, October 22, 2005, p. 14; Warwick McKibbin, "Global macroeconomic consequences of pandemic influenza" (Executive Summary), The Brookings Institution, available at: http:// www.brookings.edu/views/papers/ mckibbin/200602.htm, last visited February 27, 2006.

73. "Sitting Ducks," THE ECONOMIST, April 16, 2005, p. 35; "The Dying Swan," THE ECONOMIST, April 8, 2006, p. 56.

74. "Global health: A shot of transparency," THE ECONOMIST, August 12, 2006, p. 65; "EU bans live birds ... from Turkey," NEWS @ EU, October 13, 2005, p. 3.

75. "A shot of transparency," op. cit.; "The dying swan," op. cit.; Andrew Bounds, "Smugglers boost threat of human flu crisis," FINANCIAL TIMES, April 17, 2006, p. 6; "Sitting Ducks," op. cit.; "Avian flu: Ominous," THE ECONOMIST, February 25, 2005, p. 12.

76. Nicholas Wade, "Studies suggest pandemic isn't imminent," THE NEW YORK TIMES, March23, 2006, p. A 18.

77. "Preparing for a pandemic," THE ECONOMIST, September 24, 2005, p. 95; Elizabeth Rosenthal, "Wealthier nations buy up bird flu drugs," SEATTLE POST-INTELLIGENCER, September 19, 2005, p. A2.

78. "The maladies of affluence," THE ECONOMIST, August 11, 2007, p. 49.

79. David Stipp, "The coming war against bird flu," FORTUNE, March 7, 2005, p. 115; "On a wing and a scare," *op. cit.*; "Preparing for a pandemic," *op. cit.*

80. Aaron Cosbey, Luke Peterson & Laszio Pinter, "Environmental Health and International Trade," International Institute for Sustainable Development, March 31, 2005.

81. "Rescuing environmentalism," THE ECONOMIST, April 23, 2005, p. 11; "The dirty sky," THE ECONOMIST, June 10, 2006, p. 10; BUCKMINSTER FULLER, OPERATING MANUAL FOR SPACESHIP EARTH (Clarion, 1969) pp. 85–95. Since 1990, greenhouse gas emissions have dropped in the European Union, despite economic growth of 32 percent. "Climate change: More effort needed to reduce greenhouse gases," NEWS @ EU, June 29, 2006, p. 3.

82. Progressive Policy Institute, "World marine fish catch: 80 million tons a year" available at: ppi_admin@dlcppi.org, last visited August 23, 2006; "EU calls for action against destructive fishing methods," NEWS @ EU, November 27, 2006, p. 4.

83. A collective action problem is a situation in which everyone in a given group has a choice between two alternatives and where, if everyone chooses the alternative that was best for them individually, the outcome will be worse for everyone than if they were all to choose the other alternative. As this pertains to pollution, ignoring emissions may appear to be the most individually profitable choice for a given factory owner. However, when all factory owners make that same choice, the resulting pollution harms them all more than if they had all chosen to pollute less in the beginning.

84. "Rescuing environmentalism," THE ECONOMIST, April 23, 2005, p. 11; John Lloyd, "Cultivating the world," FINANCIAL TIMES, September 20, 2000, p. 12.

85. Found at http://americas.irc-online.org/am/1409, last visited April 5, 2006.

86. "Millennium ecosystem assessment reveals 'strain' on earth," 9 BRIDGES No. 11, April 6, 2005, p. 7.

87. Richard Steiner, "The real clear and present danger," SEATTLE POST-INTELLIGENCER, May 30, 2004, p. F1.

88. "Rescuing environmentalism," *op. cit.*; "In focus: Energy and the environment," THE BROOKINGS ALERT, June 17, 2005, available at: brookings_alert-

117216@webserv.brookings.edu, last visited June 20, 2005; "Cultivating the world," *op. cit.*

89. "A great wall of waste," The Economist, August 21, 2004, pg. 55; Richard McGregor, "Beijing clouds the pollution picture," Financial Times, August 3, 2007, p. 2.

90. "Green guise," The Economist, March 26, 2005, pg. 42.

91. Progressive Policy Institute, "The world's five smokiest cities: New Delhi, Cairo, Calcutta, Tianjin, Chongqing," available at: ppi_admin@dlcppi.org, last visited August 17, 2006; Sarah Schafer, "China's coal addiction," Newsweek, October 28, 2002, p. 44R; James Harding, "China emerging as bad boy in pollution stakes," Financial Times, December 9, 1997, p. 4; John Vidal, "Climate change and pollution are killing millions, says [World Bank] study," The (UK) Guardian, October 6, 2005, p. 1; "Up to their necks in it," The Economist, July 19, 2008, p. 49.

92. "Environmental health and international trade," *op. cit.*, section 2. 1. 3; "The real and present danger," *op. cit.*

93. "The greening of China," The Economist, October 22, 2005, p. 43; Denis Hayes, "Making China green," Seattle Post-Intelligencer, August 21, 2005, p. D1; "EU and China in landmark climate change partnership," News @ EU No. 81, September 13, 2005, p. 1; "China emerging as bad boy in pollution stakes," *op. cit.*

94. *Id.*; "More hot air," The Economist, January 14, 2006, p. 46; "Carry on Kyoto," The Economist, October 9, 2004 p. 13; Vanessa Houlder, "Climate deal leaves U.S. isolated," Financial Times, July 24, 2001, p. 1; Eugene Linden, "Cloudy with a chance of chaos," Fortune, January 23, 2006 p. 134; "Environmental decay may prompt refugee surge," The Kitsap Daily, October 12, 2005, p. 10.

95. "This is a challenge that requires a 100 percent effort; ours, and the rest of the world's. The world's second-largest emitter of greenhouse gases is China. Yet, China was entirely exempted from the requirements of the Kyoto Protocol. India and Germany are among the top emitters. Yet, India was also exempt from Kyoto.... America's unwillingness to embrace a flawed treaty should not be read by our friends and allies as any abdication of responsibility. To the contrary, my administration is committed to a leadership role on the issue of climate change.... Our approach must be consistent with the long-term goal of stabilizing greenhouse gas concentrations in the atmosphere." Found at http://www.whitehouse.gov/news/releases/2001/06/20010611-2.html; last visited February 9, 2006.

96. "Rescuing environmentalism," The Economist, April 23, 2005, p. 11.

97. "Soot, smoke and mirrors," The Economist, November 18, 2006, p. 54; "The hot air of hypocrisy," The Economist, March 22, 2008, p. 62.

98. "Pricking the global conscience," THE ECONOMIST, December 17, 2005, p. 77; "UN Climate change conference: 'the end of the beginning,'" EUROPA NEWSLETTER No. 71, December 20, 2005, p. 3; "EIB gives [euro] 500 million to support climate change mitigation in China," NEWS @ EU, December 7, 2007, p. 4.

99. "Better than Kyoto," THE ECONOMIST, June 25, 2005, p. 13; "G8 reaches deal on climate change, but without binding targets," 9 BRIDGES No. 25, July 13, 2005, p. 13; "An alternative to Kyoto," THE ECONOMIST, July 30, 2005, p. 39.

100. "Don't despair," THE ECONOMIST, December 10, 2005, p. 11; Brendan Case, "Climate change becomes serious business," SEATTLE TIMES, October 2, 2005, p. I1; "Upset about offsets," THE ECONOMIST, August 5, 2006, p. 53; "Can business be cool?" THE ECONOMIST, June 10, 2006, p. 59.

101. Andres Bounds, "EU seeks binding cap on greenhouse gases," FINANCIAL TIMES, November 28, 2007, p. 2; "Bali Climate Conference: The next two years will tell," 7 BRIDGES ICTSD, November–December, 2007, p. 14; Fiona Harvey & John Aglionby, "Who bears the load?" FINANCIAL TIMES, December 18, 2007, p. 7; "The greening of America," THE ECONOMIST, January 27, 2007, p. 9; Fiona Harvey & Andrew Ward, "Sacrifice the planet or the economy, Rice tell leaders," FINANCIAL TIMES, September 28, 2007, p. 6; "Feeling the heat," THE ECONOMIST, May 14, 2005, p. 66; Francesco Guerrera, "GE 'green' sales soar to $12 bn," FINANCIAL TIMES, May 24, 2007, p. 15. A brief history of the run-up to Bali can be found at: Sharon Begley, "The truth about denial," NEWSWEEK, August 13, 2007, p. 20.

102. David Sandalow, "Climate change: Beyond Bali," available at: http://www.brookings.edu/opinions/2007/1217, last visited December 18, 2007; (Untitled charts), FINANCIAL TIMES, November 28, 2007, p. 2.

103. "Poorest hit hardest by climate change," 11 BRIDGES No. 13, April 18, 2007, p. 10; Martin Wolf, "Why the climate change wolf is so hard to kill off," FINANCIAL TIMES, December 15, 2007, p. 15; "EU ministers tackle economic challenges of climate change," NEWS @ EU, February 14, 2008, p. 2.

104. Fiona Harvey, "UN panel: Urgent call to adapt to climate change," FINANCIAL TIMES, April 7–8, 2007, p. 3; Seth Borenstein, "Last word on climate change is ours, scientists say," SEATTLE TIMES, April 8, 2007, p. A8; Martin Wolf, "In spite of economic skeptics, it is worth reducing climate change risk," FINANCIAL TIMES, February 7, 2007, p. 11; Gideon Rachman, "Climate change is not a global crisis—that is the problem," FINANCIAL TIMES, April 17, 2007, p. 13; Fiona Harvey, "World faces more disease, starvation and mass migration," FINANCIAL TIMES, April 7–8, 2007, p. 3; Fiona Harvey & Gernot Wagner, "13 years to turn round global warming," FINANCIAL TIMES, May 5–6, 2007, p. 3; "They came, they jawed, they failed to conquer," THE ECONOMIST, July 12, 2008, p. 68.

105. For example, Marc Gunther, "The green machine," FORTUNE, August 7, 2006, p. 42; Marc Gunther, "Cops of the global village," FORTUNE, July 27, 2005, p. 158; "Flawed campaign threatens world's poor," FINANCIAL TIMES, November 23, 1999, p. 14; "Regulating chemicals: No thanks, we're European," THE ECONOMIST, November 26, 2005, p. 77.

106. "Warning: 50% surge in energy demand by 2030," SEATTLE POST-IN-TELLIGENCER, November 8, 2005, p. C3; "Under powering [India]," THE ECON-OMIST, September 24, 2005, p. 83; Robert Samuelson, "The dawn of new oil era?" NEWSWEEK, April 4, 2005, p. 37; "Nervous energy," THE ECONOMIST, January 7, 2006,p. 61.

107. "Oil's dark secret," THE ECONOMIST, August 12, 200, p. 55; "Drill-seeking," THE ECONOMIST, July 8, 2006, p. 28; Ed Crooks, "Norway begins drilling in arctic waters to assess oil prospects," FINANCIAL TIMES, November 26, 2007, p. 1; Daniel Yergin, "Questions of oil," in "The World in 2006," THE ECONOMIST, circa December 15, 2005, p. 115.

108. Gideon Rachman, "The world has two energy crises but no real an-swers," FINANCIAL TIMES, August 10 2007, p. 11; Joseph Fitchett, "Achilles heel: An increasingly conspicuous [EU] energy gap," TRANSATLANTIC, May/June, 2006, p. 16; Richard McGregor, "China set to miss target for energy efficiency," FINANCIAL TIMES, February 17–18, 2007, p. 3; Fiona Harvey, "Study finds profit in cutting emissions," FINANCIAL TIMES, February 14, 208, p. 4.

109. Brad Foss, "Nations rich in energy assert power," SEATTLE POST-IN-TELLIGENCER, May 3, 2006, p. A 10; Carola Hoyos, "Will the lights go out?" FINANCIAL TIMES (Energy: Special Report), May 30, 2006, p. 1; "Nervous en-ergy," op. cit.; "Questions of oil," op. cit.; Progressive Policy Institute, "Energy: Now 18 cents of each dollar of U.S. imports," available at: ppi_admin.main.dlc@ppionline.org, last visited January 16, 2008.

110. "Nations rich in energy assert power," op. cit.; "Will the lights go out?" op. cit.

111. BUCKMINSTER FULLER, OPERATING MANUAL FOR SPACESHIP EARTH, op. cit., pp. 123–125.

112. "Can business be cool?" op. cit.; "Don't despair," op. cit.; Casper Hen-derson, "Natural step to sustainability," FINANCIAL TIMES, January 7, 1998, p. 12.

113. Robert Bassman, "Living with high energy prices," TRANSATLANTIC, January/February 2006, p. 20; see generally, "Technology Quarterly," in THE ECONOMIST, June 10, 2006, particularly pp. 11–12, 18–20 and 30–32; Geof-frey Colvin, "Nuclear is back—not a moment too soon," FORTUNE, May 30, 2005, p. 57; Andrew Bounds, "EU set to agree tough climate targets," FINANCIAL TIMES, March 9, 2007, p. 2; Fareed Zakaria, "A cure for oil addicts and "Its not

star wars," both in NEWSWEEK, August 6, 2007, p. 34 and October 1, 2007, p. 40, respectively; "The future of energy," THE ECONOMIST, June 12, 2008, p. 17.

114. Available at: http://www.globalexchange.org/campaigns/cafta/Agriculture.html.

115. See, for example, "How green was my valley," THE ECONOMIST, April 29, 2006, p. 39; "From hand to mouth," THE ECONOMIST, October 8, 2005, p. 55; "The real clear and present danger," *op. cit.*; Kim Barker, "Opium production 'staggering' [in Afghanistan]," THE SEATTLE TIMES, September 3, 2006, p. A10.

116. Clive Cookson, "In deep water," FINANCIAL TIMES, July 28–29, 2001, p. 7; "World marine fish catch: 80 million tons a year," *op. cit.*; "Turtle wars," in "Where next?" (A survey of World Trade), THE ECONOMIST, October 3, 1998, p. 22; "The real and present danger," *op. cit.*

117. Elizabeth Grossman, "Mountain of high-tech trash presents a world of problems," SEATTLE POST-INTELLIGENCER, August 20, 2006, p. D1; Fiona Harvey, "Reduction should be the target" and Ross Tieman, "Europe leads as rubbish is recycled into global business," both in "Special Report: Waste & the environment', FINANCIAL TIMES, April 18, 2007, pp. 2 and 3, respectively.

118. "Rescuing environmentalism," *op. cit.*; "EU trade-environment proposal receives cool reception at WTO," 10 ITR 533 (March 28, 2002), p. 34.

119. Robert Mignin & Steven Miller, "Developing Global Employment Policies and Procedures," in DENNIS CAMPBELL & OTHERS (eds.), INTERNATIONAL EMPLOYMENT LAW (Transnational Publishers, 1999), p. 67; Jeffery Sachs, "Weapons of mass salvation," THE ECONOMIST, October 26, 2002, p. 71; "Economic focus: A modest undertaking," THE ECONOMIST, March 6, 2004, p. 68; "U.S. signs free-trade pact with Jordan that includes labor, environment rules"; "IP standards in the U.S.-Peru FTA: Health and environment," 10 BRIDGES ICTSD No. 1, January–February, 2006, p. 17; John Browne & Nick Butler, "We had an International Carbon Fund," FINANCIAL TIMES, May 16, 2007, p. 11; Progressive Policy Institute, "The Antarctic ozone hole is no longer growing," available at: ppi_admin@dlcppi.org, last visited April 25, 2007.

Chapter IX

1. Matthew Green, "Nigeria ministers sacked in graft probe," FINANCIAL TIMES, March 27, 2008, p. 6; "Corruption and the law: Barefaced," THE ECONOMIST, December 23, 2006, p. 18.

2. "Judge or be judged," THE ECONOMIST, July 29, 2006, p. 68; "Congo: The results came with a bang," THE ECONOMIST, August 26, 2006, p. 39; "Legal reform and development: The law poor," THE ECONOMIST, June 7, 2008, p. 87.

3. "Water, sanitation and poverty: Clean water is a right," THE ECONOMIST, November 11, 2006, p. 67.

4. The United Nations estimates that 40 percent of African nations' financial portfolios are invested abroad. "Special Report: Aid to Africa: The $25 billion question." THE ECONOMIST, July 2, 2005, p. 25.

5. Federico Bonaglia & Kiichiro Fukasaku, "Export diversification in low-income countries: An international challenge after Doha" (Technical Paper No. 209) DEV/DOC (2003)07, OECD Development Center (Paris) 2003, p. 21; See also UNDP. 2005 HUMAN DEVELOPMENT REPORT, March 26, 2006 (New York), pp. 129–33, available at: http://hdr.undp.org/reports/global/2005. Progressive Policy Institute, "America's farm policies and their effects on international trade," and "Two-thirds of American farmers receive no subsidies," both available at: ppi_admin@dlcppi.org, last visited July 25, 2007. World farm subsidies for OECD countries amounted to $272 billion in 2005; including $130 billion for the European Union, $50 billion for Japan, and $40 billion for the U.S. "World Bank makes farming priority in drive on poverty," FINANCIAL TIMES, October 20–21, 2007, p. 2.

6. Progressive Policy Institute, "Unemployment rates are higher in the Middle East," available at: ppi_admin@dlcppi.org, last visited September 11, 2006.

7. USAID, "Foreign aid in the national interest: Promoting freedom, security, and opportunity," Washington, D.C., 2002: 4.

8. World Trade Organization, "Ministerial Conference, Fourth Session, Doha, 9–14 November 2001, document WT/MIN(01)/DEC/W/1 (14 November 2001), Point 13.

9. "Irresistible attraction," THE ECONOMIST, in "A survey of migration," November 2, 2002, p. 5.

10. "UNCTAD governing body highlights need for [developing countries] 'policy space'," 10 BRIDGES No. 34, October 18, 2006, p. 4; "The European Consensus on Development" (Joint Statement by the Council and the Representatives of the Governments of the Member States meeting within the Council, the European Parliament and the Commission), Brussels, December 20, 2005, p. 3.

11. Independent Evaluation Group (IEG), "Improving the World Bank's Development Effectiveness: What Does Evaluation Show?" World Bank (Washington, D.C.) March 26, 2006.

12. According to the USAID, $33.6 billion in private international assistance went to developing countries in 2000, more than one-half of it in individual remittances. The public share (40%) consisted of ODA $9.9 billion and all other U.S. government aid of $12.7 billion. USAID, FOREIGN AID IN THE NATIONAL INTEREST, "Chapter 6: The Full Measure of Foreign Aid," Table 6.1, P. 131 (Washington, D.C., 2002).

13. For example, "The Kashmir earthquake: A double tragedy," THE ECON-OMIST, October 15, 2005, p. 12; "World mobilizes to aid US victims," BBC News, 2 September 2005; 26 March 2006, available at: http://news.bbc.co.uk/1/hi/world/americas/4210264.stm.

14. OCED, DAC MEMBERS; NET OFFICIAL DEVELOPMENT ASSISTANCE IN 2004, "Table 1. Statistical Annex of the 2005 Development Co-Operation Report, March 26, 2006.

15. "Special Report: Aid to Africa," *op. cit.*

16. "Foreign aid in the national interest," *op. cit.*, chart 6.3, p. 134; "EU determined to play key role in achieving MDG's," EUROPA NEWSLETTER (Development Special), August 11, 2005, p. 2.

17. "EU agrees on funding for development cooperation," NEWS @ EU, October 31, 2006, p. 2; "ACP, UK anxious about EU demands in EPA talks," 10 BRIDGES No. 34, October 18, 2006, p. 1; "Doubling EU development aid," EUROPA NEWSLETTER (Development Special), *op. cit.*, p. 4; Erik Reinert, "Balancing aid and development to prevent 'welfare colonialism'," available at: http://www.paecon.net/PAEReview/issue30/Reinert30.htm, last visited October 2, 2005.

18. Lael Brainard, "Transforming foreign aid for the 21st Century," The Brookings Institution, available at: http://www.brookings.edu/comm/events/20060522. htm, last visited June 29, 2006.

19. See generally, "Report of the National Advisory Commission on Civil Disorders" ("Kerner Commission Report"), Washington, D.C.: GPO, 1968.

20. "China, beware," THE ECONOMIST, October 13, 2007, p. 15; "China's growing pains," THE ECONOMIST, August 21, 2004, p. 11; Paul Krugman, "Challenging Conventional Wisdom," in POP INTERNATIONAL (MIT Press, 1996), pp. 143–144.

21. United Nations General Assembly, "55/2. United Nations Millennium Declaration," Document A/RES/55/2 (September 18, 2000), especially point 19. Despite some "unprecedented progress" (chiefly in Asia) and some "unacceptable delays" (in sub-Saharan Africa) it is unlikely that the UN will meet these goals. "United Nations Summit: World gathering in New York in September," EUROPA NEWSLETTER No. 64, September 8, 2005, p. 9. A more modest (and more affordable) proposal by a Danish think tank might be more realistic. "Economic focus: A modest undertaking," THE ECONOMIST, March 6, 2004, p. 68; Gary Poole, "$50 billion Question: World, where to begin?" THE NEW YORK TIMES, June 5, 2004, p. A15.

22. Information available on Europa World, at: http://www.europaworld.com/entry/10_un_ibrd and .2208, respectively, last visited November 6, 2006.

23. "Developing nicely," THE ECONOMIST, October 21, 2006, p. 85.

24. "Kirchner and Lula: Different ways to give the Fund the kiss off" and "Nestor unbound," both in THE ECONOMIST, December 24, 2005, pp. 49 and 14, respectively; "The Chavez play," THE ECONOMIST, October 28, 2006, p. 86.

25. "No easy answers on effect of freer capital-IMF paper," THE KITSAP DAILY, August 22, 2006, p. 5; "Monetary misquotations," THE ECONOMIST, August 26, 2006, p. 56; "Monetary fund approves reforms," SEATTLE POST-IN-TELLIGENCER, September 19, 2006, p. C6; International Monetary Fund, "IMF Board of Governors approves quota and related governance reforms," Press release No. 061205 (September 18, 2006); "Corruption: Wolfowitz's new war," THE ECONOMIST, March 4, 2006, p. 12.

26. Abraham Lustgarten, "China's stock boom," FORTUNE, October 2, 2006, p. 159.

27. "Bad loans made good," THE ECONOMIST, October 1, 2005, p. 70; Andrew Balls & Chris Giles, "Doubters assent to details of debt plan," FINANCIAL TIMES, September 26, 2005, p. 10; Joanna Chung, "Shackles severed—how the developing world is striving to free itself of debt," FINANCIAL TIMES, February 9, 2007, p. 9.

28. "UNCTAD unveils 2006 World Investment Report," 10 BRIDGES No. 34, October 18, 2006, p. 6; Progressive Policy Institute, "Three-Quarters of foreign direct investment in China is Asian," available at: ppi_admin@dlcppi.org, last visited April 17, 2006.

29. "[U.S.] Senate approves Africa/CBI trade bill," (BNA) 5/12/2000 BTD d5 (May 12, 2000); "G8 leaders agree on [euro] 41.9 billion package for Africa," EUROPA NEWSLETTER No. 61, July 14, 2005, p. 2; "New UNCTAD report backs calls for a 'Marshall Plan' for Africa," 10 BRIDGES No. 32, October 4, 2006, p. 8; Joanna Chung, "Investors dive into the heart of Africa's markets," FINANCIAL TIMES, November 19, 2007, p. 19; "Southern Africa to push for greater economic integration," 10 BRIDGES No. 35, October 25, 2006, p. 7; "Africans tired of being seen as the world's beggars," THE KITSAP DAILY, October 31, 2006, p. 4.

30. "Special Report: Aid to Africa: The $25 billion question," THE ECONO-MIST, July 2, 2005, p. 25; "Development aid spending fell in 2006," 11 BRIDGES No. 12, April 4, 2007, p. 5; Homi Kharas, "Short term fixes for development assistance," available at: http://www.brookings.edu/opinions/2008/0410, last visited April 21, 2008; "Promises, promises," THE ECONOMIST, July 12, 2008, p. 86; Hugh Williamson, "African affront as the 'rich club' leaves aid pledges unmet," FINANCIAL TIMES, October 15, 2007, p. 7.

31. See generally, OECD, "The Paris Declaration [on Aid Effectiveness]" (March 2, 2005), available at: http://www.oecd.org/documentprint, last visited October 23, 2006; "Development aid-delivering more, better, faster" (com-

menting on the The European Consensus on Development, *op. cit.*), Europa Newsletter No. 76, March 9, 2006, p. 4; IMF, Steven Radelet & others, "Aid and Growth," 42 Finance & Development No. 3 (September 2005); "Foreign aid: The non-aligned movement," The Economist, April 7, 2007.

32. USAID, "Foreign Aid in the National Interest," *op. cit.*, table 6.1, p. 131.

33. "Since the mid-1990s, FDI has become the largest component of external financing to developing countries." This investment "plays a significant role in the economic growth of the host country when accompanied by sound domestic policies and greater openness." World Bank, Global Development Finance 2000, Vol. 1: "Analysis and Summary Tables" (Washington, D.C. 2000) p. 42.

34. China has been making significant investments in Africa's oil resources, which has resulted in capital to build national infrastructure: "[r]ailways in Angola, roads in Rwanda, a port in Gabon and a dam in Sudan." Declan Walsh, "Sudan at the head of global sweep to mop up world's oil resources." Guardian Unlimited, November 9, 2005, available at: http://www.guardian.co.uk/china/story/0,,1637389,00.html, last visited April 2, 2006; Chinese companies also have recently acquired a number of foreign enterprises, including IBM's personal computer division, partly for their brand appeal, but also for their engineering expertise, "a ready-made distribution channel," and "to get their hands on the most modern internal processes, systems and strategic thinking." "Special report: Chinese companies abroad—The dragon tucks in," The Economist, July 2, 2005, pp. 34–5; "Building BRICs of growth," The Economist, June 7, 2008, p. 88.

35. Stephen Fidler, "FDI inflow 'is good for growth.'" Financial Times, April 11, 2001, p. 15.

36. "Middle-age spread," The Economist, December 17, 2005, p. 76.

37. "Emerging economies: Climbing back." The Economist, January 21, 2006, p. 69; World Bank, World Development Report 2005: A Better Investment Climate For Everyone (New York, Oxford University Press 2004), p. 5; "Special report/Business in Africa: The flicker of a brighter future," The Economist, September 9, 2006, p. 60.

38. Accordingly, "the central trend in American foreign direct investment has been a comparative increase in U.S. investment in Europe and a relative decline in investment in Latin America." Edward Gresser, "Race to the … Top?" Progressive Policy Institute, March, 2000, pp. 5–7; "Globalization with a third-world face." The Economist, April 9, 2005, p. 66.

39. In 2003, India reported only $4.7 billion in FDI, less than a tenth of what China attracted in 2002. "A survey of India: The flip side," The Economist, February 21, 2004, p. 16; "Wal-Mart still waits," The Economist, July 16, 2005, p. 39.

40. For example, the Chinese government estimates that a quarter of China's gold deposits could not be developed without foreign technologies. "China's gold rush: cracking the vault." THE ECONOMIST, October 15, 2005, p. 67; "Chinese companies: Over the Great Wall." THE ECONOMIST, November 5, 2005, p. 71.

41. "Doing business in China: Fools rush in." THE ECONOMIST, August 7, 2004, p. 50; Progressive Policy Institute, "Three-quarters of foreign direct investment in China is Asian," *op.cit.*

42. "The business of giving" (A survey of wealth and philanthropy), THE ECONOMIST, February 25, 2006, pp. 1–11; "The new powers in giving," THE ECONOMIST, July 1, 2006, p. 63; Bethany McLean, "The power of philanthropy," FORTUNE, September 18, 2006, p. 82; Tom Paulson, "Gates keys projects on global health," SEATTLE POST-INTELLIGENCER, October 31, 2005, p. A7.

43. William Kole, "Migrants send billions home," SEATTLE TIMES, August 19, 2007, p. A18; Progressive Policy Institute, "A quarter of Haitian GDP comes from remittances," available at: ppi_admin@dlcppi.org, last visited October 31, 2006; "Open up" in "A special report on migration," THE ECONOMIST, January 5, 2008, p. 3; Andrew Taylor, "OCED states host 75m migrants," FINANCIAL TIMES, February 21, 2008, p. 2; Mark Stevenson, "Mexicans working in U.S. sending less money home," SEATTLE POST-INTELLIGENCER, July 31, 2008, p. A8.

44. "Trade's bounty," THE ECONOMIST, December 4, 2004, p. 80.

45. Most of the external finance that middle income countries receive from OECD countries comes from trade, "which is followed by foreign direct investment, other private flows and remittances all ahead of ODA." OECD, "DAC DEVELOPMENT CO-OPERATION REPORT 2005: STATISTICAL ANALYSIS," Graph A.1.3, March 26, 2006, available at: http://thesius.sourceoecd.org/vl=4211586/cl=11/nw=1/rpsv/dac/a01.htm; U.S. Department of Agriculture, "Average applied agricultural tariffs for selected countries and years," Economic Research Service, Washington, DC, December, 2002, available at: http://www.ers.usda.gov/db/Wto/WtoTariff_database/StandardReports/tariffT5.xls, last visited March 26, 2006. "Agricultural Trade: Reaping a Rich Harvest from Doha," 41 FINANCE & DEVELOPMENT No. 4 (Dec. 2004) p. 34. For example, the average agricultural tariff bindings in Sub-Saharan Africa is 75 percent, while in South Asia it is 113 percent. U.S. Department of Agriculture, "Mean and median WTO bound tariffs, by region and commodity group." U.S. Department of Agriculture, Economic Research Service, Washington, DC, December 2002, available at: http://www.ers.usda.gov/db/Wto/WtoTariff_database/StandardReports/tariffT2.xls, last visited March 26, 2006.

46. "How the world has (and hasn't) changed," THE ECONOMIST, October 27, 2001, p. 11; Martin Wolf, "How trade can help the world," FINANCIAL TIMES, October 3, 2001, p. 15; David Dollar & Aart Kraay, "Growth is Good

for the Poor" (The World Bank, 2001) available at: www.worldbank.org/research/growth; Progressive Policy Institute, "Pakistan's exports have doubled since 2001" and "Life expectancy in Botswana has fallen 29 years since 1990)," both available at: ppi_admin@dlcppi.org, last visited July 13, 2006 and September 11, 2006, respectively.

47. Jane Drake-Brockman, "New WTO Round launched at Doha," 5 APEC ECONOMIES NEWSLETTER No. 12 (December 12, 2001), available at: http://apsem.anu.edu.au; "Analysts see precedent for delay in WTO talks, shift in balance of power [after Cancun]," 20 ITR 1538 (September 18, 2003); "WTO Ag Chair's new text: Gradual progress on market access, 'headline numbers' unchanged," 12 BRIDGES No. 5, February 13, 2008, p. 1.

48. Kym Anderson & Will Martin, "Agricultural Trade Reform and the Doha Development Agenda," World Bank, 2006 (Washington, D.C.) pp. 348, 385; Under current commitments, the U.S. is allowed to "spend up to $19.1 billion on farm-production subsidies, which heavily distort trade," "The EU can spend over $75 billion." "The Doha trade round: A stopped clock ticks again." THE ECONOMIST, October 15, 2005, p. 76.

49. WTO, "A Summary of the Final Act of the Uruguay Round," available at: http://www.wto.org/english/docs_e/legal_e/ursum_e.htm#aAgreement, last visited March 26, 2006.

50. A study found that the gains from liberalizing trade in agriculture would "virtually disappear" with just two percent of agricultural tariff lines in developed countries (and four percent in developing countries) being classified as sensitive or special. Christopher Neal, "Tariff reform could deliver annual global gains of $300 billion by 2015, says World Bank study." World Bank (Press Release No: 2006/147/DEC) November 9, 2005.

51. "Agricultural Trade Reform and the Doha Development Agenda," *op. cit.*

52. Brian Reidl, "Another year at the federal trough: Farm subsidies for the rich, famous, and elected jumped again in 2002," The Heritage Foundation (Backgrounder No. 1763) March 26, 2006; "Agriculture trade: Patches of light." THE ECONOMIST, June 7, 2001, p. 69; "Japan's farmers: Facing the scythe?" THE ECONOMIST, May 28, 2005, p. 46.

53. "Growth Is Good for the Poor," *op.cit.*, citing 149 episodes in which per capita GDP grew by at least 2 percent, and noting that poor persons' income increased in 131 of those episodes, p. 5; Agriculture employs 68 percent of the work force in low-income countries and one-quarter in middle-income countries. Melinda Ingco & John Nash, "Agriculture and the WTO: Creating a trading system for development," World Bank, 2004 (Washington, D.C.) p. 2.

54. WTO, "Non-trade concerns: agriculture can serve many purposes," available at: http://www.wto.org/english/tratop_e/agric_e/negs_bkgrnd

17_agri_e.htm, last visited March 26, 2006. For the countries of West and Central Africa, U.S. cotton subsidies have resulted in a revenue loss of nearly US$250 million annually. "Agriculture and the WTO: Creating a trading system for development," *op. cit.*, p. 9; Fareed Zakaria, "Realism and responsibility," NEWSWEEK, June 20, 2005, p. 42.

55. "DSU roundup: US cotton; China auto parts; US shrimp ad duties," 10 BRIDGES No. 30, September 20, 2006, p. 7.

56. For example, the United States insistence that shrimp imported into the country be caught with nets with sea turtle excluders. Nets that Asian shrimpers say are too expensive for them to afford. "WTO members question dispute body on good faith finding in shrimp turtle case," 18 ITR 1896 (November 29, 2001).

57. Progressive Policy Institute, "America's tariffs hit Cambodia and Bangladesh hardest," available at: ppi_admin@dlcppi.org, last visited February 22, 2007; "Review of EU trade policy reveals 'substantial' barriers to imports remains," 11 BRIDGES No. 8, March 7, 2007, p. 3; Alan Beattie, "EU has a mixed record over trade and aid," FINANCIAL TIMES, March 27, 2007, p. 5.

58. "WTO mini-ministerial ends in collapse," BRIDGES DAILY UPDATE No. 10, July 30, 2008, p. 1.

59. "Doha doldrums: Others should act," 10 BRIDGES ICTSD No. 6, September/October 2006, p. 1, available at: www.ictsd.org; "With round in disarray, Mandelson proposes carving out 'development package'," 10 BRIDGES No. 27, July 26, 2006, p. 6.

60. "[General Council]: Members endorse recommendations on aid for trade," 10 BRIDGES No. 33, October 11, 2006, p. 3; "Aid for Trade endorsed at World Bank and IMF meetings," 10 BRIDGES ICTDS No. 6, September/October 2006, p. 9, available at: www.ictsd.org, last visited November 14, 2006.

61. "Farm subsidies: Uncle Sam's hat," THE ECONOMIST, September 9, 2006, p. 35; "The EU makes market access for developing countries both simpler and fairer," EUROPA NEWSLETTER, August 11, 2005, p. 7; "Trade and Africa: Emerging deals," THE ECONOMIST, February 21, 2004, p. 73; "CAFTA-DR narrowly wins House vote, signed into law," 9 BRIDGES No. 28, August 3, 2005, p. 3; "Peru: Free traders," THE ECONOMIST, July 1, 2006, p. 34.

62. "India, Brazil, South Africa strengthen south-south cooperation," 8 BRIDGES No. 9, March 11, 2004, p. 5; "UNCTAD governing body highlights need for 'policy space'," *op.cit.*

63. For example, the EU's "everything but arms" program for the 48 poorest nations; or its ACP program for 77 former colonies. "[European] Commission proposes duty-free access for imports from 48 poorest nations," 17

ITR 1480, (September 28, 2000); "Falling out of favor," THE ECONOMIST, May 28, 2005, p. 78. Or the U.S. African Growth and Opportunity Act. "President says 35 African countries eligible for trade benefits under AGOA," 19 ITR 72 (January 10, 2002). "Talking the talk," THE ECONOMIST, July 17, 2004, p. 14.

64. "Chinese textile exports surge; US, EU to invoke textile safeguard," 9 BRIDGES No. 11, April 6, 2005, p. 1.

65. Progressive Policy Institute, "US, EU, Canada join forces to challenge China on auto parts," 10 BRIDGES No. 30, September 20, 2006, p. 6; "Trade disputes have become rarer," August 9, 2006, available at: ppi_admin@dlcppi.org, last visited September 11, 2006.

66. "Vietnam: Changing gear," THE ECONOMIST, November 26, 2005, p. 49; "Vietnam is the WTO's 150th member," available at: ppi_admin@dlcppi.org, last visited, November 10, 2006.

67. "Uruguay to challenge U.S. rice subsidies," 9 BRIDGES No. 28, August 3, 2005, p. 14; US anti-dumping duties on shrimp face new challenge [from India]," 10 BRIDGES No. 40, November 29, 2006, p. 9.

68. "Trade facilitation talks continuing despite impasse elsewhere," 10 BRIDGES No. 26, July 20, 2006, p. 6; "Trade facilitation talks focus on co-operation and technical assistance," 9 BRIDGES No. 28, August 3, 2005, p. 11.

69. "Ready for warfare in the aisles" and "China: Something new [government R & D]," both in THE ECONOMIST, August 5, 2006, pp. 59 and 38, respectively; "India: The next wave," THE ECONOMIST, December 17, 2005, p. 57; "India's acquisition spree: Circle the wagons," THE ECONOMIST, October 14, 2006, p. 69; "In search of elusive domestic demand," THE ECONOMIST, October 15, 2005, p. 44; East, west and the gap between," THE ECONOMIST, November 26, 2005, p. 63.

70. "The tiger in front" and "The flipside," both in THE ECONOMIST (A survey of India and China), March 5, 2005, pp. 3 and 16, respectively; "Change, please [Mexico]," THE ECONOMIST, July 1, 2006, p. 10; "Who leads Latin America?" THE ECONOMIST, September 30, 2006, p. 11; "Not always with us," THE ECONOMIST, September 17, 2005, p. 13; "Africa's economy: A glimmer of light at last?" THE ECONOMIST, June 24, 2006, p. 51.

71. "Opening the door" and "the longest journey," both in THE ECONOMIST, November 2, 2002, p. 11 and (A survey of migration) p. 3, respectively; Judy Dempsey, "Polish workers exodus creates labor shortage," SEATTLE TIMES, November 9, 2006, p. A 26; "The brain-drain cycle," THE ECONOMIST, December 10, 2005, p. 57. See generally, "Open up" (A special report on migration), THE ECONOMIST, January 5, 2008.

72. "The EU makes market access for developing countries both simpler and fairer" and "Focus on Africa," both in EUROPA NEWSLETTER (Development

Special), August 11, 2005, p. 4; William Wallis, 'China's pledge of $20bn for Africa will eclipse other donors," FINANCIAL TIMES, May 18, 2007, p. 1; "A glimmer of light at last?" THE ECONOMIST, June 24, 2006, p. 51; Progressive Policy Institute, "Africa's trade has nearly tripled since 2002," available at: ppi_admin.main.dlc@ppionline.org, last visited February 6, 2008.

73. "Not always with us" and "New thinking about an old problem," both in THE ECONOMIST, September 17, 2005, pp. 13 and 36, respectively; "Dreaming of glory" (A special report on Brazil), THE ECONOMIST, April 14, 2007.

74. "The EU and food aid: The case of Mali and Niger," EUROPA NEWSLETTER (Development Special) *op. cit.*, p. 6; Progressive Policy Institute, "A tenth of Haitian GDP comes from garment exports," available at: ppi_admin@dlcppi.org, last visited December 8, 2006.

75. "Brazil to grant duty-and quota-free market access to LDC exports," 10 BRIDGES No. 41, December 6, 2006, p. 3; "China vows to ramp up aid, investment, trade with Africa," 10 BRIDGES No. 37, November 8, 2006, p. 1.

76. David Kirkpatrick, "I'd like to teach the world to type," FORTUNE, November 28, 2005, p. 63; "Food for thought," THE ECONOMIST, July 31, 2004, p. 67; "Ladders out of poverty," THE ECONOMIST (A survey of South Africa), April 8, 2006, p. 9; "Fruit that falls far from the tree," THE ECONOMIST, November 5, 2005, p. 86.

77. "Thinking for themselves," THE ECONOMIST (A survey of patents and technology), October 22, 2005, p. 14; Steven Levy, "Shanghai starts up," NEWSWEEK, June 12, 2006, p. 61; Thomas Friedman, "Chinese inventors dream of Ferraris," SEATTLE POST-INTELLIGENCER, November 6, 2005, p. D4; Geoffrey Colvin, "From knock off bags to knockout brands," FORTUNE, June 27, 2005, p. 52.

78. "Emerging-market indicators: competitiveness," THE ECONOMIST, September 30, 2006, p. 110.

79. THE ECONOMIST, "Pocket World in Figures" (2006 ed.), p. 61.

80. Rik Kirkland, "Will the U.S. be flattened by a flatter world?" FORTUNE, June 27, 2005, p. 47.

81. Trineesh Biswas, "LDC rising: The growth of technical capacity," 7 BRIDGES TRADE NEGOTIATION INSIGHTS ICTSD, No. 3 (April 2008), p. 11.

82. "U.N. agency warns that e-commerce could widen countries' development gap," 18 ITR 1900 (November 29, 2001); David Kirkpatrick, "Tech into plowshares," FORTUNE, October 15, 2001, p. 211; "G-8 seeks to spread use of computers, internet as part of developing country focus," 17 ITR 1152 (July 27, 2000); The DOT Force plan (May 11, 2001) is available at: www.dotforce.org/reports; "WSIS meeting changes little on internet governance or digital divide funding," 9 BRIDGES No. 40, November 23, 2005, p. 13; "Getting bet-

ter all the time," THE ECONOMIST (A survey of technology and development), November 21, 2001, p. 3.

83. "Shadows at Europe's heart," THE ECONOMIST, October 14, 2006, p. 56; "World made no headway to halve number of hungry—UN," THE KITSAP DAILY, October 31, 2006, p. 10.

84. "UNCTAD governing body highlights need for 'policy space'," *op. cit.*; "DSU roundup: US cotton, China auto parts; US shrimp [anti-dumping] duties," *op. cit.*

85. "The next green revolution," THE ECONOMIST, February 23, 2008, p. 81; Salamander Davoudi, "GM crop use to double by 2015, study finds," FINANCIAL TIMES, February 13, 2008, p. 3; "Microfinance: Time to take the credit," THE ECONOMIST, March 17, 2007, p. 16.

86. "[South Africa] going global," THE ECONOMIST, July 15, 2006, p. 59; "Not yet, say the Arabs," THE ECONOMIST, July 22, 2006, p. 79; "Africa's economy: A glimmer of light at last?" THE ECONOMIST, June 24, 2006, p. 51.

87. See generally, CLYDE PRESTOWITZ, THREE BILLION NEW CAPITALISTS (Basic Books, 2005); "Recalculating China's GDP: Clipping the dragon's wings," THE ECONOMIST, December 22, 2007, p. 68.

88. Richard Steiner, "The real clear and present danger," SEATTLE POST-INTELLIGENCER, *op.cit.*

89. Henrik Rasmussen, "Free trade fights global poverty," SEATTLE POST-INTELLIGENCER, November 22, 2006, p. B7; David Dollar & Aart Kraay, "Growth Is Good for the Poor" (World Bank, Development Research Group) March 2001, p. 2; "Good morning at last," THE ECONOMIST, August 5, 2006, p. 37; "Africa trade has nearly tripled since 2002," *op.cit.*

90. "East African countries vow to create customs union," 15 ITR 292 (February 18, 1998); "Africans tried of being seen as the world's beggars," *op. cit.*; "Keep chasing," THE ECONOMIST (A survey of South Africa), April 8, 2006, p. 12; "Bigger spenders," THE ECONOMIST, July 1, 2006, p. 36; "Economic growth: Why the rich must get richer," THE ECONOMIST, November 12, 2005, p. 87.

91. "In the twilight of Doha," THE ECONOMIST, July 29, 2006, p. 63.

92. "Latin America: The return to populism," THE ECONOMIST, April 15, 2006, p. 39.

93. "Emerging market multinationals: Wind of change," THE ECONOMIST, January 12, 2008, p. 12; Progressive Policy Institute, "Indonesia marks 10 years of political reform this year," available at: ppi_admin.main.dlc@ppionline.org, last visited March 13, 2008; Progressive Policy Institute, "Ghana has cut malnutrition rates by 75 percent since 1992," available at: http://www.ppionline.org, last visited July 24, 2007.

94. "Moscow's boom: Building a new Rome," THE ECONOMIST, August 26, 2006, p. 44; "Technology in China: The allure of low technology," THE ECONOMIST, December 20, 2003, p. 99; Brad Foss, "Nations rich in energy assert power," SEATTLE POST-INTELLIGENCER, May 3, 2006, p. A10; "New friendships and petropuzzles," THE ECONOMIST, January 20, 2006, p. 70; "Don't mess with Russia," THE ECONOMIST, December 16, 2006, p. 11.

95. "Least-developed countries seek seat at WTO table," 2 BRIDGES ICTSD No. 2 (March 2008), p. 3.

96. "Opening the door," THE ECONOMIST, November 2, 2002, p. 11; "Managing immigration: Ministers stress the need for solidarity and common rules," EUROPA NEWSLETTER No. 89, September 29, 2006, p. 2.

97. Progressive Policy Institute, "WTO members account for 96 percent of trade," available at: ppi_admin@dlcppi.org, last visited April 17, 2006; "Vietnam looks set to join WTO," 10 BRIDGES No. 34, October 18, 2006, p. 6.

98. "Cuba: Big brother's shadow," THE ECONOMIST, August 2, 2008, p. 42.

99. Progressive Policy Institute, "World exports reached $12.5 trillion in 2005," available at: admin@newsmail.dlc.org, last visited November 28, 2006.

100. John Authers, "We must learn how to learn from emerging markets," FINANCIAL TIMES, March 1–2, 2008, p. 12; "The new face of hunger," THE ECONOMIST, April 19, 2008, p. 32.

Chapter X

1. Progressive Policy Institute, "The world has become more peaceful," December 21, 2005, available at: http://www.ppionline.org, last visited January 5, 2007; Charles J. Hanley, "Number of wars in world drops to new low," SEATTLE POST-INTELLIGENCER, June 29, 2006, p.A7; "Somewhere over the rainbow," THE ECONOMIST, January 26, 2008, p. 27

2. Jonathan Wheathy, "Brazil enjoys the real benefits of stability," FINANCIAL TIMES, September 24, 2007, p. 5; Joanna Chung, "Sub-Saharan Africa confident it can attract investment," FINANCIAL TIMES, May 2, 2007, p. 27; Progressive Policy Institute, "Indonesia marks 10 years of political reform," available at: ppi_admin.main.dlc@ppionline.org, last visited March 13, 2008.

3. "Afghanistan: The illusion of empire lite," THE ECONOMIST, June 24, 2006, p. 13.

4. "South Africa: Fear factor," THE ECONOMIST, August 5, 2006, p. 43; Jonathan Katzenellenbogen, "Crime and red tape deter Chinese capital," BUSINESS DAY, November 2, 2006, p. 5.

5. Marilyn Geewax, "South Africa's economy thrives despite shadow of AIDS," HOUSTON CHRONICLE, October 28, 2006, p. 7.

6. Mohammed Ayoob, "Defining Security: A Subaltern Realist Perspective," CRITICAL SECURITY STUDIES: CONCEPTS AND CASES (Michael C.Williams & Keith Krause, eds., London, 2003), p. 126; Fareed Zakaria, "The limits of democracy," NEWSWEEK, January 29, 2007, p. 35.

7. "Apocalypse, maybe: Taiwan may be a time bomb, but one on a very long fuse," THE ECONOMIST, November 5, 1998, p.S6.

8. "Democracy in the Arab world: Not yet, thanks," THE ECONOMIST, June 29, 2006, p. 42; Progressive Policy Institute, "Ten of the Western Hemisphere's 35 nations are monarchies," available at: http://www.ppionline.org, last visited December 29, 2006; Xan Smiley, "Plenty of seeds, but still a long way to fruition," THE WORLD IN 2006, THE ECONOMIST, December 15, 2005, p. 53.

9. "Somalia: Islamists half-ready for holy war," THE ECONOMIST, October 14, 2006, p. 49.

10. "Ethiopia and Somalia: The rumbling rumors of war," THE ECONOMIST, December 2, 2006, p. 64; Jeffrey Gettleman, "Somali forces retake capital from Islamists," NEW YORK TIMES, December 29, 2006, p.A1; "Somalia: Thank you and goodbye," THE ECONOMIST, January 6, 2007, p. 10; "Somalia: A failed state that threatens the region," THE ECONOMIST, April 7, 2007, p. 43; "Somalia: Continuing to fail," THE ECONOMIST, July 5, 2008, p. 58.

11. "Burma junta fuels poverty, claims UN," FINANCIAL TIMES, July 13, 2007, p. 4.

12. "Congo's constitutional agenda: A ray of hope in the heart of Africa," ECONOMIST.COM, December 19, 2005, available at: http://www.economist.com, last visited March 22, 2007.

13. Barney Jopson, "Talks to end Kenyan crisis suspended," FINANCIAL TIMES, February 27, 2008, p. 4.

14. "Congo: A wilderness that may become a state," THE ECONOMIST, November 23, 2006, p. 62; Rebecca Bream, "Stability temps mining companies back to Congo," FINANCIAL TIMES, February 21, 2007, p. 5.

15. Id.; William Wallis & Fred Robarts, "UN sees its Congo peacekeeping operations descend into disarray," FINANCIAL TIMES, December 22–23, 2007, p. 1.

16. Eric Jansson & Neil MacDonald, "Last fight will shape the future," FINANCIAL TIMES/Kosovo, May 30, 2006, p. 1; "Kosovo: To block a nation's birth," NEWSWEEK, March 3, 2008, p. 10.

17. "A hero at home, a villain abroad," THE ECONOMIST, July 14, 2007, p. 40.

18. "Vietnam to join WTO on 11 January," 10 BRIDGES No. 42, December 13, 2006, p. 13.

19. "Order in the jungle," THE ECONOMIST, March15, 2008, p. 83; see generally, KENNETH DAM, THE LAW-GROWTH NEXUS: THE RULE OF LAW AND ECONOMIC DEVELOPMENT (Brookings, 2006), p. 14 and 228; "Legal reform and development: The law poor," THE ECONOMIST, June 7, 2008, p. 87.

20. "Wolfowitz's new war: Corruption," THE ECONOMIST, March 4, 2006, p. 55; Noah J. Smith, "Trade policy: China working to improve quality of judges, Supreme Court chief says," 19 ITR 455 (March 14, 2002).

21. "Three-quarters of nations perceived as corrupted," SEATTLE POST-INTELLIGENCER, November 7, 2006, p.A3; Transparency International, "2006 Corruption Perceptions Index," November 6, 2006, available at: www.transparency.org, last visited March 22, 2007.

22. Martin Wolf, "Corruption in the spotlight," FINANCIAL TIMES, September 16, 1997, p. 15; Patti Waldmeir, "Bribery is not just a cost of doing business," FINANCIAL TIMES, March 5, 2007, p. 8; "Rules of the road," THE ECONOMIST, May 5, 2007, p. 92.

23. "Doing business in China: Brick wall," THE ECONOMIST, September 24, 2005, p. 12; Donald C. Clarke, "Economic development and the rights hypothesis: The rights problem," 51 AM. J. COMP. L. 89, 94 note 25 (2003); "Not the best way to clean up," THE ECONOMIST, April 21, 2007, p. 43.

24. Id.; Chris Rugaber, "International agreements: Use of bribes by OECD nations continues despite agreement; China and Russia worst," 19 ITR 906 (May 23, 2002); Steven R. Weisman, "Before visit to China, a rebuke," NEW YORK TIMES, December 12, 2006, p.C1; Andrew Yeh, "China sets up agency to crack down on corruption," FINANCIAL TIMES, February 14, 2007, p. 3.

25. "The diddle kingdom," THE ECONOMIST, July 7, 2007, p. 63; Geoff Dyer, "China executes ex-chief of food and drug watchdog for bribery," FINANCIAL TIMES, July 11, 2007, p. 1.

26. Andrew Jack, "Putin vows to increase funding for legal system," FINANCIAL TIMES, November 28, 2000, p. 2; Rugaber, op.cit.; "Richer, bolder— and sliding back," THE ECONOMIST, July 15, 2006, p. 23.

27. Martin Wolf, "As long as it is trapped, the bear will continue to growl," FINANCIAL TIMES, February 21, 2007, p. 13; "A bear at the throat," THE ECONOMIST, April 14, 2007, p. 58; Jonathan Eyal, "European appeasement will worsen Russian aggression," FINANCIAL TIMES, May 18, 2007, p. 9; Catherine Belton, "Russia forced into new arms race, says Putin," FINANCIAL TIMES, February 9–10, 2008, p. 3; "Geopolitics (1): A bowl of alphabet soup," THE ECONOMIST, August 9, 2008, p. 55.

28. Martin Wolf, "Corruption in the spotlight," FINANCIAL TIMES, September 16, 1997, p. 15; "Corruption in South-East Asia: Who will watch the watchdogs?" THE ECONOMIST, February 21, 2004, p. 39.

29. "Argentina's Economy: Crawling back to daylight," THE ECONOMIST, December 6, 2003, p. 32; "France's failure: The biggest lesson in the French riots is that more jobs are needed," THE ECONOMIST, November 12, 2005, p. 11.

30. "Coalitions of the unwilling," THE ECONOMIST, October 21, 2006, p. 25; Progressive Policy Institute, "Unemployment rates are highest in the Middle East," available at: www.ppionline.org, last visited January 5, 2007; "Moderates and rejectionists: The Palestinian test case," THE ECONOMIST, October 21, 2006, p. 28.

31. Robert Samuelson, "Terror's economics," NEWSWEEK, August 28, 2006, p. 57; Fareed Zakaria, "The arrogant empire," NEWSWEEK, March 24, 2003, p. 17.

32. "South African land: Should reform be faster or steadier?" THE ECONOMIST, July 9, 2005, p. 38; "Fear factor," op.cit.

33. Alec Russell & Tony Hawkins, "Zimbabwe's defiant dictator', FINANCIAL TIMES, February 24–25, 2007, p. 7; "Toppling a tyrant," THE ECONOMIST, March 17, 2007, p. 14; "Zimbabwe: Back to the dark ages," THE ECONOMIST, May 19, 2007, p. 49; "No welcome, no let-up," THE ECONOMIST, August 11, 2007, p. 37.

34. "A test case for Africa," THE ECONOMIST, March 31, 2007, p. 15; "The hogwash of quiet diplomacy," THE ECONOMIST, April 7, 2007, p. 44; "Zimbabwe: Africa's shame," THE ECONOMIST, July 5, 2008, p. 57. A power-sharing deal for Zimbabwe was finally brokered by South Africa's president Mbeki in September, 2008. But it is unlikely to be the end of conflict there. Celia Dugger and Alan Cowell, "Mugabe, opposition leader sign power-sharing deal," Seattle Post-Intelligencer, September 16, 2008, p. A4.

35. Mark Mulligan & Victoria Burnett, "Spanish PM pays price after bomb derails Eta peace talks," FT.COM (January 3, 2007) available at: http://www.ft.com, last visited January 7, 2007; "Mediterranean rivals," THE ECONOMIST, November 4, 2006, p. 64; John Kay, "A poor view of poverty: Although the capitalist model of development is not perfect, it is the only one we have," FINANCIAL TIMES, July 25, 2001, p. 9.

36. "Globalization and the rise of inequality: Rich man, poor man," THE ECONOMIST, January 20, 2007, p. 50; "Somewhere over the rainbow," THE ECONOMIST, January 26, 2008, p. 27.

37. "Venezuela: With Marx, Lenin and Jesus Christ," THE ECONOMIST, January 13, 2007, p. 33; "Ecuador: Banana republic," THE ECONOMIST, October 21, 2006, p. 48; "Wanted: a champion for privatization," THE ECONOMIST, October 28, 2006, p. 18; "Bolivia: Friends, not clones," THE ECONOMIST, June 9, 2007, p. 41; Benedict Mander, "Delistings could be death knell for Venezuela," FINANCIAL TIMES, May 9, 2007, p. 25; "Ecuador's Rafael Correa: Tightening his grip," THE ECONOMIST, April 21, 2007, p. 39.

38. Hal Weitzman, "Reform on hold as divisions in Bolivia deepen," FI-
NANCIAL TIMES, January 27, 2007, p. 4; Ian James, "Chavez follows Cuba's
path to nationalize industries," SEATTLE POST-INTELLIGENCER, January 9, 2007,
p.A6; "Brazil's elections: When victory spells defeat," THE ECONOMIST, October 7, 2006, p. 43; "Bolivia: Friends, not clones," *op.cit.*; "Brazil: Should try
harder," THE ECONOMIST, April 14, 2007, p. 14.

39. Joanna Chung & Hal Weitzman, "Debt decision surprises bond market," FINANCIAL TIMES, February 16, 2007, p. 4; "Nicaragua: 'Twixt Washington and Caracas," THE ECONOMIST, January 13, 2007, p. 34; "The United States
and Nicaragua: Dealing with Daniel," THE ECONOMIST, November 11, 2006, p.
15; "Brazil: Should try harder," *op.cit.*; "Bolivia: Friends not clones," *op.cit.*;
"Ecuador's Rafael Correa: Tightening his grip," *op.cit.*

40. Maria Salinas, "Latin America leans to the left," SEATTLE POST-INTEL-
LIGENCER, October 22, 2006, p.D5; Andy Webb-Vidal, "Venezuela prepares to
act over inflation as price caps on food staples fail," FINANCIAL TIMES, February 9, 2007, p. 6.

41. "Mercosur: A turning point?" THE ECONOMIST, July 7, 2007, p. 40

42. "Somewhere over the rainbow," *op.cit.*

43. Mark Turner, "World looks away as Iraqis flood nearby states," FINAN-
CIAL TIMES, February 15, 2007, p. 7; "Sudan: No end in sight to Darfur's mis-
ery," THE ECONOMIST, July 8, 2006, p. 40; "Somalia: A failed state that threatens
the region," THE ECONOMIST, April 7, 2007, p. 43; Alec Russell, "Pretoria hosts
secret Zimbabwe talks," FINANCIAL TIMES, May 22, 2007, p. 6; John Thornhill,
"Sarkozy and Brown unite on Darfur," FINANCIAL TIMES, July 21–22, 2007, p.
2; Edith Lederer, "Girls tell U.N. panel of grim struggles," SEATTLE TIMES,
March 4, 2007, p. A14.

44. "Sanctions: History lessons," THE ECONOMIST, October 21, 2006, p. 70; But
c.f., Helene Cooper, "N. Korea shares documents on three nuclear campaigns,"
SEATTLE POST-INTELLIGENCER, May 9, 2008, p. A13; "Saddam Hussein: The blun-
dering dictator" THE ECONOMIST, January 6, 2007, p. 43; "America in the Middle East: Arming its friends and talking peace," THE ECONOMIST, August 4, 2007,
p. 39; "How to win the war within Islam," THE ECONOMIST, July 19, 2008, p. 16.

45. "World looks away as Iraqis flood nearby states," *op.cit.*; Alfred de Mon-
tesquiou, "Darfur conflict spills into Chad," SEATTLE POST-INTELLIGENCER,
April 2, 2007, p. A.7; Alec Russell, "At 17, A goodbye note and then over the
wire from Zimbabwe's shambles," FINANCIAL TIMES, March 24–25, 2007, p. 4.

46. Ron Asmus, "Nato must go global to have a meaningful purpose," FI-
NANCIAL TIMES, February 7, 2007, p. 11; "A chance for a safer world," THE
ECONOMIST, January 6, 2007, p. 9; "Sudan: Peacekeepers into the fray," THE ECON-
OMIST, March 15, 2008, p. 58.

47. "Colonial baggage," THE ECONOMIST, February 9, 2008, p. 60; William Wallis, "Plea for more Somalia peacekeepers," FINANCIAL TIMES, December 17, 2007, p. 3.

48. Andrew England, "Hu urges Sudan to act on Darfur crisis," FINANCIAL TIMES, February 4, 2007, p. 4; Gideon Rachman, "The hard evidence that China's soft power policy is working," FINANCIAL TIMES, February 20, 2007, p. 13; Mure Dickie, "China tempers military pact by seeking Sudan peace move," FINANCIAL TIMES, April 4, 2007, p. 1; James Blitz, "Sudan arms sale claims exaggerated, says China," FINANCIAL TIMES, February 23–24, 2008, p. 4; Barney Jopson, "China wins permit to look for oil in Somalia," FINANCIAL TIMES, July 14–15, 2007, p. 4.

49. "EU disappointed at Iran nuclear move," NEWS @ EU, August 12, 2005; "More nuclear talks with Iran urged," SEATTLE POST-INTELLIGENCER, September 20, 2005, p. A3; Mahir Uthman, "UK Arabic paper considers Blair's prospects as Quartet Mideast envoy," British Broadcasting Corporation, July 13, 2007; "Patience pays off with North Korea," FINANCIAL TIMES, July 21, 2007, p. 6.

50. "America, Europe and the management of danger: A hazardous comparison," THE ECONOMIST, March 1, 2008, p. 61.

51. "The United States in the Middle East: Weakness or a new realism?" THE ECONOMIST, April 28, 2007, p. 51; "NATO in Afghanistan: No rush for the exit, yet," THE ECONOMIST, July 14, 2007, p. 44; "The hobbled hegemon," THE ECONOMIST, June 30, 2007, p. 29; "Charlemange: Defensive gestures," THE ECONOMIST, July 26, 2008, p. 64.

52. "The United States in the Middle East: Weakness—or a new realism?" op.cit.; Demetri Sevastopulo, "Pentagon calls truce with march of globalization," FINANCIAL TIMES, July 6, 2007, p. 3; "The hobbled hegemon," op.cit.

53. Norimitsu Onishi, "Bomb by bomb, Japan sheds military restraints," NEW YORK TIMES, July 23, 2007, p. 1; David Pilling & Victor Mallet, "Japan weighs bigger role as peacekeeper," FINANCIAL TIMES, February 25, 2008, p. 5.

54. John D. Sparks & Gilbert Gates, "The power game," NEWSWEEK, December 22, 2003, p.E17; "The future of NATO: The test in Afghanistan," THE ECONOMIST, November 25, 2006, p. 12; "Charlemange: Defensive gestures," op.cit.

55. Edward Luce, "Support for terror falls in Muslim countries," FINANCIAL TIMES, July 25, 2007, p. 4; "Must they be wars without end?" THE ECONOMIST, December 15, 2007, p. 13; Peter Wehner, "Al-Queda is losing war of minds," FINANCIAL TIMES, March 5, 2008, p. 13; "Ghana has cut malnutrition rates by 75 percent since 1992," July 18, 2007, available at: http://www.ppi online.org, last visited July 24, 2007.

56. "The nuclear black market: Still in business," THE ECONOMIST, May 5, 2007, p. 74; "Nuclear trafficking: A radioactive subject," THE ECONOMIST, Feb-

ruary 3, 2007, p. 60; "Nuclear proliferation: Why not just blow your whistle?" THE ECONOMIST, March 1, 2008, p. 62.

57. For example Peter Marsh, "ABB helps with 'suspect payment' [bribery] investigations in several countries," FINANCIAL TIMES, July 27, 2007, p. 13; "Spain and ETA: Bombers return," THE ECONOMIST, January 6, 2007, p. 44; Vanda Felbab-Brown, "Tackling transnational crime: Adapting U.S. national security policy," available at: http://www.brookings.edu, last visited April 24, 2008.

58. Jack Goldsmith "The global convergence on terror," FINANCIAL TIMES, August 1, 2007, p. 11; Mark Turner, "UN panel close to framing a law on state aggression," FINANCIAL TIMES, February 6, 2007, p. 6. See generally, "After Bush: A special report on America and the World," THE ECONOMIST, March 29, 2008.

59. "Crime in Mexico: The tough get going," THE ECONOMIST, January 27, 2007, p. 33; "An early harvest for Calderon," THE ECONOMIST, April 7, 2007, p. 33; "European defense ministers review EU-led peace operations and military capabilities," EUROPA NEWSLETTER No. 90, October 13, 2006, p. 5; "Australia and Europe join forces to combat international crime," NEWS @ EU, February 21, 2001, p. 2; "NATO must go global to have a meaningful purpose," FINANCIAL TIMES, February 7, 2007, p. 11.

Chapter XI

1. There are far too many of these books to list them all. However, a representative sample might include: BRUCE RICH, MORTGAGING THE EARTH (Beacon Press, 1994); GEORGE SOROS, THE CRISIS OF GLOBAL CAPITALISM: OPEN SOCIETY ENDANGERED (BBS/Public Affairs, 1998); Robin Board, ed., GLOBAL BACKLASH (Rowman & Littlefield, 2002); AMY CHUA, WORLD ON FIRE, (Doubleday, 2003); BARRY LYNN, END OF THE LINE (Doubleday, 2005); RAPHAEL KAPLINSKY, GLOBALIZATION, POVERTY AND INEQUALITY (Cambridge University Press, 2005); DANIEL COHEN, GLOBALIZATION AND ITS ENEMIES (MIT Press, 2006). Some more-objective books have been written as well. For example: JAGDISH BHAWATI, IN DEFENSE OF GLOBALIZATION (Oxford University Press, 2004); and MARTIN WOLF, WHY GLOBALIZATION WORKS (Yale University Press, 2004).

2. UNESCO, Joseph Stiglitz: The Subtle Truth about Globalization, THE NEW COURIER, No. 1, October 2002, W.W. Norton & Company, (2006), pp. xv–xvi.

3. Edward Gresser, "Trading in Myth," BLUEPRINT MAGAZINE, February 9, 2006, available at: http://www.ppionline.org, last visited April 4, 2007.

4. See, e.g., "Black & Decker will move some operations overseas," N.Y. TIMES, January 30, 2002, p. C5.

5. Peter Preston, "Don't blame papers over Europe," THE OBSERVER, June 24, 2007, p. 12; David Ellis, "Toyota to build new SUV plant in Mississippi," cnnmoney.com, February 27, 2007, available at: http://money.cnn.com/, last visited May 13, 2007; "Lou Dobbs is wrong!," available at: http://www.ppi online.org, last visited April 23, 2007.

6. "American's fear of China," THE ECONOMIST, May 19, 2007, p. 9; Chris Giles, "Poll reveals backlash in wealthy countries against globalization," FINANCIAL TIMES, July 23, 3007, p. 1; "Hillary Clinton is wrong on trade," FINANCIAL TIMES, December 4, 2007, p. 14.

7. Robert Samuelson, "Globalization's Achilles' heel," NEWSWEEK, July 21, 2008, p. 53; "The perils of protection," THE ECONOMIST, December 9, 2006, p. 80; Paul Betts, "The losing battle to defend champions," FINANCIAL TIMES, April 20, 2007, p. 1; "Asia-Pacific finance ministers warn of growth threat from protection," FINANCIAL TIMES, August 4–5, 2007, p. 4; Adam Thompson, "Mexicans riled by threats to ditch trade accord," FINANCIAL TIMES, March 4, 2008, p. 4.

8. "Somewhere over the rainbow," THE ECONOMIST, January 26, 2008, p. 27; Chris Woodyard, "Which is more American?" USA TODAY, March 22, 2007, p. B1.

9. LESTER C. THUROW, THE ZERO-SUM SOCIETY: DISTRIBUTION AND THE POSSIBILITIES FOR ECONOMIC CHANGE (Basic Books, 1990), pp. 11–12.

10. Robert Samuelson," China's wrong turn on trade," NEWSWEEK, May 14, 2007, p. 55; John Authers, " 'Decoupled' US maintains a grip on world economy," FINANCIAL TIMES, May 19–20, 2007, p. 12.

11. George F. Russell, Jr., "The power of globalization," NBR ANALYSIS, Vol. 16, No. 2, November 2005, p. 7.

12. Id. at pp. 7–8.

13. "Shock to the system," THE ECONOMIST, December 24, 2005, p. 88; "The lessons of history," THE ECONOMIST, July 14, 2007, p. 58.

14. Pranab Bardhan, "Capitalism: One size does not suit all," YaleGlobal.com, December 7, 2006, available at: http://yaleglobal, last visited May 13, 2007; Danny Leipziger & Michael Spence, "Globalisation's losers need support," FINANCIAL TIMES, May 15, 2007, p. 11.

15. "The hobbled hegemon," THE ECONOMIST, June 30, 2007, p. 32; Ralph Atkins, "China exports more to the EU than the US for the first time," FINANCIAL TIMES, March 28, 2007, p. 2; "Come in number one, your time is up," THE ECONOMIST, April 14, 2007, p. 12; "America's fear of China," op.cit.

16. THE ECONOMIST, "Pocket World in Figures" (Profile Books, 2007), pp. 26, 130, 234; Albert Keidel, "The limits of a smaller, poorer China," FINANCIAL TIMES, November 14, 2007, p. 11.

17. Geoffrey Colvin, "The U.S. is in decline—and that's a good thing," FORTUNE, February 21, 2005, p. 58; "Still No. 1," THE ECONOMIST, June 30, 2007, p. 11; "U.S. image sinks, yet American goods keep selling," THE KITSAP DAILY, July 20, 2007, p. 4; Richard McGregor, "China affirms dollar's global reserve status," FINANCIAL TIMES, August 3, 2007, p. 4. See generally, FAREED ZAKARIA, THE POST-AMERICAN WORLD (W. W. Norton, 2008).

18. Michiyo Nakamoto, "China overtakes US in trade with Japan," FINANCIAL TIMES, April 26, 2007, p. 5; Jamil Anderlini, "Chinese bourses eclipse all of Asia," FINANCIAL TIMES, May 10, 2007, p. 1; Gideon Rachman, "As America looks the other way, China's rise accelerates," FINANCIAL TIMES, February 13, 2007, p. 13.

19. Robin Kwong, "China on course to lead world IPO league," FINANCIAL TIMES, July 5, 2007, p. 1.

20. The alternative engine, THE ECONOMIST, Oct. 21, 2006, pp. 79–81; Sheridan Prasso, "China's new cultural revolution," FORTUNE, May 28, 2007, p. 91; Robert J. Samuelson, "The world's powerhouse," NEWSWEEK, May 31, 2004, p. 57.

21. "The great game is Asia," THE ECONOMIST, March 31, 2007, p. 14; Mure Dickie & David Pilling, "Wen speech lauds Chinese ties with Japan," FINANCIAL TIMES, April 13, 2007, p. 5; Roula Khalaf & Others, "The great bridge of China: how energy-hungry Beijing hews its Mideast links," FINANCIAL TIMES, February 12, 2007, p. 13; Stefan Wagstyl, "How the west can win again in central Asia," FINANCIAL TIMES, August 27, 2007, p. 7.

22. "Chinese seal deal for 42 787 Jets," SEATTLE POST-INTELLIGENCER, August 11, 2005, p. C1.

23. Progressive Policy Institute, "Trade fact of the week," available at: ppi_admin@dlcppi.org, last visited November 16, 2005.

24. "General Motors: Rising in the East," THE ECONOMIST, April 28, 2007, p. 76.

25. Richard McGregor, "China plans a policy switch on massive foreign reserves," FINANCIAL TIMES, January 22, 2007, p. 1; "China moves from hunter to gatherer," FINANCIAL TIMES, August 22, 2007, p. 2; Jamil Anderlini, "Chinese overseas listings set to increase," FINANCIAL TIMES, May 11, 2007, p. 19; Jing Huang, "China-US relationship not a zero-sum game," CHINA DAILY, May 28, 2007 available at: http://www.brookings.edu, last visited July 24, 2007.

26. Tony Tassell, "Fear of overheating in Chinese economy transmits a shudder," FINANCIAL TIMES April 20, 2007, p. 24; Richard McGregor, "Untamed," FINANCIAL TIMES, May 22, 2007, p. 7; "China's inflation sparks fear for economy," FINANCIAL TIMES, August 14, 2007, p. 3; "Bubbly asset prices hold a nasty surprise for China," FINANCIAL TIMES, August 23, 2007, p. 26; Peter

Marsh, "Fatigue fears over China's exports," FINANCIAL TIMES, May 23, 2007, p. 18; Richard McGregor, "China's good corporate citizens find their voice," FINANCIAL TIMES, February 26, 2007, p. 3; Peter Marsh, "US to lose role as world's top manufacturer by 2020," FINANCIAL TIMES, May 24, 2007, p. 8.

27. WILL HUTTON, THE WRITING ON THE WALL (Little, Brown, 2007), cited by Martin Wolf, "China, cracked," FINANCIAL TIMES, February 3–4, 2007, p. W7.

28. Richard McGregor, "Beijing clouds the pollution problem," FINANCIAL TIMES July 3, 2007, p. 2; "Polluted China rivers threaten 'sixth' of population," THE KITSAP DAILY, August 27, 2007, p. 10; Richard McGregor, "China's prosperity brings income gap," FINANCIAL TIMES, August 9, 2007, p. 2; Geoff Dyer, "Chinese regulator warns food safety could threaten social stability," FINANCIAL TIMES, July 10, 2007, p. 1; Richard McGregor, "If you are Chinese, try very hard not to be ill," FINANCIAL TIMES, August 30, 2007, p. 9.

29. "China acts on food safety after pet poisoning," THE KITSAP DAILY, May 10, 2007, p. 3; "China shuts down 5 drug makers," SEATTLE TIMES, July 8, 2007, P. A15; "Government bans exports of lead-tainted toys," SEATTLE POST INTELLIGENCER, August 10, 2007, p. 2; Richard McGregor, "Beijing group to tackle product safety," FINANCIAL TIMES, August 18–19, 2007, p. 5.

30. "Capturing talent," THE ECONOMIST, August 18, 2007, p. 59; Andrew Taylor, "Toymakers face further attack over working conditions," FINANCIAL TIMES, August 22, 2007, p. 6; Richard McGregor, "OCED sees obstacles to China's high tech drive," FINANCIAL TIMES, August 28, 2007, p. 3; Jamil Anderlini, "China's strong earnings growth inflated by stock market bull run," FINANCIAL TIMES, August 28, 2007, p. 13; Clay Chandler, "Rolling the dice on China's banks," FORTUNE, December 25, 2006, p. 181.

31. Richard McGregor, "China power: Long march to modernization begins," FINANCIAL TIMES, August 10, 2007, p. 3; "Wen hits at failure to cut pollution," FINANCIAL TIMES, May 9, 2007, p. 2; Geoff Dyer, "Beijing sets aside $1bn to restore faith in food safety," FINANCIAL TIMES, August 9, 2007, p. 2.

32. Geoff Dyer, "The rise of China: Faced with a steep learning curve," FINANCIAL TIMES, April 23, 2007, p. 6; Jamil Anderlini & Geoff Dyer, "Wary welcome for China labor law," FINANCIAL TIMES, July 2, 2007, p. 6; Geoff Dyer, "Beijing cracks down on insider trading," FINANCIAL TIMES, May 24, 2007, p. 27; Mure Dickie, "Chinese-FBI joint crackdown nets $500 in pirated software," FINANCIAL times, July 25, 2007, p. 1.

33. "US files WTO complaints against China over counterfeiting, trade barriers" and "China IP case: Additional countries join US challenge," both in 11 BRIDGES Nos. 13 and 16, April 18, 2007, p. 6 and May 9, 2007, p. 14, respectively; Richard McGregor & Eoin Callan, "China hits out as US launches trade cases," FINANCIAL TIMES, April 11, 2007, p. 1; Richard McGregor, "Chinese

inflation reaches 11-year high," FINANCIAL TIMES, December 12, 2007, p. 2; "Doing business in China: 850,000 lawsuits in the making," THE ECONOMIST, April 12, 2008, p. 74; "China facing scrutiny on multiple fronts at WTO," 11 BRIDGES No. 35, October 17, 2007, p. 7.

34. Richard McGregor, "Beijing unveils big government shake-up," FINANCIAL TIMES, April 28–29, 2007, p. 2; Mure Dickie & Geoff Dyer, "China shifts on currency band ahead of US talks," FINANCIAL TIMES, May 19–20, 2007, p. 1; Andrew Wood, "China's savers are poised to go global," FINANCIAL TIMES, August 28, 2007, p. 21; Florian Gimbel & Jamil Anderlini, "China to relax curbs of foreign investment," FINANCIAL TIMES, May 12–13, 2007, p. 2; "China roars but its still too young to be calling all the shots," FINANCIAL TIMES, March 1, 2007, p. 28; Richard McGregor, "Protest groups grab their chance to put pressure in China," FINANCIAL TIMES, August 6, 2007, p. 4.

35. POCKET WORLD IN FIGURES, 2007 ed. (THE ECONOMIST, 2006), p. 26

36. "India trade policy review lauds growth but calls for further reforms," 11 BRIDGES No. 19, May 30, 2007, p. 6; Peter Marsh, "Multinational managers in India rival US for skill," FINANCIAL TIMES, July 13, 2007, p. 3; "Democracy's drawbacks," THE ECONOMIST, Oct. 29, 2005, pp. 23–26; Tim Sullivan, "India's tech firms hunting for help," SEATTLE TIMES, April 8, 2007, p. E1.

37. "India overheats," THE ECONOMIST, February 3, 2007, p. 11; Jo Johnson, "A confident new country" and Shawn Donnan, "Behemoths strut their stuff," both in "India: Special Report," FINANCIAL TIMES, August 15, 2007, pp. 1 and 5, respectively; "India's economy: Turning sour," THE ECONOMIST, August 2, 2008, p. 43; Andrew Jack & Amy Yee, "China may prove a hard pill for India to swallow," FINANCIAL TIMES, August 31, 2007, p. 16.

38. See generally, THOMAS C. FISCHER, THE UNITED STATES, THE EUROPEAN UNION, AND THE "GLOBALIZATION" OF WORLD TRADE (Greenwood, 2000), Chapters 11: "Japan: Asia's Disintegrating Colossus" and 12: "China: The Middle Kingdom in the Middle," pp. 145–177; "Pocket World in Figures," op.cit., p. 26; Geoff Dyer, "Chinese stock market bigger than Japan's," FINANCIAL TIMES, August 29, 2007, p. 23.

39. "Financial services in Japan: Serious, honest," THE ECONOMIST, May 12, 2007, p. 83; Mariko Sanchanta, "Japanese PM plans to cut ports' red tape," FINANCIAL TIMES, April 25, 2007, p. 5; "The Japan syndrome," THE ECONOMIST, May 12, 2007, p. 45; "Gaijin at the gates," THE ECONOMIST, August 18, 2007, p. 53; Michiyo Nakamoto, "One-way street," FINANCIAL TIMES, March 3, 2008, p. 7.

40. Mure Dickie & David Pilling, "Warm words, old wounds: How China and Japan are starting to march in step," FINANCIAL TIMES, April 9, 2007, p. 9; Jo Johnson, "Abe hails ties with India as 'crucial'," FINANCIAL TIMES, August 21, 2007, p. 6.

41. Homi Kharas, "Ten years after the East Asian crisis: A Resurgent and restructured region," The Brookings Institution, June 27, 2007, available at: http://www.brookings.edu, last visited July 9, 2007; Louise Lucas, "Heady Asian party shows no signs of abating," FINANCIAL TIMES, July 1, 2007, p. 12; Mariko Sanchanta, "Tokyo plans for Asian 'open skies'," FINANCIAL TIMES, March 31/April1, 2007, p. 5.

42. Seth Mydans, "Fervor for capitalism sweeps Vietnam," INTERNATIONAL HEARD TRIBUNE, April 27, 2006, p. 1.

43. Lawrence Summers, "History holds lessons for China and its partners," FINANCIAL TIMES, February 26, 2007, p. 15; Chris Giles, "Wrong lessons from Asia's crisis," FINANCIAL TIMES, July 2, 2007, p. 7; Andrew Taylor, "Asian economies near 'demographic cliff'," FINANCIAL TIMES, August 13, 2007, p. 4; Brooke Masters & Rebecca Knight, "Concern over talent shortage," FINANCIAL TIMES, August 13, 2007, p. 3.

44. "Charlemagne: The puny economic powerhouse," THE ECONOMIST, Dec. 10, 2005, p. 60.

45. European Council, Presidency Conclusions, Brussels, 25–26 March 2004, point 7; "Strength to strength," THE ECONOMIST, April 28, 2007, p. 86; "Can Europe's recovery last?" THE ECONOMIST, July 14, 2007, p. 11; "The non-functioning myth," THE ECONOMIST, April 14, 2007, p. 64; David Oakley, "Euro-bonds issuance hits record levels," FINANCIAL TIMES, February 9, 2007, p. 23; "European Commission, Europe closes transatlantic innovation gap," available at: http://ec.europa.EU/news, last visited March 1, 2007; Chris Giles, "Globalization 'a blessing' for west Europe," FINANCIAL TIMES, February 26, 2008, p. 6; Tony Barber & Ralph Atkins, "Eurozone still on track after global turmoil," FINANCIAL TIMES, September 5, 2007, p. 2; "Europe's monetary policy: The wages of sin," THE ECONOMIST, August 2, 2008, p. 75; "Commission welcomes negotiations for FTAs with India, Korea and ASEAN," NEWS @ EU, May 2, 2007, p. 4; Tony Barber, 'Stumbling towards mutual [EU-China] understanding," FINANCIAL TIMES, November 27, 2007, p. 2; "The Mediterranean Union: Sarko's southern dream," THE ECONOMIST, July 19, 2008, p. 61.

46. Jonathan Wheatley, "Brazil moves to top of emerging market index," FINANCIAL TIMES, February 29, 2008, p. 25.

47. Paul Laudicina, Moises Naim & David Bosco, "The Globalization Index," FOREIGN POLICY, Oct. 19, 2006, available at: YaleGlobal online, http://yale global.yale.edu/article.print? id=8313, last visited May 13, 2007.

48. "A giant stirs," THE ECONOMIST, June 12, 2004, pp. 34–35.

49. Belo Horizonte, "Slow! Government obstacles ahead," THE ECONOMIST, June 17, 2006, p. 41; Jonathan Wheatly, "Brazil 'must lift barriers' to investment in infrastructure," FINANCIAL TIMES, March 1, 2007, p. 6.

50. "A wannabe Chavez short of oil," THE ECONOMIST, September 1, 2007, p. 30; "Venezuela's Chavez Grabs $30 Billion Oil Field in Orinco River Basin," May 1, 2007, available at: http://www.cnbc.com/id/18415992, last visited May 14, 2007; "The beginning of the end for Hugo Chavez," THE ECONOMIST, December 8, 2007, p. 12.

51. "Mercosur: A turning point?" THE ECONOMIST, July 7, 2007, p. 40; "A shrug not a shudder," THE ECONOMIST, August 25, 2007, p. 67; Michael Mackenzie, "Latin America stands tall amid market highs," FINANCIAL TIMES, May 15, 2007, p. 26; "Latin American economies: Up from the bottom of the pile" and "Chile: Destitute no more," both in THE ECONOMIST, August 18, 2007, pp. 10 and 23, respectively.

52. Marla Dickerson & Carlos Martinez, "Bombardier gives boost to Mexico's aerospace industry," SEATTLE TIMES, May 27, 2007, p. G4; Adam Thompson, "Mexico closer on tax reform," FINANCIAL TIMES, August 24, 3007, p. 2; "Pocket World in Figures," op.cit., p. 26.

53. Neil Buckley, "Putting the state back in charge," FINANCIAL TIMES (Special Report: Russia), April 20, 2007, p. 1; Stephen Hanson, "The WTO and Russian Politics," in National Bureau of Asian Research, Special Report No. 12 (March 2007), "Russia and the WTO: A Progress Report," pp. 7–12.

54. "Putin's people," THE ECONOMIST, August 25, 2007, p. 11; "Russia and the west: No divide, no rule," THE ECONOMIST, May 19, 2007, p. 12; Isabel Gorst, "Putin increases missile defense rhetoric," FINANCIAL TIMES, August 13, 2007, p. 1; "Don't mess with Russia," THE ECONOMIST, December 16, 2006, p. 11; Abraham Lustgaten, "Shell shake down," FORTUNE, February 5, 2007, p. 93; "Do you want Putin's paw on the pipe?" THE ECONOMIST, January 13, 2007, p. 12.

55. "'Frank' discussions help forge strong EU-Russia partnerships," NEWS @ EU, May 30, 2007, p. 3; "Enter, pursued by a bear," THE ECONOMIST, September 15, 2007, p. 67; Tony Barber, "Energy at heart of EU bids to build ties with neighbors," FINANCIAL TIMES, September 4, 2007, p. 4.

56. "Don't mess with Russia," op.cit.; Ed Crooks, "Lukoil plans $9bn European acquisition spree," FINANCIAL TIMES, September 13, 2007, p. 21; Wolfgang Proissi & Ed Crooks, "Russia faces EU energy barriers," FINANCIAL TIMES, August 30, 2007, p. 1; Stefan Wagstyl & others, "Russia rejects tougher stance on Iranian nuclear programme," FINANCIAL TIMES, September 13, 2007, p. 5; "Russia and the world: Talk, don't shout," THE ECONOMIST, February 17, 2007, p. 15.

57. "Putting the state back in charge," op.cit.; Neil Buckley, "Putin urges business chiefs to modernize," FINANCIAL TIMES, February 7, 2007, p. 2; Quentin Peel, "Putin takes to the world stage in search of business," FINAN-

CIAL TIMES, February 14, 2007, p. 2; Catherine Belton, "Russia torn over how to invest its oil riches," FINANCIAL TIMES, September 18, 2007, p. 7; Martin Wolf, "As long as it is trapped, the bear will continue to growl," FINANCIAL TIMES, February 21, 2007, p. 13.

58. Joanna Chung, "Sub-Saharan Africa confident it can attract investment," FINANCIAL TIMES, May 2, 2007, p. 27; Nicol Innocenti & Carola Hoyos, "Africa launches a union to fight war and poverty," FINANCIAL TIMES, July 10, 2002, p. 1; "African Union," EUROPA WORLD YEARBOOK, Volume 1, pp. 157 *et seq*; Joseph Schatz, "Zimbabwe issues are left unresolved," SEATTLE TIMES, August 19, 2007, p. A 20; "Commission holds joint meeting with African Union in Addis Ababa" and "The EU and Africa: Investing in humanitarian aid," both in EUROPA NEWSLETTER, No. 90 (October 13, 2006), pp. 3 and 4 respectively.

59. William Wallis, "Highest stakes for a generation," FINANCIAL TIMES (Nigeria: Special Report), July 12, 2007, p. 1; "Ghana has cut malnutrition rates by 75 percent since 1992," (July 18, 2007) available at: http://www.ppi online.org, last visited July 24, 2007; Kate Burgess & William Wallis, "Africa becomes sunny proposition for funds," FINANCIAL TIMES, August 10, 2007, p. 13; "South Africa's economy: How to spend it," THE ECONOMIST, February 24, 2007, p. 88.

60. "Israel and Palestine: Still campaigning for co-existence," THE ECONOMIST, September 1, 2007, p. 37; "Cold Turkey: Why some emerging markets may suffer from withdrawal," THE ECONOMIST, August 4, 2007, p. 63; Simeon Kerr, "Oil states cash to dip, says IMF," FINANCIAL TIMES, May 14, 2007, p. 6; *cf*. "'Bubble economy' defies gravity," FINANCIAL TIMES (Special Report: Dubai), June 24, 2007, p. 1.

61. Roula Khalaf & Gillian Tett, "Backwater sector moves into global mainstream," FINANCIAL TIMES (Special Report: Islamic Finance), May 23, 2007, p. 1; Simeon Kerr, "With cash to burn, China and Mideast eye each other's riches," FINANCIAL TIMES, September 6, 2007, p. 5.

62. "India's acquisition spree: Circle the wagons," THE ECONOMIST, October 14, 2006, p. 69.

63. Chris Noon, "Volvo buys Ingersoll-Rand unit," Forbes.com, February 27, 2007, available at: http://www.forbes.com, last visited May 21, 2007.

64. See "The dragon tucks in," THE ECONOMIST, July 2, 2005, pp. 54–56; "Over the great wall," THE ECONOMIST, November 5, 2005, p. 71.

65. Michael R. Fancher, "Globalization story is one that touches way in which we live," THE SEATTLE TIMES, August 8, 2004, p. A2.

66. "Home, sweet home—for some," THE ECONOMIST, August 13, 2005, p. 37.

67. International Labour Office & Secretariat of the World Trade Organization, "Trade and Employment: Challenges for Policy Research," 2007, pp. 87–90.

68. "Doha: Draft ag text meets lukewarm response," 11 BRIDGES No. 27, July 25, 2007, p. 1; "WTO mini-ministerial ends in collapse," BRIDGES DAILY UPDATE No. 10, July 30, 2008; "EU face[s] calls for farm reform at WTO," THE KITSAP DAILY, July 21, 2008, p. 8.

69. Elizabeth Becker & Todd Benson, "How Brazil trumped U.S. on cotton aid," INTERNATIONAL HERALD TIMES, May 5, 2004, p. 15.

70. George F. Russell, Jr., "The Power of Globalization," NBR ANALYSIS, op.cit., p. 19.

71. "Draft NAMA agreement text criticized by many developing countries," 11 BRIDGES No. 28 (August 1, 2007), p. 4.

72. "So near and yet so far" and "The Doha round ... and round ... and round," both in THE ECONOMIST, August 2, 2008, pp. 14 and 71, respectively; "U.S.-Laos trade has grown ten-fold since 2004," available at: ppi_admin@dlcppi.org, last visited September 7, 2007; The World Bank (Development Research Group), "Growth is good for the poor," March 2001, pp. 1–3.

73. "The future of globalisation," THE ECONOMIST, July 29, 2006, p. 11.

74. Richard Steiner, "The real clear and present danger," SEATTLE POST-INTELLIGENCER, May 30, 2004, pp. F1–F4.

75. Roula Khalaf & Others, "The great bridge of China: how energy-hungry Beijing hews its Mideast links," FINANCIAL TIMES, February 12, 2007, p. 13; Charles Hanley, "Global-warming summit beckons world leaders," SEATTLE POST-INTELLIGENCER, September 24, 2007, p. A2; "The future of energy," THE ECONOMIST, June 21, 2008, p. 17.

76. "High food prices leave developing countries struggling to cope," 12 BRIDGES No. 14, April 23, 2008, p. 1.

77. World Trade Organization, "Understanding the WTO: The Organization, Members and Observers," available at: http://www.wto.org, last visited May 21, 2007; "WTO members account for 96 percent of trade," available at: ppi_admin@dlcppi.org, last visited November 2, 2005.

78. "The IMF reports on a wonderful world," FINANCIAL TIMES, April 12, 2007, p. 12; Scheherazade Daneshkhu, "OECD Report: Global balance but domestic finances on edge," FINANCIAL TIMES, May 25, 2007, p. 2; "A good time for a squeeze," THE ECONOMIST, August 4, 2007, p. 9.

79. "The United States has initiated only 10 anti-dumping cases this year," available at: ppi_admin@dlcppi.org, last visited November 30, 2005.

80. Edward Gresser, "Healthy Factories, Anxious Workers," PPI Policy Report, February 2007, p. 4.

81. "The U.S. commercial services trade surplus reached $100 billion last year," available at: ppi_admin@dlcppi.org, last visited February 28, 2007.

82. Michael Liedtke, "Chinese to buy $4.3 billion in American tech products," Seattle Post-Intelligencer, May 10, 2007, p. D1.

83. Edward Gresser, "Healthy Factories, Anxious Workers," *op.cit.*, p. 5.

84. Martin Crutsinger, "Port issue spurs debate on foreign ownership," Seattle Post-Intelligencer, Mar. 20, 2006, p. A2.

85. Edward Gresser, "Lou Dobbs is wrong!" *op.cit.*; Bernard Simon, "Further Toyota push in America," Financial Times, February 28, 2007, p. 18.

86. Michael O'Hanlon, "National Security and Foreign Ownership," Brookings Analysis & Commentary, February 15, 2007; "Dubai Ports to sell U.S. operations to AIG unit," The Kitsap Daily, December 12, 2006, p. 5; Norma Cohen, "Nasdaq to sell LSE stake to boost OMX bid," Financial Times, August 21, 2007, p. 1; David Wighton, "Citi buys into Banco de Chile," Financial Times, July 20, 2007, p. 13; David Ibison, "Volvo buys Ingersoll Rand unit for $1.3 bn," *op.cit.*; Roger Blitz, "Dubai in $5 bn deal with MGM Mirage," Financial Times, August 23, 2007, p. 16; Adrian Michaels, "Rome's approach scares Telecom Italia suitors," Financial Times, April 19, 2007, p. 16; Jamil Andrelini, "Foreign investors fear China law to curb monopolies," Financial Times, August 31, 2007, p. 5; "Foreign investment: Love me, love me not," The Economist, July 12, 2008, p. 36; "Study of CFIUS finds increase in filings following Dubai Ports World controversy," 24 ITR No. 5, February 1, 2007, p. 161.

87. Peter Larsen, "Activity soars beyond western horizons," Financial Times (Special Report: Corporate Finance) February 28, 2007, p. 2; Raphael Minder, "Asia cross-boarder M&A running at double of last year," Financial Times, July 31, 2007, p. 16; "India's acquisitive companies: Marauding maharajahs," The Economist, March 31, 2007, p. 71; Neil Buckley, "Russian M&As surge to $71 bn record," Financial Times, April 2, 2007, p. 6; Lina Saigol & James Politi, "M&A volume tops $1,000 bn," Financial Times, March 30, 2007, p. 13; "Global M&A market takes a tumble," Financial Times, September 28, 2007, p. 19.

88. Tomoeh Murakami Tse, "NYSE, Tokyo exchange announce partnership; Markets pledge to cooperate on trading technology; Deal could be first step toward a merger," The Washington Post, February 1, 2007, p. D3; "Stock exchanges: Flying in formation," The Economist, February 3, 2007, p. 76; "Buy, buy, buy," The Economist, May 26, 2007, p. 75.

89. Progressive Policy Institute, "Currency trading totals $3 trillion a day," available at: ppi_admin@dlcppi.org, last visited March 14, 2007; Roberto F. De Campo, "A single currency for Asia: Is it time?," Given at 37th ADB Annual Meeting, May 14, 2004, p. 10–12; Wolfgang Munchau, "Asian monetary integration poses many questions," Financial Times May 7, 2007, p. 9.

90. Richard Milne, "Bosch urges carmakers to agree on parts," FINANCIAL TIMES, September 13, 2007, p. 16; Wolfgang Munchau, "Cross-boarder banks require a single regulator," FINANCIAL TIMES, April 2, 2007, p. 13; Bertrand Benoit & James Mackintosh, "Hedge funds to meet G7 on greater openness," FINANCIAL TIMES, April 11, 2007, p. 1; Brooke Masters, "Watchdogs step up global tracking of insider trading," FINANCIAL TIMES, February 15, 2007, p. 1; John Smith, "Wanted: a guardian of the world's financial system," FINANCIAL TIMES, April 13, 2007, p. 13.

91. Robert Bruce, "Giant step is taken towards a single global [accounting] standard," FINANCIAL TIMES, May 3, 2007, p. 19; "Tax reform: Overhauling the old jalopy," THE ECONOMIST, August 4, 2007, p. 61; Anuj Gangahar, "Trading surge set to test systems," FINANCIAL TIMES, March 5, 2007, p. 19.

92. "Transatlantic aviation: Chocks away," THE ECONOMIST, April 7, 2007, p. 61; "US and EU announce final design for GPS-Galileo common civil signal," NEWS @ EU, August 1, 2007, p. 2; Tobias Buck, "Brussels threatens Americans with reciprocal travel restrictions," FINANCIAL TIMES, August 8, 2001, p. 1.

93. Patti Waldmeir, "Bribery is not just a cost of doing business," FINANCIAL TIMES, March 5, 2007, p. 8; Progressive Policy Institute, "Piracy rates have dropped," March 28, 2007, available at: ppi_admin@dlcppi.org, last visited March 29, 2007.

94. See THOMAS C. FISCHER, "A New Era in World Trade," in THE UNITED STATES, THE EUROPEAN UNION, AND THE "GLOBALIZATION" OF WORLD TRADE: ALLIES OR ADVERSARIES? 63 (Quorum Books, 2000); Anne-Marie Slaughter, "The Real New World Order: The State Strikes Back," 76 FOREIGN AFFAIRS, p. 183.

95. "Flights to Europe face new emissions rules," USA TODAY, December 21, 2006, p. 4B.

96. Daniel Pruzin, "Trade officials see improvement in WTO impasse over Singapore issues," 21 ITR No. 19 (May 6, 2004), p. 764; Marcus Wallenberg & Guy Sebban, "Doha must not fail," SOUTH CHINA MORNING POST, June 29, 2006, p. 14.

97. "The Real New World Order: The State Strikes Back," op.cit.

98. Fareed Zakaria, "The end of the end of history," NEWSWEEK, September 24, 2001, p. 70.

99. Rik Kirkland, "Will the U.S. be flattened by a flatter world?" FORTUNE, June 27, 2005, p. 47.

100. Robert J. Samuelson, "The world is still round," NEWSWEEK, July 25, 2005, p. 49.

101. "Why the rich must get richer," THE ECONOMIST, November 12, 2005, p. 87 (review of BENJAMIN J. FRIEDMAN, THE MORAL CONSEQUENCES OF ECONOMIC GROWTH).

102. "Brains, not bullets," THE ECONOMIST, October 27, 2007, p. 15.

103. Fareed Zakaria, "America's new balancing act," NEWSWEEK, August 6, 2001, p. 37.

104. Samuel P. Huntington, "The Lonely Superpower," FOREIGN AFFAIRS, March/April 1999, pp. 35–37; Colin Bradford, "Restoring America's leadership legitimacy," available at: http://www.brookings.edu, last visited July 24, 2007; Philip Stephens, "America is still indispensable but it must work with others," FINANCIAL TIMES, November 2, 2007, p. 9.

105. "EU citizens favourable to globalisation," EUROPA NEWSLETTER, No. 23, November 25, 2003.

106. "Ag, NAMA talks continue, with revised texts expected mid-November," 11 BRIDGES No. 37 (October 31, 2007), p. 1; Progressive Policy Institute, "Two-thirds of American farmers receive no subsidies," available at: ppi_admin@dl cppi.org, last visited August 26, 2007.

107. "US and EU announce final design for GPS-Galileo common civil signal," *op.cit.*; Jeremy Grant, "Transatlantic regulatory harmony is in the air," FINANCIAL TIMES, September 26, 2007, p. 11; Andrew Bounds, "US and EU to set date for transatlantic trade zone," FINANCIAL TIMES, February 20, 2007, p. 2.

108. Philip Stephens, "Good manners, but still very different views of the world," FINANCIAL TIMES, April 27, 2007, p. 9; Irwin Stelzer, "Brussels is right to restrict dominant companies," FINANCIAL TIMES, September 12, 2007, p. 11.

109. John Thornhill, "OECD hits at protectionist Europe," FINANCIAL TIMES, September 21, 2007, p. 3; Peggy Hollinger, "Europe's big companies sheltered from hostile bids," FINANCIAL TIMES, February 28, 2007, p. 23.

110. Geoffrey Colvin, "Saving America's socks—but killing free trade," FORTUNE August 22, 2005, p. 38.

111. See THOMAS C. FISCHER, "Chapter 12: Japan: Asia's Disintegrating Colossus," in THE UNITED STATES, THE EUROPEAN UNION, AND THE "GLOBALIZATION" OF WORLD TRADE: ALLIES OR ADVERSARIES? (Quorum Books 2000), p. 145.

112. David J. Lynch, "Some would like to build a wall around U.S. economy," USA TODAY, March 15, 2006, p. B2.

113. Chris Giles, "Economists' rule change puts US on top of the world," FINANCIAL TIMES, November 1, 2007, p. 2.

114. "Don't just bash the bureaucrats," THE ECONOMIST, October 15, 2005, p. 56; "Winners and losers," THE ECONOMIST, March 1, 2008, p. 56.

115. "Wooing the world" in "After Bush: A special report on America and the world," THE ECONOMIST, March 29, 3008, p. 12; Fareed Zakaria, "What the world is hearing," NEWSWEEK, March 10, 2008, p. 45.

116. "Europe's despot dilemma," THE ECONOMIST, October 13, 2007, p. 58; "Commissioner sees enlargement as instrument of EU soft power," NEWS @ EU, October 24, 3007, p. 2; "EPA's: Vision, faith or blindness," 6 BRIDGES ICTSD No. 6, October 2007, p. 1.

117. "Overweight but under powered," THE ECONOMIST, September 8, 2007, p. 56; "France and Iran: Let's keep squeezing them harder," THE ECONOMIST, September 22, 2007, p. 60; Ben Hall & James Blitz, "Sarkozy fears defensive Brown will resist push for EU military," FINANCIAL TIMES, November 12, 2007, p. 4; "Commission proposes global alliance to help developing countries most affected by climate change," NEWS @ EU, September 19, 2007, p. 3; Andrew Bounds, "Europe will use tariffs in subsidy fight with China," FINANCIAL TIMES, November 15, 2007, p. 2; "Euro area unemployment down to 7.3%," NEWS @ EU, November 11, 2007, p. 6; Tony Barber, "Poll backs bigger EU global role," FINANCIAL TIMES, September 7, 2007, p. 4.

118. "America, Europe and the management of danger: A hazardous comparison," THE ECONOMIST, March 1, 2008, p. 61; "The EU treaty: What Lisbon contains," THE ECONOMIST, October 27, 2007, p. 60.

119. "Why Japan keeps failing," THE ECONOMIST, February 23, 2008, p. 33; "U.S., Japan to simplify patent process, fight piracy," THE KITSAP DAILY, January 9, 2007, p. 4; Mariko Sanchanta, "Japan to align anti-monopoly powers with west," FINANCIAL TIMES, October 17, 2007, p. 2; "Looking to the future, stuck in the present," THE ECONOMIST, November 17, 2007, p. 32; John Burton, "Sino-Japanese thaw gathers pace," FINANCIAL TIMES, November 21, 2007, p. 7; David Pilling & Victor Mallet, "Japan weighs bigger role as peace keeper," op.cit.

120. Mure Dickie, "China agrees to set up U.S. military hotline," FINANCIAL TIMES, November 6, 2007, p. 3; Doug Cameron, "Caterpillar to increase output with China plant," FINANCIAL TIMES, August 29, 2007, p. 16; Jamie Anderlini, "China warns exporters could 'be devastated' by U.S. slowdown," FINANCIAL TIMES, November 16, 2007, p. 1.

121. Progressive Policy Institute, "Chinese direct investment abroad has grown twenty-fold since 2000," available at: ppi_admin@dlcppi.org, last visited October 29, 2007; Jon Boone & Geoff Dyer, "Chinese group wins rights to Afghan copper." FINANCIAL TIMES, November 21, 2007, p. 7; William Wallis & Rebecca Bream, "Alarm over China's Congo deal," FINANCIAL TIMES, September 20, 2007, p. 7; Alec Russell & Others, "$5bn S African bank deal signals China's ambition," FINANCIAL TIMES October 26, 2007, p. 1; Joe Quinlan, "China's capital finds new targets across south-east Asia," FINANCIAL TIMES, November 14, 2007, p. 24; Sundeep Tucker, "Asian companies fail to grasp green issues," FINANCIAL TIMES, September 25, 3007, p. 19; "Asia 'complacent'

on governance," FINANCIAL TIMES, September 24, 2007, p. 20; Alec Russell, "US business frets over China's Africa expansion," FINANCIAL TIMES, November 20, 2007, p. 6.

122. Daniel Dombey, "China pulls out of UN meeting on [Iran] sanctions," FINANCIAL TIMES, November 17–18, 2007, p. 3.

123. "Disputes involving China on the increase at the WTO," No. 6 BRIDGES ICTSD, October 2007, p. 10; "WTO sets up dispute panel to decide U.S. challenge to Chinese IP enforcement," 24 ITR 38 (September 27, 2007); "China subsidy consultations fail to ease trade tensions with US, Mexico," 11 BRIDGES No. 11, March 28, 2007, p. 8; Chris Giles & Others, "G7 considers tougher language on renminbi," FINANCIAL TIMES, October 20–21, 2007, p. 2.

124. Richard McGregor, "An intimidating but brittle colossus," FINANCIAL TIMES, (Special Report), October 9, 2007, p. 1; "Taking the waters," FINANCIAL TIMES, July 24, 2007, p. 11; Richard McGregor, "Beijing freezes state-controlled prices as inflation fuels discord," FINANCIAL TIMES, September 20, 2007, p. 1; "Corruption poses 'lethal threat' to China," FINANCIAL TIMES, October 11, 2007, p. 4; "China: Beware of demob," THE ECONOMIST, November 10, 2007, p. 49.

125. Cf. Peter Marsh, "China trade body backs check on steel emissions," FINANCIAL TIMES, October 10, 2007, p. 9. But then this can be seen as a self-protective measure to curb corrosive pollution.

126. "The making of a neo-KGB state," THE ECONOMIST, August 25, 2007, p. 25; Josef Hebert, "U.S., Russia agree on safe disposal of weapons-grade plutonium," SEATTLE POST-INTELLIGENCER, November 20, 2007, p. A6; "Moscow signals it's ready for more missile talks," SEATTLE POST-INTELLIGENCER, November 27, 2007, p. A2; Phillip Stephens, "The west must resist Putin's claim on the old Soviet space," FINANCIAL TIMES, November 23, 2007, p. 11; "Putin accuses U.S. of meddling in Russian vote," THE KITSAP DAILY, November 27, 2007, p. 3.

127. Roman Olearchyk & Catherine Belton, "Gazprom threat to cut gas to Ukraine," FINANCIAL TIMES, October 3, 2007, p. 1; Martin Wolf, "Welcome to the new world of run away energy demand," FINANCIAL TIMES, November 14, 2007, p. 11; "Don't mess with Russia," THE ECONOMIST, December 16, 2006, p. 11.

128. Neil Buckley, "The paradox of Russia's retreat from democracy," FINANCIAL TIMES, November 17–18, 2007, p. 9; "Industry's vanguard: Russia plans grand projects....," FINANCIAL TIMES, November 15, 2007, p. 15; Neil Buckley, "Investing in Russia: Too good to resist," FINANCIAL TIMES (Special Report), October 2, 2007,p. 1; "Russia foreign policy: Last tango in Tehran," THE ECONOMIST, October 20, 2007, p. 69; Neil Buckley & Andrew England, "Putin visits Qatar amid talk of 'gas Opec'," FINANCIAL TIMES, February, 13, 2007, p.

5; Ed Crooks, "Exxon Mobil attacks US energy drive," FINANCIAL TIMES, November 13, 2007, p. 2; "Russia and the west: Out to do business, or out for a scrap?" THE ECONOMIST, November 17, 2007, p. 68; Catherine Belton, "Russia forced into new arms race, says Putin," FINANCIAL TIMES, February 9–10, 2008, p. 3; Martin Wolf, "Why Putin's rule threatens both Russia and the west," FINANCIAL TIMES, February 13, 2008, p. 9.

129. Joe Leaky, "Tata plans to double its capacity by 2015," FINANCIAL TIMES, May 18, 2007, p. 17; "India puts research under microscope," FINANCIAL TIMES, October 12, 2007, p. 6; Jo Johnson, "Food prices eat away at reputations of reformers," FINANCIAL TIMES, February 28, 2007, p. 3; Amy Yee, "Indian microfinance is attracting big business," FINANCIAL TIMES, October 12, 2007, p. 21; Progressive Policy Institute, "A Chinese-made DVD player contains almost 400 Western, Japanese, and Korean patents," available at: http://www.ppi online.org, last visited July 5, 2007; "Howling at the moon," THE ECONOMIST, November 10, 2007, p. 16.

130. "Politics in Brazil: Laws for the lawmakers," THE ECONOMIST, November 10, 2007, p. 47; "Brazil & U.S. square off on subsidies," BRIDGES ICTSD, No. 5 (August 2007), p. 5.

131. Alan Beattie, "Developing countries rule out Doha plans for big tariff cuts," FINANCIAL TIMES, October 10, 2007, p. 2; Hugh Williamson & Barney Jopson, "Ethiopia promises troops for Darfur," FINANCIAL TIMES, October 5, 2007, p. 6.

132. Roula Khalaf & Others, "Arabian funds eye distressed US assets," FINANCIAL TIMES, November 20, 2007, p. 2; John Gapper, "Be thankful for canny Arab wealth," FINANCIAL TIMES, November 29, 2007, p. 11.

133. Colin Bradford & Johannes Linn, "Reform of Global Governance: Priorities for Action," available at: http://www.brookings.edu/papers/2007, last visited October 30, 2007.

134. UN General Assembly, "55/2. United Nations Millennium Declaration," Document A/RES/55/2, signed September 8, 2000; released September 18, 2000. Jeffrey Sachs, "Weapons of mass salvation," THE ECONOMIST, October 26, 2002, p. 71; "The eight Commandments," THE ECONOMIST, July 7, 2007, p. 25. For a progress report regarding what the UN Millennium project has achieved up until 2005, see: JEFFERY SACHS, INVESTING IN DEVELOPMENT: A PRACTICAL PLAN TO ACHIEVE THE MILLENNIUM GOALS (Earthscan; London 2005).

135. Michael Casey, "Poor nations want help to fight global warming," SEATTLE POST-INTELLIGENCER, December 6, 2007, p. A3; Mure Dickie & Jo Johnson, "Beijing and Delhi resist calls to cap their CO_2," FINANCIAL TIMES, December 5, 2007, p. 3; Fiona Harvey, "UN focuses emissions reduction burden on in-

dustrialized nations," Financial Times, November 28, 2007, p. 1; "UN climate summit in Bali underway," 11 Bridges No. 42, December 5, 2007, p. 4.

136. "Mission impossible" and "Peace keeping: Call the blue helmets," both in The Economist, January 6, 2007, pp. 20 and 22, respectively.

137. Javier Blas & Jenny Wiggins, "UN warns it cannot afford to feed the world on its budget," Financial Times, July 16, 2007, p. 1.

138. "Fighting for survival," (Special report: United Nations), The Economist, November 20, 2004, p. 25; "When your only weapon is blame," The Economist, November 24, 2007, p. 64.

139. See generally, "Chapter 14: Metamorphosing the GATT: the World Trade Organization (WTO)," in Thomas C. Fischer, The United States, The European Union, and the "Globalization" of World Trade (Quorum, 2006), pp. 201–210.

140. "How the WTO works," available at: http://www.unicc.org/wto/wto works, last visited April 9, 1996; Kathrin Hille, "Taiwan acts to avoid WTO dispute," Financial Times, April 26, 2007, p. 5; Progressive Policy Institute, "The WTO has considered 369 disputes," available at: ppi_admin@dlcppi.org, last visited December 6, 2007.

141. Nagesh Kumar, "Building a development-friendly world trading system," Bridges ICTSD No. 5, August 2007, available at: www.icsd.org, p. 3; "Chronicle of a clash foretold," Bridges ICTSD No. 6, October 2007, available at: www.ictsd.org, p. 1; "WTO negotiators look to 2008, though Doha deal prospects remain slim," 11 Bridges No. 42, December 5, 2007, p. 1; "Members submit revised proposals on trade facilitation," 11 Bridges No. 34, October 10, 2007, p. 15.

142. The most recent assessment of the WTO's future is: World Trade Organization Consultative Board, The Future of The WTO (2004), Peter Sutherland, Chair. E-mail address: publications@wto.org.

143. Marcela Sanchiz, "Will IMF, World Bank get the message?" Seattle Post-Intelligencer, May 16, 2007, p. B6; "The IMF: Funding the fund," The Economist, February 3, 2007, p. 75; "Kahn do," The Economist, November 3, 2007, p. 88; Chris Giles, "Credit squeeze and criticisms deepen crisis of [IMF] legitimacy," Financial Times, October 22, 2007, p. 4.

144. Robert Zoellick, "Globalization must be all inclusive," Financial Times (Special Report: World Economy), October 17, 2007, p. 16; Krishna Guha, "Private sector to join forces with World Bank on aid," Financial Times, October 18 2007, p. 2; Hugh Williamson & Chris Giles, "Donations show World Bank is back in action," Financial Times, December 15–16, 2007, p. 2; Chris Giles, "World Bank makes farming priority in drive on poverty," Financial Times, October 20–21, 2007, p. 2.

145. "Economic focus: Divine intervention," THE ECONOMIST, March 29, 2008, p. 100; "Global warming: Struggling to save the planet," THE ECONOMIST, June 2, 2007, p. 63.

146. Chris Giles, "OECD calls for pace of reforms to be maintained," FINANCIAL TIMES, February 14, 2007, p. 5; "Central banks make joint assault," FINANCIAL TIMES, December 13, 2007, p. 1.

147. James Blitz & Stephen Fidler, "Putin poised to freeze arms pact as assertiveness grows," FINANCIAL TIMES, December 12, 2007, p. 6; "Predictions of its death are premature," THE ECONOMIST, November 25, 2006, p. 24; "NATO's Afghan test," FINANCIAL TIMES, February 4, 2008, p. 6; Ron Asmus, "NATO must go global to have a meaningful purpose," FINANCIAL TIMES, February 7, 2007, p. 11; Matthew Green & Andrew Bounds, "Delay in deploying Darfur force casts shadow on Lisbon," FINANCIAL TIMES, December 8–9, 2007, p. 5; "A ray of light in the dark defile" (Briefing: The state of NATO), THE ECONOMIST, March 29, 2008, p. 33.

148. "With allies like these," THE ECONOMIST, April 5, 2008, p. 65; "Redrawing the MAP in Europe," THE ECONOMIST, April 12, 2008, p. 57.

149. "What a way to run the world" and "Who runs the world: Wrestling for influence," both in THE ECONOMIST, July 5, 2008, pp. 13 and 33, respectively; Raghuram Rajan, "Why it takes small groups to solve global problems," FINANCIAL TIMES, May 16, 2007, p. 11; "White House, Democrats reach deal on bilateral FTAs," 11 BRIDGES No. 17, May 16, 2007, p. 3.

150. See generally, THE POST-AMERICAN WORLD, *op.cit.*

151. "World economy: Stronger China," THE ECONOMIST, September 29, 2007, p. 14; Raphael Minder, "East Asia's surge forecast to continue," FINANCIAL TIMES, November 16, 2007, p. 3; "The great American slowdown," THE ECONOMIST, April 12, 2008, p. 13; David Pillings, "Big import rise dents Japanese trade gap," FINANCIAL TIMES, August 23, 2007, p. 4; "The U.S. trade deficit is falling," October 13, 2007, available at: ppi_admin@dlcppi.org, last visited, November 1, 2007; Martin Wolf, "Big challenges lie ahead for the emerging economies," FINANCIAL TIMES, October 10, 2007, p. 9.

152. A recent Economist article called the U.S. "the world's indispensable power." "A la recherche du temps perdu," in "After Bush: A special report on America and the world," THE ECONOMIST, March 29, 2008, p. 15; Progressive Policy Institute, "American manufacturing is not dying," available at: ppi_admin@dlcppi.org, last visited February 15, 2007; Gillian Tett, "Dollar loses grip on Asian debt sector," FINANCIAL TIMES, November 20, 2007, p. 31; Wolfgang Munchau, "Early steps towards an assertive Eurozone," FINANCIAL TIMES, November 19, 2007, p. 13; Scheherazade Daneshkhu, "Global balance, but domestic finances on edge," FINANCIAL TIMES, May 25, 2007, p. 2; Tony Bar-

ber, "Brown's absence makes Brussels's heart ponder," FINANCIAL TIMES, December 13, 2007, p. 4.

153. Christopher Bowe, "Call for big pharma to reconnect with the world," FINANCIAL TIMES, September 28, 2007, p. 4.

154. Jagdish Bagwati, "The free trade consensus lives on," FINANCIAL TIMES, October 10, 2007, p. 9.

155. Hugh Williamson & Alex Barker, "EU 3 in credit crisis talks," FINANCIAL TIMES, December 18, 2007, p. 3; "Smart power is a smart investment," FINANCIAL TIMES, November 12, 2007, p. 10.

156. "Amid new talks, Russia could complete WTO accession this year," 12 BRIDGES No. 6, February 20, 2008, p. 9; "EU opens talks with Asian countries," 23 ITR No. 36 (September 14, 2006), p. 1330; Anna Fifield & Eoin Callan, "S Korea and US in landmark accord," FINANCIAL TIMES, April 3, 2007, p. 2.

157. Tim Hindle, "The third age of globalization', in THE ECONOMIST, THE WORLD IN 2004, circa December 15, 2003, p. 97.

158. For example, "Come in number one, your time is up," THE ECONOMIST, April 14, 2007, p. 12; Alan Webber, "From afar, America resembles a 2nd-rate power," USA TODAY, October 18, 2007, p. 15A; Peter Marsh, "US to lose role as world's top manufacturer by 2020," FINANCIAL TIMES, May 24, 2007, p. 8.

159. In "2006 Overview," p. 1 Annex I. "U.S. Trade in 2006," Office of the United States Trade Representative, '2007 Trade Policy agenda and 2006 Annual Report," available at: http://www.ustr.gov, last visited October 9, 2007; "American manufacturing is not dying," op.cit.

160. THE ECONOMIST, POCKET WORLD IN FIGURES (2007 Edition), pp. 26, 62, 96 and 30, respectively; Stephen Ohlemacher, "41 nations top U.S life expectancy," SEATTLE TIMES, August 12, 2007, p. A4.

161. Robert Samuelson, "Globalization to the rescue?" NEWSWEEK, October 29, 2007, p. 41.

162. Robert Samuelson, "Globalization's Achilles' heel," NEWSWEEK, July 21, 2008, p. 53; Peter March, "US to lose role as world's top manufacturer by 2020," op. cit.; Robert Samuelson, "The economics of the rat race," NEWSWEEK, July 30, 2001, p. 37; Fareed Zakaria, "What the world is hearing," NEWSWEEK, March 10, 2008, p. 45; Nina Easton, "Make the world go away," FORTUNE, February 4, 2008, p. 105.

163. THOMAS L. FRIEDMAN, THE WORLD IS FLAT: A BRIEF HISTORY OF THE TWENTY FIRST CENTURY (Farrar, Straus and Giroux, 2005), p. 5. But the author himself confesses that it is not, at pp. 44–45.

164. Geoffrey Colvin, "The U.S. is in decline—and that's a good thing," FORTUNE, February 21, 2005, p. 58; Chris Giles, "Economists' rule change put US on top of world," FINANCIAL TIMES, November 1, 2007, p. 2; Stefan Theil

& Others, "Seeing the bright side," NEWSWEEK, June 12, 2006, p. 64; Justin Baer & Francesco Guerrera, "US groups find overseas cushion," FINANCIAL TIMES, October 24, 2007, p. 15; Michiyo Nakamoto & John Reed, "GM regains position as worlds largest carmaker from Toyota," FINANCIAL TIMES, October 23, 2007, p. 17; "Globalization to the rescue?" *op.cit.*

165. Fareed Zakaria, "How long will America lead the world?" NEWSWEEK June 12, 2006, p. 40; "Testing all engines," THE ECONOMIST, February 4, 2006, p. 65; "Switching engines," THE ECONOMIST, February 24, 2007, p. 18; Daniel Pimlott & Krisha Guha, "[US] economy surges on the back of exports," FINANCIAL TIMES, November 30. 2007, p. 1; Martin Wolf, "Why the credit squeeze is a turning point for the world," FINANCIAL TIMES, December 12, 2007, p. 11; "From Mao to the mall," THE ECONOMIST, February 16, 2008, p. 86; Richard Milne & John Reed, "Ghosn sees sales shift to emerging markets," FINANCIAL TIMES, March 5, 2008, p. 21; Clyde Prestowitz's book, THREE BILLION NEW CAPITALISTS: THE GREAT SHIFT OF WEALTH AND POWER TO THE EAST (Basic Books, 2005), may be a bit too optimistic, however; "Emerging markets: The decoupling debate," THE ECONOMIST, March 8, 2008, p. 79; "Hard to decouple from the US train," FINANCIAL TIMES, October 13, 2007, p. 6; "Globalization's Achilles' heel," *op.cit.*

166. Phillip Stephens, "A global response is needed to the shifting world order," FINANCIAL TIMES, November 30, 2007, p. 11; Richard McGregor & George Parker, "China's trade surplus hits record high," FINANCIAL TIMES, July 11, 2007, p. 2; "Discord over implementation record marks China's five-year anniversary in WTO," 10 BRIDGES No. 43, December 20, 2006, p. 5.

167. "U.S.-Laos trade has grown ten-fold since 2004," available at: ppi_admin@dlcppi.org, last visited September 6, 2007; Martin Wolf, "A divided world of economic success and political turmoil," FINANCIAL TIMES, January 31, 2007, p. 11.

168. "How long will America lead the world?" *op.cit.*

169. "On the hiking trail," THE ECONOMIST, September 2, 2006, p. 66; "A foreign affair," THE ECONOMIST, October 22, 2005, p. 81.

170. Danny Leipziger & Michael Spence, "Globalization's losers need support," FINANCIAL TIMES, May 15, 2007, p. 11; Jamil Anderlini & Mure Dickie, "Bold activists hold Beijing to account," FINANCIAL TIMES, December 27, 2007, p. 2; Tom Mitchell & Geoff Dyer, "Labour laws set to raise costs in China," FINANCIAL TIMES, January 2, 2008, p. 2; "How fit is the panda?" THE ECONOMIST, September 29, 2007, p. 75; Robin Kwong & Ed Crooks, "PetroChina to take 'every opportunity' to expand abroad," FINANCIAL TIMES, March 20, 2008, p. 15.

171. "On credit watch," in "A special report on the world economy," THE ECONOMIST, October 20, 2007, p. 26; Wolfgang Munchau, "Brace for Act II when

the crisis goes global," FINANCIAL TIMES, September 17, 2007, p. 11; "The rules of the game', in "A special report on financial centers," THE ECONOMIST, September 15, 2007, p. 16; Gillian Tett & Others, "'Super fund' helps calm markets," FINANCIAL TIMES, October 16, 2007, p. 1; "A global response is needed to the shifting world order," *op.cit.*

172. Ian Mackintosh, "Vital steps on the road to common global standards," FINANCIAL TIMES, October 25, 2007, p. 19 (concerning accountancy); Progressive Policy Institute, "Currency trading totals $3 trillion a day," available at: ppi_admin@dlcppi.org, last visited March 14, 2007.

173. "Sovereign-wealth funds: The world's most expensive club," THE ECONOMIST, May 26, 2007, p. 79; Ruth Sunderland, "Sovereign funds set to rule the markets," THE OBSERVER, June 24, 2007, p. B3; Martin Wolf, "We are living in a brave new world of state capitalism," FINANCIAL TIMES, October 17, 2007, p. 11; "Chinese direct investment abroad has grown twenty-fold since 2000," available at: admin@newsmail.dlc.org, last visited October 29, 2007; Richard McGregor, "China sovereign wealth fund to follow strictly 'politics-free' goals," FINANCIAL TIMES, October 17, 2007, p. 1; Lawrence Summers, "Sovereign funds shake the logic of capitalism," FINANCIAL TIMES, July 30, 2007, p. 9; Tony Barber & George Parker, "EU demands more transparency over sovereign investments," FINANCIAL TIMES, September 28, 2007, p. 1.

174. Simeon Kerr, "Gulf Arabs flex muscles for buyouts," FINANCIAL TIMES, September 12, 2007, p. 4; John Willman, "Big spenders: How sovereign funds are stirring up protectionism," FINANCIAL TIMES, July 30, 2007, p. 9; "Dubai Ports [forced] to sell U.S. operations to AIG unit," THE KITSAP DAILY, December 12, 2006, p. 5; Jeremy Grant, "Washington agrees over vetting foreign acquisitions," FINANCIAL TIMES, May 17, 2007, p. 6; "Chinese outbound investment: Dealing with sinophobia," THE ECONOMIST, July 12, 2008, p. 72.

175. Sundeep Tucker, "China's IPO juggernaut thunders on," FINANCIAL TIMES, December 19, 2007, p. 17.

176. George Parker & Others, "Barroso tells EU leaders to avoid protectionism," FINANCIAL TIMES, January 30, 2008, p. 2; "What the world is hearing," *op.cit.*; "Somewhere over the rainbow," *op.cit.*; "The World Bank's 'Doing Business' report: Unblocking business," THE ECONOMIST, September 17, 2005, p. 77.

177. Chris Giles & Krishna Guha, "Global turmoil strengthens case for multilateral action," FINANCIAL TIMES, October 19, 2007, p. 2; Krishna Guha, "IMF to heed new global players," FINANCIAL TIMES, November 3–4, 2007, p. 4; "Building a development-friendly world trading system," 5 BRIDGES ICTSD (August 2007) p. 3; James Boughton & Colin Bradford, "Global governance: New players, new rules," 44 (IMF) FINANCE AND DEVELOPMENT No. 4 (December, 2007).

178. Eoin Callan, "US accuses Doha dissidents," FINANCIAL TIMES, September 7, 2007, p. 5; "Chronicle of a clash foretold," 6 BRIDGES ICTSD (October 2007), p. 1; "Members submit revised proposals on trade facilitation," 11 BRIDGES No. 34, October 10, 2007, p. 15; "Adios to poverty, hola to consumption," THE ECONOMIST, August 18, 2007, p. 21; "Exports and the economy: a few good machines," THE ECONOMIST, March 15, 2008, p. 35; "WTO mini-ministerial: The day after," BRIDGES DAILY UPDATE No. 11, July 30, 2008. See generally, JOHN JACKSON, SOVEREIGNTY, THE WTO AND CHANGING FUNDAMENTALS OF INTERNATIONAL LAW (Cambridge University Press, 2006).

179. Progressive Policy Institute, "The WTO has considered 369 disputes," available at: http://www.ppion-line.org, last visited December 11, 2007; Kathrin Hille, "Taiwan acts to avoid WTO dispute," FINANCIAL TIMES, April 26, 2007, p. 5; "WTO backs US in banana dispute," FINANCIAL TIMES, February 9–10, 2008, p. 2; Frances Williams, "US told to cut cotton subsidies," FINANCIAL TIMES, December 19, 2007, p. 4; "Interim WTO ruling goes against China in auto parts dispute," 12 BRIDGES No. 6, February 20, 2008, p. 8; "Improving the WTO enforcement mechanism: Toward a more balanced regime for all members," 2 BRIDGES ICTSD, p. 11.

180. A Danish "think tank" that proposed to address the "daunting challenges" of climate change, war, disease, financial instability and more—and prioritize them—came up with the following list: climate change; communicable diseases; armed conflict; education; financial instability; governance and corruption; malnutrition and hunger; population and migration; sanitation and water; and subsidies and trade barriers. "A modest undertaking," THE ECONOMIST, March 6, 2004, p. 68.

181. "The world economy: In search of an insurance policy," THE ECONOMIST, February 16, 2008, p. 12; Daniel Dombey, "China eyes free trade and fair play," FINANCIAL TIMES, February 15, 2008, p. 2; "Global push to tackle food crisis," 12 BRIDGES No. 15, April 30, 2008, p. 4. Cf. "Central banks: A dangerous divergence," THE ECONOMIST, March 22, 2008, p. 83; Paul Taylor, "Battle lines are drawn for the future of 4G," FINANCIAL TIMES, February 13, 2008, p. 15.

182. "Cleaning up," THE ECONOMIST, June 2007, p. 13; "Global warming: [Congress] getting the message, at last," THE ECONOMIST, November 17, 2007, p. 35; Sundeep Tucker, "Asian companies fail to grasp green issues," FINANCIAL TIMES, September 25, 2007, p. 19; Mure Dickie & Jo Johnson, "Beijing and Delhi resist calls to cap their CO2," FINANCIAL TIMES, December 5, 2007, p. 3; "The arctic ozone hole is no longer growing," available at: ppi-admin@dl-cppi.org, last visited April 25, 2007.

183. "Brazil's government suspends exports of rice to guarantee domestic supplies" and "International organizations call for lifting of food export re-

strictions to ease crisis," both in 25 ITR 18 (May 1, 2008), pp. 656 and 636, respectively.

184. Kevin Allison, "Immigration curbs are damaging US economy, Gates warns," FINANCIAL TIMES, March 8, 2007, p. 6; Chris Giles, "Immigrants boost British and Spanish economies," FINANCIAL TIMES, February 20, 2007, p. 3; "Global migration: Keep the borders open," THE ECONOMIST, January 5, 2008, p. 8.

185. David Lynch, "Some would like to build wall around U.S. economy," USA TODAY, March 15, 2006, p. B1; "Somewhere over the rainbow," *op.cit.*; "What the world is hearing," *op.cit.*

186. Geoff Colvin, "A recession of global dimensions?" FORTUNE, February 4, 2008, p. 18; "OCED: Dangers of globalization real, but perceptions exaggerated," 11 BRIDGES No. 23, June 27, 2007, p. 6.

187. Robert Samuelson, "Globalization to the rescue?" *op.cit.*; "The number of 'globalized' workers has quadrupled since 1980," and "World exports reached $12.5 trillion in 2005," both available at: ppi_admin@dlcppi.org, last visited August 29, 2007, and November 15, 2006, respectively; Philip Siekman, "The big myth about U.S. manufacturing," FORTUNE, October 2, 2000, p. 244; John Willman, "US leads way as global R&D spending rises 10%," FINANCIAL TIMES, November 12, 2007, p. 2; Geoffrey Colvin, "The imagination economy," FORTUNE, July 10, 2006, p. 53; "Unhappy America," THE ECONOMIST, July 26, 2008, p. 15.

188. "The new face of hunger," THE ECONOMIST, April 19, 2008, p. 32; "The evolution of everyday life," THE ECONOMIST, August 14, 2004, p. 69; see generally, World Bank, Commission on Growth and Development, "The Growth Report: Strategies for Sustained Growth and Inclusive Development" (also referred to as the "Spence Report"), May, 2008.

Index